WITHDRAWN

Adjustment
in Africa

A World Bank Policy Research Report

Adjustment in Africa

Reforms, Results,
and the Road Ahead

Published for the World Bank
OXFORD UNIVERSITY PRESS

AVG 1058 - 6/2

Oxford University Press

OXFORD   NEW YORK   TORONTO
DELHI BOMBAY CALCUTTA MADRAS KARACHI
KUALA LUMPUR SINGAPORE HONG KONG TOKYO
NAIROBI DAR ES SALAAM CAPE TOWN
MELBOURNE AUCKLAND

and associated companies in

BERLIN   IBADAN

© *1994 The International Bank for Reconstruction*
and Development / THE WORLD BANK
1818 H Street, N.W.
Washington, D.C. 20433, U.S.A.

Published by Oxford University Press, Inc.
200 Madison Avenue, New York, N.Y. 10016

Manufactured in the United States of America
First printing February 1994

The boundaries, colors, denominations, and other information shown on the map in this vol-
ume do not imply on the part of the World Bank Group any judgment on the legal status of
any territory or the endorsement or acceptance of such boundaries.

Library of Congress Cataloging-in-Publication Data

Adjustment in Africa : reforms, results, and the road ahead.
    p. cm. — (A World Bank policy research report)
  Includes bibliographical references.
   ISBN 0-19-520994-X
   1. Structural adjustment (Economic policy)—Africa, Sub-Saharan.
I. World Bank. II. Series.
HC800.A55258   1993
338.967—dc20
                                               93-47887
                                                 CIP

ISSN *1020-0851*

∞ *Text printed on paper that conforms to the American National Standard for Permanence*
of Paper for Printed Library Materials, Z39.48-1984

Contents

Boxes

Text figures

Text tables

Appendix tables

Foreword

A BROAD-BASED PATTERN OF RAPID ECONOMIC GROWTH IS vital to reducing poverty in Sub-Saharan Africa. Many African countries have undertaken structural adjustment programs to reverse the economic decline of the 1980s and accelerate growth. GDP per capita growth remains low, however, raising troubling questions about the extent and efficacy of the policy reform efforts. For this reason, the Development Economics Vice Presidency conducted a study to assess how much policy reform has taken place in Africa, how successful it has been, and how much more remains to be done. This report, *Adjustment in Africa: Reforms, Results, and the Road Ahead,* summarizes the findings of that research. A companion report, *Adjustment in Africa: Lessons from Country Case Studies* (Husain and Faruqee forthcoming), documents reform efforts in seven countries.

Adjustment programs are necessary but not enough to raise economic growth. As discussed at length in *Sub-Saharan Africa: From Crisis to Sustainable Growth* (World Bank 1989a), investments in human capital and infrastructure, efforts to build the economic institutions necessary to a well-functioning market economy, and initiatives to increase technical capacity must also continue apace. This report, with its focus on adjustment, is intended to complement other World Bank publications dealing with the various facets of Africa's long-term development strategy.

Adjustment in Africa reviews the policy reforms typically included in African adjustment programs during the second half of the 1980s and analyzes their relation to economic performance. The evidence shows that progress has been mixed, and that in every African country, key reforms are still incomplete.

There are rewards to adjustment, however, as countries that have come the furthest in implementing good policies—particularly good macroeconomic policies—have enjoyed a resurgence of growth. But the level of per capita growth, even among the countries that have adjusted the most, is still below what is needed for rapid poverty reduction.

Where do adjustment programs go from here? The report concludes that in the macroeconomic, trade, and agricultural sectors, the major task is to move forward with the current approach to policy reform. In the financial and public enterprise sectors, some rethinking of strategy is called for. This report highlights the role that adjustment needs to play in improving the policy environment for the provision of basic social services and protecting the environment.

Government ownership of an economic reform program is a prerequisite for its success. But ownership must not stop with the government. Political leaders must build a broad-based consensus on the need for reform so that adjustment programs are not derailed by powerful interest groups. One of the major challenges for the next generation of adjustment programs is for governments and donors alike to find ways of widening ownership and building consensus.

This study is the second in a series of Policy Research Reports, which are intended to bring to a broad audience the results of World Bank research on development policy issues. As reports on policy issues, these books should help us take stock of what we know—and what we do not know. While remaining accessible to nonspecialists, they should contribute to the debate among academics and policymakers about appropriate public policy objectives and instruments for developing economies. And as research documents, these books may also provoke debate, both within the Bank and outside, concerning the analytic methods used and the conclusions drawn.

Adjustment in Africa is a product of the staff of the World Bank, and the judgments made herein do not necessarily reflect the view of the Board of Directors or the governments they represent.

Michael Bruno
Vice President Development Economics
and Chief Economist
The World Bank

The Report Team

CHRISTINE W. JONES AND MIGUEL A. KIGUEL WERE THE PRINcipal authors of the report. Lant Pritchett and Michael Walton collaborated closely and made important contributions. Takamasa Akiyama, Elliot Berg, Tyler Biggs, Lawrence Bouton, Gerald Caprio, Yoon Je Cho, Wilfrido Cruz, William Easterly, Ibrahim Elbadawi, Faezeh Foroutan, Ronald Johannes, Ross Levine, John Nash, Jo Ann Paulson, David Sahn, Hafeez Shaikh, and the Fiscal Affairs Department of the International Monetary Fund contributed to particular sections. Francisca Castro and Heidi Zia provided research assistance. Lawrence H. Summers played a leading role in the initial stages of the report's preparation. The work was carried out under the general direction of Nancy Birdsall and completed under Michael Bruno.

Bruce Ross-Larson was the principal editor. The editorial-production team for the report was led by Kathryn Kline Dahl. Lawrence MacDonald provided additional editorial input. The support staff was headed by Cecilia Guido-Spano and included Julia Baca, Milagros Divino, Raquel Luz, Anna Marañon, Rebecca Martin, and Christopher Rollison.

Acknowledgments

T HIS REPORT WAS PREPARED IN CLOSE COLLABORATION WITH the World Bank's Africa Region. Special thanks are due to the Africa Region country economists, whose input was essential to assessing the extent of policy reforms. Under the direction of Ishrat Husain, the lead economists of the Africa Region—Lawrence Hinkle, Peter Miovic, Ulrich Thumm, Ajay Chhibber, François Laporte, and Gene Tidrick—made valuable comments and contributions, as did the Africa Technical Department under the guidance of Kevin Cleaver and Michel Wormser. Philip Birnbaum provided liaison with the donors participating in the Bank's Special Program of Assistance for Africa (SPA). The strong support of Edward V. K. Jaycox is much appreciated.

Preparation of this report drew on the seven country case studies of adjustment coordinated by Ishrat Husain (Husain and Faruqee forthcoming). The report also benefited from research from the African Economies in Transition Project managed by Jo Ann Paulson and from the Trade Policy Expansion Project directed by John Nash. Takamasa Akiyama, Mark Blackden, Ajay Chhibber, Graeme Donovan, Alan Gelb, Alfred Gulstone, Rebecca Hanson, Brendan Horton, Steven Jaffee, Chad Leechor, John Nash, John Page, Paul Popiel, Mustapha Rouis, Shala Torabi, and Rogier van den Brink contributed material for boxes and tables in the report.

Many individuals inside and outside the World Bank provided valuable comments. Particular thanks are due to those Bank staff outside the Africa Region who commented on various drafts: Alan Gelb, Magdi Iskander, Pierre Landell-Mills, Johannes Linn, Gobind Nankani, John Nellis, John Page, and Lyn Squire. External reviewers included Paul Collier, Gerald Helleiner, Tony Killick, Benno Ndulu, Ademola Oyejide, Jorn Rattsoe, and representatives of the SPA donors, the Economic Commission for Africa, and the Organization of African Unity; the usual disclaimer absolving them of responsibility for the contents of the report applies.

Definitions and Data Notes

Country Groups

Analytical groups. This book focuses on twenty-nine Sub-Saharan countries with a population of 500,000 or more in mid-1991, reasonable social stability, and adjustment programs in place during 1987–91. If no other group is specified, the text and data refer to these countries: Benin, Burkina Faso, Burundi, Cameroon, the Central African Republic, Chad, Congo, Côte d'Ivoire, Gabon, The Gambia, Ghana, Guinea, Guinea-Bissau, Kenya, Madagascar, Malawi, Mali, Mauritania, Mozambique, Niger, Nigeria, Rwanda, Senegal, Sierra Leone, Tanzania, Togo, Uganda, Zambia, and Zimbabwe.

These African adjusters are sometimes classified into subgroups:

- *Countries with flexible exchange rates:* Burundi, The Gambia, Ghana, Guinea, Guinea-Bissau, Kenya, Madagascar, Malawi, Mauritania, Mozambique, Nigeria, Rwanda, Sierra Leone, Tanzania, Uganda, Zambia, and Zimbabwe.
- *Countries with fixed exchange rates:* Benin, Burkina Faso, Cameroon, the Central African Republic, Chad, Congo, Côte d'Ivoire, Gabon, Mali, Niger, Senegal, and Togo.
- *Low-income countries* are those with a gross national product (GNP) per capita of $610 or less in 1990. They are Benin, Burkina Faso, Burundi, the Central African Republic, Chad, The Gambia, Ghana, Guinea, Guinea-Bissau, Kenya, Madagascar, Malawi, Mali, Mauritania, Mozambique, Niger, Nigeria, Rwanda, Sierra Leone, Tanzania, Togo, Uganda, and Zambia.
- *Middle-income countries* are those with a GNP per capita of more than $610 but less than $7,620 in 1990. They are Cameroon, Congo, Côte d'Ivoire, Gabon, Senegal, and Zimbabwe.
- *Oil exporters:* Cameroon, Congo, Gabon, and Nigeria.

Occasionally, this book also presents data for the following analytical groups:

■ *Other developing countries:* For convenience, low- and middle-income countries are sometimes referred to as developing countries. Classification by income does not, however, imply a judgment about development status. The composition of "other developing countries" varies depending on the availability of data.

■ *Other adjusting countries* refers to developing countries outside Sub-Saharan Africa with adjustment programs during 1987–91.

■ The *high-performing Asian economies* are Hong Kong; Indonesia; Japan; the Republic of Korea; Malaysia; Singapore; Taiwan, China; and Thailand.

Geographic groups. The geographic groupings used in this report are not intended to be comprehensive lists of all countries in a particular region. Furthermore, complete data may not be consistently available for all countries in each group. Where coverage differs significantly from the standard definitions that follow, those differences are indicated.

■ *Sub-Saharan Africa* comprises World Bank borrowers south of the Sahara: Angola, Benin, Botswana, Burkina Faso, Burundi, Cameroon, Cape Verde, the Central African Republic, Chad, Comoros, Congo, Côte d'Ivoire, Djibouti, Equatorial Guinea, Ethiopia, Gabon, The Gambia, Ghana, Guinea, Guinea-Bissau, Kenya, Lesotho, Liberia, Madagascar, Malawi, Mali, Mauritania, Mauritius, Mozambique, Namibia, Niger, Nigeria, Rwanda, São Tomé and Principe, Senegal, Seychelles, Sierra Leone, Somalia, Sudan, Swaziland, Tanzania, Togo, Uganda, Zaire, Zambia, and Zimbabwe. In this report, the term "Africa" refers to Sub-Saharan Africa.

■ *East Asia and the Pacific* comprises China, Fiji, Indonesia, the Republic of Korea, Malaysia, Papua New Guinea, the Philippines, the Solomon Islands, Thailand, and Vanuatu.

■ *Latin America and the Caribbean* comprises Argentina, the Bahamas, Barbados, Belize, Bolivia, Brazil, Chile, Colombia, Costa Rica, the Dominican Republic, Ecuador, El Salvador, Grenada, Guatemala, Guyana, Haiti, Honduras, Jamaica, Mexico, Nicaragua, Panama, Paraguay, Peru, St. Vincent and the Grenadines, Suriname, Trinidad and Tobago, Uruguay, and Venezuela.

■ *The Middle East* comprises the Islamic Republic of Iran, Iraq, Israel, Jordan, Oman, the Syrian Arab Republic, and the Republic of Yemen.

■ *North Africa* comprises Algeria, Egypt, Morocco, and Tunisia.

- *South Asia* comprises Bangladesh, India, Myanmar, Nepal, Pakistan, and Sri Lanka.

Data Notes

HISTORICAL DATA IN THIS BOOK MAY DIFFER FROM THOSE IN other World Bank publications if more reliable data have become available, if a different base year has been used for constant price data, or if countries have been classified differently.

Additionally, in this book:

- *Billion* is 1,000 million.
- *Trillion* is 1,000 billion.
- *Dollars* are current U.S. dollars unless otherwise specified.
- *Growth rates* are based on constant price data.
- *Net transfers* equal net transfers on debt (loan disbursements minus amortization minus interest) plus grants (excluding technical assistance) plus International Monetary Fund net transfers.
- Ratios reported over a multiyear period are annual averages unless otherwise specified.

Acronyms and Abbreviations

CFA franc	Currency known in West Africa as the "franc de la Communauté financière d'Afrique" and known in Central Africa as the "franc de la Coopération financière en Afrique centrale"
EPZ	Export processing zone
FAO	Food and Agriculture Organization of the United Nations
GDP	Gross domestic product
GNP	Gross national product
HPAEs	High-performing Asian economies
IMF	International Monetary Fund
NTB	Nontariff barrier
OGL	Open general license
REER	Real effective exchange rate
RPP	Real producer price of agricultural exports
SPA	Special Program of Assistance for Africa
VAT	Value-added tax

Overview

I N THE AFRICAN COUNTRIES THAT HAVE UNDERTAKEN AND
sustained major policy reforms, adjustment is working. But a
number of countries have yet to implement the reforms needed
to restore growth. And even among the strongest adjusters, no
country has gone the full distance in restructuring its economy.

Of the twenty-nine countries studied in this report, the six
with the most improvement in macroeconomic policies between
1981–86 and 1987–91 enjoyed the strongest resurgence in economic
performance.[1] They experienced a median increase of almost 2 percentage points in the growth rate of gross domestic product (GDP) per capita,
bringing their median rate of growth up from a negative level to an
average 1.1 percent a year during 1987–91. The increase in their industrial and export growth rates was even more striking. And agricultural
growth also accelerated in the countries that taxed their farmers less. By
contrast, countries that did not improve their policies saw their median
GDP growth fall to a level of –2 percent a year, in all likelihood increasing the number of the poor.

Policy reforms have been uneven across sectors and across countries.
The countries studied here have generally been more successful in improving their macroeconomic, trade, and agricultural policies than their
public and financial sectors. Almost two-thirds of the countries managed to put better macroeconomic and agricultural policies in place by
the end of the 1980s. Improvements in the macroeconomic framework
also enabled countries to adopt more market-based systems of foreign
exchange allocation and fewer administrative controls over imports.

However, reforms remain incomplete. No African country has
achieved a sound macroeconomic policy stance—which in broad terms
means inflation under 10 percent, a very low budget deficit, and a com-

petitive exchange rate. In a third of the countries, macroeconomic policies actually deteriorated over the decade. Furthermore, countries are still taxing their farmers heavily, through marketing boards and/or overvalued exchange rates. Most countries have further to go in eliminating nontariff barriers and adopting a moderate, tariff-based level of protection. Social spending, while not showing an overall decline during the adjustment period, is misallocated within the health and education sectors. And the politically difficult reform of the public enterprise and financial sectors lags well behind.

Moreover, there is considerable concern that the reforms undertaken to date are fragile and that they are merely returning Africa to the slow-growth path of the 1960s and 1970s. At the same time, there is hope that Africa, like East Asia thirty years ago, will move onto a faster development track. For that to happen, more progress will be required in macroeconomic reform—to provide a stable environment in which economic activity can flourish. Much more progress in trade, agricultural, and regulatory reform will also be needed—to create a favorable climate for business so that Africa can join the world economy. And growth with equity will call for strong political resolve to tackle money-losing public enterprises and bloated bureaucracies—to free up the resources needed to improve basic health and education services for the poor.

Adjustment alone will not put countries on a sustained, poverty-reducing growth path. That is the challenge of long-term development, which requires better economic policies *and* more investment in human capital, infrastructure, and institution-building, along with better governance. But development cannot proceed when inflation is high, the exchange rate overvalued, farmers overtaxed, vital imports in short supply, prices and production heavily regulated, key public services in disrepair, and basic financial services unavailable. In such cases, fundamental restructuring of the economy is needed to make development possible. The objective of structural adjustment programs thus is to establish a market-friendly set of incentives that can encourage the accumulation of capital and more efficient allocation of resources.

This report addresses three questions: How much did adjusting African countries change their policies? Did their policy reforms restore growth? And what is the road ahead for adjustment? In answering these questions, the report advances the debate on adjustment by providing the most comprehensive data so far on policy changes in Sub-Saharan Africa. It takes a careful look at whether reforms are paying off, and it identifies the areas where the adjustment strategy needs to be redirected. The report shows that African countries have made great strides in improving policies and restoring growth, but that they still have a long way to go in adopting the policies needed to move onto a faster growth path and reduce poverty.[2]

Policies Are Getting Better

THE TWENTY-NINE AFRICAN COUNTRIES EXAMINED HERE drew up adjustment programs in the 1980s—programs intended to improve the poor policies that were the primary cause of the 15 percent fall in Africa's GDP per capita between 1977 and 1985. The outcomes? Macroeconomic reforms have spurred external competitiveness while keeping inflation low. Trade reforms have increased access to the imports needed for growth. And the reduced taxation of agriculture has helped the poor while encouraging production and exports.

- On the macroeconomic front, six of the adjusting countries had a large improvement in policies, nine a small improvement, and eleven a deterioration.[3] As a whole, they cut their budget deficits (by a median of 1.9 percent of GDP between 1981–86 and 1990–91) and reduced inflation to moderate levels. And the countries with flexible exchange rates (those outside the CFA franc zone) depreciated the real effective exchange rate by 50 percent and reduced the premium on the parallel market for foreign exchange (from a median of 60 percent during 1981–86 to 25 percent during 1990–91).
- In trade, many countries have substantially reduced the number of imports subject to nontariff barriers and begun to rationalize the tariff structure. Most of the flexible exchange rate countries have moved to more automatic systems of granting foreign exchange licenses.
- In agriculture, two-thirds of the adjusting countries are taxing their farmers less. Despite huge declines in real export prices, policy changes have increased real producer prices for agricultural exporters in ten countries. Of the fifteen governments that had major restrictions on the private purchase, distribution, and sale of

major food crops before adjustment, thirteen have withdrawn from marketing almost completely.

For public enterprises and financial enterprises, however, there have been few policy changes.

- African governments have sold off only a small share of their assets. The value of privatizations in Nigeria between 1988 and 1992 was less than 1 percent of that in Argentina, Malaysia, or Mexico, even after adjusting for Nigeria's smaller GDP.[4] Explicit and implicit financial flows to public enterprises are still high. But one encouraging trend is that governments have stopped expanding their public enterprise sectors.
- In most African countries, the financial sector, despite reform efforts, is still heavily burdened by public sector demands for credit—with the central government alone (excluding public enterprises) absorbing more than 30 percent of domestic credit.

Better Policies Pay Off

THERE HAS BEEN MUCH TALK ABOUT THE COSTS OF ADJUSTment, less about the substantial benefits. Most countries that improved their policies have returned to positive rates of GDP per capita growth. This turnaround shows that adjustment policies work when implemented properly. And although GDP per capita growth rates remain low, it is unreasonable to expect that African countries would quickly match the rapid rise of the best performers in Asia and elsewhere. Even before the macroeconomic crisis of the early 1980s, Sub-Saharan Africa was growing more slowly than other regions.

As we have noted, the six adjusting countries with the most improved macroeconomic policies had a median increase in GDP per capita growth of almost 2 percentage points between 1981–86 and 1987–91 (figure 1). That compares with an increase of 1.5 percentage points for those countries with less improved policies and a decline of 2.6 percentage points for those with a deterioration in policies. The median increase in export growth was almost 8 percentage points for countries with the most improved macroeconomic policies, while in countries with policy

Figure 1 Median Changes in Average Annual Growth Rates of Adjusting African Countries between 1981–86 and 1987–91

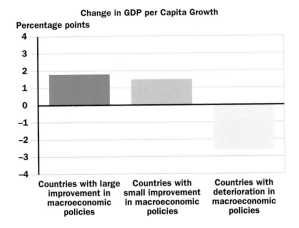

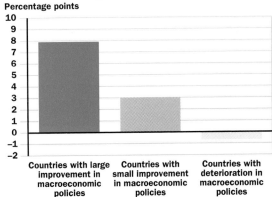

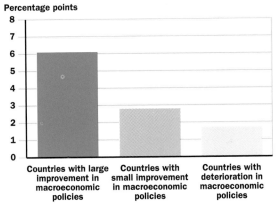

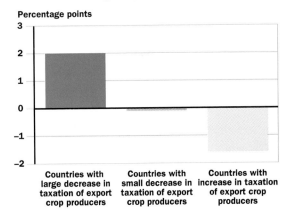

Note: See source tables for a listing of countries in each group.
Sources: Table 5.1 and appendix tables A.19, A.21, and A.22.

Policy reforms paid off in higher growth rates in income, exports, industry, and agriculture.

deteriorations, export growth declined 0.7 percentage points. For the best performers, industrial growth accelerated by more than 6 percentage points, compared with 1.7 percentage points in countries with deteriorating policies. And countries that substantially reduced the taxation of export crop farmers increased median agricultural growth by 2 percentage points, while countries that taxed farmers more saw growth fall by 1.6 percentage points.

Policy packages to address the adverse external shocks and severely overvalued real exchange rates of the early 1980s had high payoffs. Countries that brought about a real depreciation of 40 percent or more between 1981–86 and 1987–91—all of them with flexible exchange rates—had a median increase in GDP per capita growth of 2.3 percentage points. Countries that had appreciations—all of them with fixed exchange rates—suffered a median decline of 1.7 percentage points.

These results demonstrate the payoffs to improving policies. What about the payoffs to good policies? Countries that maintained or ended up with fair or adequate macroeconomic policies during 1987–91 did better than countries with poor or very poor policies (figure 2). The median rate of GDP per capita growth in countries with the better macroeconomic policy stance was 0.4 percent a year between 1987 and 1991—low but at least positive, and a turnaround from annual declines of about 1 percent a year in the early 1980s. By contrast, in countries with poor or very poor macroeconomic policies, median GDP per capita growth fell 2.1 percent a year on average. The extent of government intervention in markets also made a difference in growth. Countries that limited their intervention in markets had median GDP per capita growth of almost 2 percent during 1987–91, compared with declines of more than 1 percent for the countries that intervened more extensively.

Countries with better policy stances had faster GDP per capita growth.

Figure 2 Policy Stance and Median GDP per Capita Growth in Adjusting African Countries

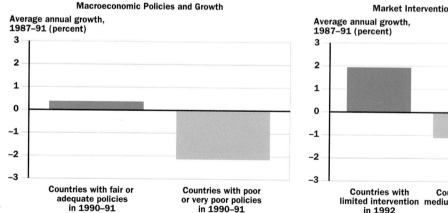

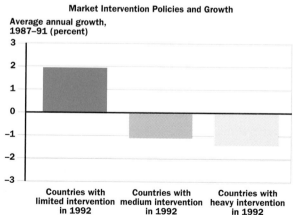

Note: See source tables for a listing of countries in each group.
Sources: Table 5.1 and appendix table A.13.

External Transfers Helped

Increases in external transfers (a median rise of 2.4 percent of GDP between 1981–86 and 1987–91) also contributed to faster growth. Sixteen countries benefited from higher external transfers. Countries with increases in external transfers (a median increase of 0.6 percent of GDP) had a median increase in GDP per capita growth of 1.2 percentage points. Those with reductions (a median decrease of 0.6 percent of GDP) suffered a small slowdown in GDP per capita growth. External transfers relieved import constraints, financed investment, and smoothed consumption—just what they are intended to do. But overall, policy reforms were more strongly associated with increases in growth rates than external transfers were.

The Impact of Adjustment on the Poor and the Environment

In African countries that have undertaken some reforms and achieved some increase in growth, the majority of the poor are probably better off and almost certainly no worse off. The poor are mostly rural, and as producers, they tend to benefit from agricultural, trade, and exchange rate reforms and from the demonopolization of important commercial activities. As consumers, both the urban and the rural poor tend to be hurt by rising food prices. But adjustment measures have seldom had a major impact on food prices in either the open market or the parallel market, which supplies most of the poor. Where rationing was widespread, as in Tanzania, real prices for key consumer goods have even fallen. Similarly, the layoffs of public sector employees, who are among those hardest hit by adjustment, have not generally added to the number of poor people. Many of those who lost their jobs were able to find other work, often by returning to rural areas.

The absence of empirical studies makes it difficult to document any clear and specific link between adjustment reforms and environmental changes in Sub-Saharan Africa. To the extent that policy reforms have encouraged sound pricing of energy, fertilizer, and water resources, they have reduced wasteful distribution and consumption. Not all distortions have been eliminated, however, and there is still much room for progress in instituting appropriate systems of natural resource pricing and taxation.

Policies Are Not Good—Yet

DESPITE THE EFFORTS TO IMPROVE THE MACROECONOMIC environment, open up markets, and strengthen the public and financial sectors, most African countries still lack policies that are sound by international standards. Even Africa's best performers have worse macroeconomic policies than the newly industrializing economies in Asia. Few besides Ghana come close to having adequate monetary, fiscal, and exchange rate policies. And Ghana lags behind other adjusting countries elsewhere—Chile and Mexico, for example—in trade and public enterprise reform.

In trade, many African countries have, by eliminating extensive import controls, returned to the regimes they had before the crisis—helped in many cases by successful exchange rate depreciations that restored competitiveness. Other countries that never experienced a severe macroeconomic crisis, such as Kenya and Zimbabwe, have moved slowly toward import liberalization. The current policy stance in countries with flexible exchange rates is free of the heavy administrative controls that characterized the period before adjustment, but most African countries still have some nontariff barriers and high and dispersed tariffs.

The policy stance for agricultural pricing and other price controls is more difficult to quantify. Most countries have eliminated price controls and restrictions on the marketing and pricing of food staples, and many have eliminated costly subsidies for fertilizer (with no apparent reduction of fertilizer use) and liberalized its distribution. But governments continue to intervene heavily in the marketing of export crops.

The scarce evidence on public enterprise reform suggests that there has been no significant reduction in financial flows to public enterprises or in the volume of assets held by the government. Nor has there been a sustainable improvement in the efficiency of enterprises remaining public. The paucity of data partly reflects institutional weaknesses, but it probably also reflects the lack of government commitment to results.

Financial reform lags behind as well. The financial position of the banking sector is weak because of poor macroeconomic management, which induces the monetization of fiscal deficits through the banks. It is also weak because of the slow pace of reform in the public enterprise sector. And it reflects continuing government interference in the management of the financial sector. A large share of bank lending still goes to the public enterprise sector, making it more difficult for the private sector to borrow.

Although public spending on health and education did not decline in the adjustment period—an achievement given the fiscal problems of African countries—there is little evidence of an increase in that spending. Nor is there much evidence that public spending within those sectors is being reallocated away from costly tertiary programs and toward the basic services most likely to reach the poor.

The Road Ahead for Adjustment

DRAWING ON SUCCESSFUL EXPERIENCES ELSEWHERE AND taking Sub-Saharan Africa's circumstances into account, three principles can guide African governments undertaking reform programs.

- **Get macroeconomic policies right.** Keeping budget deficits small helps in controlling inflation and avoiding balance-of-payments problems. Keeping a realistic exchange rate pays off in greater international competitiveness and in supporting convertible currencies.
- **Encourage competition.** Competition means higher productivity, and firms forced to compete are more efficient than those with privileged access to credit or foreign exchange. A top priority for reform in Africa is to increase competition through domestic deregulation, trade reform, and the privatization of public enterprises.
- **Use scarce institutional capacity wisely.** Because most African countries have limited capacity to govern well, high priority should be given to reforms that minimize unnecessary government involvement in markets. For example, marketing boards should be abolished, public enterprises privatized, and import restrictions replaced by tariffs.

Many African countries are moving in the right direction with their macroeconomic, agricultural, and trade policies, and most policymakers agree on what still needs to be done. But there has been little progress in reforming public enterprises and the financial sector, and there is much less consensus on how to proceed. Reform in these sectors is particularly difficult because of the powerful vested interests that have been created through government intervention. A strong social consensus on the need to improve governance is thus a prerequisite for progress.

Moving Forward Where There Is Consensus

Getting macroeconomic policies right. Countries should continue with the current strategy: avoiding overvalued exchange rates and keeping inflation and budget deficits low. Good macroeconomic policies have paid off in East Asia, and they will pay off in Africa, too—indeed they are already starting to do so.

Most countries in the region still need to cut budget deficits and indirect fiscal losses (those covered by the banking system) in order to lessen the need for inflationary financing or additional external financing. There is little scope for cutting overall public spending in many countries, although the composition of spending can and should be improved. Increasing tax revenues is thus the best avenue for reducing deficits, but the increases should come by levying broad-based taxes that do not unduly penalize businesses and by granting fewer exemptions that favor the politically well-connected.

Domestic savings, which are low in Africa relative to other developing regions, must increase to finance investment. Eliminating large negative real interest rates is a crucial first step. But given the complexity of devising additional policies to encourage private savings, raising public savings is the best option in the short run. The surest way to increase savings in the long term is to boost growth, because growth and savings reinforce each other in a virtuous circle, with high growth leading to high saving and to higher growth.

Taxing agriculture less. In agriculture the main task is to continue reducing the taxation of farmers by liberalizing pricing and marketing and by reducing the protection of industry. Progress has been made, but countries need to do more to help farmers, and the elimination of agricultural marketing parastatals, particularly for export crops, must be high on the agenda. Liberalizing markets so that private agents can compete with parastatals and linking producer prices to world market prices may be useful transitional mechanisms in the near term. These reforms can help farmers reap the full benefit of the exchange rate depreciations, which might otherwise merely shore up the financial profitability of parastatals.

Care must be taken not to undermine market liberalization efforts with restrictive licensing procedures and other interventions that give marketing parastatals an undue competitive advantage. Traders often face a thicket of regulations for licensing, transportation, the movement of goods, trading hours and locations, and weights and measures. Eliminating these burdensome obstacles is essential for increasing profitability and production in agriculture. Simultaneous progress in the development agenda is also important. Improving the quality of public spending for transport networks, rural infrastructure, and agricultural research and extension will enhance the payoffs to improving agricultural policies.

Putting exporters first. Because exports are so beneficial for growth, countries should consider the needs of exporters carefully and apply an "exporters first" rule. One easy way for government to help exporters is to remove unnecessary policy impediments—by providing automatic access to foreign exchange, eliminating export monopolies, and facilitating access to intermediate inputs and capital goods. Governments also need to welcome foreign participation, because foreign firms can bring the contacts and production knowledge needed for penetrating global markets. But governments and international agencies should abandon the practice of trying to pick "winners"— that is, pushing particular exports—because they have consistently made poor choices in the past. Export processing zones have seldom been more effective than simple free-trade zones and bonded production areas, so it is important to find other mechanisms to help exporters avoid administrative, regulatory, and tariff impediments. A high priority is developing workable schemes to provide exporters access to duty-free inputs.

The potential for export growth is great, because African countries are starting from a very low base. Even modest success in increasing their share of world markets will translate into tremendous growth. The future is in nontraditional exports, but traditional exports still need to be part of an outward-oriented strategy. Gaining just a very small foothold in the world market for such traditional, labor-intensive goods as clothing and footwear would substantially increase the region's exports. But this does not mean that Africa should neglect its traditional export of primary commodities, even those that face limited world demand. Although the region already has a large market share in a handful of agricultural commodities, notably cocoa, it is possible to expand that share further. Good policies and investments in infrastructure and research and extension activities can help to raise the productivity of African producers and displace higher-cost producers elsewhere (as Indonesia and Malaysia have demonstrated).

Rationalizing import barriers. There has been progress in liberalizing imports, but most countries have gone only halfway. African countries should continue to eliminate nontariff barriers (NTBs) to rationalize the trade regime and increase transparency. The focus should be not on fine-tuning tariff levels but on establishing a credible schedule for substituting tariffs for NTBs. Even very high tariffs, if imposed only for a clearly limited period, can support the objectives of adjustment. The next steps on the agenda are to simplify the tariff structure, reduce the highest rates to more moderate levels, and institute a minimum tax— so long as effective systems are in place to provide exporters duty-free access to imports. These reforms can often generate enough revenue to offset a fairly substantial overall lowering of tariffs, while leading to a more competitive environment and productivity gains. Beyond that, further progress toward a low and completely uniform tariff structure should not sacrifice fiscal revenues.

Rethinking Adjustment Where There Is Less Success— and Less Consensus

Privatizing public enterprises. The efforts to privatize state corporations and to improve their performance have yielded meager results so far. African governments have resisted privatization, especially of the most important public enterprises. But the alternatives—imposing hard budget constraints, granting the enterprises greater autonomy, and putting them on a commercial footing—seldom work.

Countries elsewhere are getting around the obstacles to privatization, and their experience might be useful in Africa. Some of these countries have fostered broad-based ownership by giving private citizens vouchers for shares in public enterprises, or reserving shares for employees. Others are using various types of private investment and holding companies to improve corporate management. Nonasset divestiture—through leasing, concessions, and incentive-based performance contracts—can increase private sector management of the public utilities and other natural monopolies and improve their productivity.

Prudent financial reform. The overall approach to financial development is on target, but reforms have suffered from too much faith in quick fixes. African countries need to continue with a three-part strategy of reducing financial repression, restoring bank solvency, and improving financial infrastructure. But adjustment programs have been overly hasty in cleaning balance sheets and recapitalizing banks in an environment where institutional capacity is weak and the main borrowers (the government and public enterprises) are financially distressed. Many programs were based on the assumption that banks could improve their performance simply by removing the bad loans from their balance sheets, replacing managers, and injecting new capital to bring assets up to international standards. This usually was insufficient for several reasons: reforms were not accompanied by needed macroeconomic and structural changes, bank managers continued to be exposed to political interference, and regulatory and supervisory capacities were inadequate and could only be developed over time.

A more prudent strategy to restore bank solvency involves downsizing publicly owned banks, privatizing them where possible, and encouraging new entrants. Because most African countries lack the capacity to regulate and supervise, the challenge is to devise a financial system that offers extra cushions against risk—by setting higher-than-normal capital-adequacy ratios, relying more on foreign banks, and limiting entry to reputable banks with a solid capital base. Countries must strike a balance between the need to increase competition and the need to ensure the solvency of financial institutions.

Improving public sector management remains a major challenge for the road ahead—but one that probably extends beyond what adjustment-related policy reforms alone can accomplish. Perhaps the biggest challenge is to build a more effective civil service to provide the elements necessary for a well-functioning market economy, including a sound macroeconomic and legal framework and a system for providing basic social services consistent with the development objective of growth with equity. There is increasing recognition that adjustment programs, with their focus on containing civil service costs, have had limited success in tackling the more fundamental problems of the public sector, such as the lack of accountability and transparency, civil service employment and pay practices that are unrelated to technical competence and productivity, regressive patterns of resource mobilization, expenditures that conflict with development priorities, and the limited capacity for policy analysis. Broader approaches that address the difficult tasks of strengthening the administrative structure and creating the conditions for improved governance are thus called for.

More Adjustment—Not Less—Would Help the Poor and the Environment

Findings from Brazil, Côte d'Ivoire, and Peru show that the lack of adjustment is what most hurts the poor and most increases their number. Addressing the fundamental policy distortions that inhibit growth is thus an essential part of a strategy to reduce poverty.

The poor will benefit more from an increase in growth if spending programs to develop human resources are protected during the adjustment process, and if the policy package eliminates the distortions in labor, land, and output markets that disadvantage the poor. More could have been done, and should have been done, to reduce poverty in the context of adjustment programs. This has been changing in the past few years, as adjustment programs strive to improve public expenditure in the social sectors. But the fundamental development challenge of improving Africa's human resource base requires more than policy change—it also requires sustained investment and institution-building.

In addition to reducing poverty, adjustment programs in Sub-Saharan Africa can promote judicious use of natural resources by instituting policy reforms that affect the pricing of agricultural and forest outputs, petroleum products, energy, and so forth. But macroeconomic and broad sectoral policies are very general and cannot substitute for specific environmental interventions. Designing effective systems for environmental protection when institutional capacity is limited is no simple task. It may be preferable to give firms and communities incentives to protect the environment rather than to depend on governmental regulatory and enforcement capacity. As with poverty, many environmental problems require a combination of policy reform, investment, and institution-building.

Aid and Growth

Aid to African countries must be structured in ways that speed, rather than impede, growth. Higher income generates greater domestic savings and, in time, reduces the dependence on foreign savings. But today's large volume of aid poses dangers: it could soften budget constraints and thus finance the postponement of public sector reforms. Expanded aid flows should therefore be linked to strong reform programs and better governance. In financing country-specific adjustment programs that have a good probability of yielding substantial reforms, a key issue is to design transfer mechanisms and to allocate aid across countries and sectors so that it supports a policy and investment framework for high accumulation of capital and rising public savings. Another key issue is to design aid so that it supports reforms without adding distortions in foreign exchange or labor markets and so that it builds institutions up instead of wearing them down. One of the major challenges on the road ahead is finding ways to help governments promote widespread ownership of adjustment programs and muster support among the interest groups that have the most to gain from reforms.

Efforts by donors to bring Africa's stock of debt down to sustainable levels can, when linked to strong adjustment efforts, help countries realize the benefits of policy reforms. The debt burden of many African countries is huge, and many will have too much debt even under the very favorable debt relief proposals under consideration. So far, aid flows and concessional lending have more than offset debt service payments. But in the medium and long term, as countries adopt better policies, the debt overhang is likely to deter private investment. And the debt service burden threatens to eat away at increased export earnings and domestic savings that might otherwise be used in pursuit of long-term development objectives. For countries undertaking comprehensive and sustained policy reform, reducing the debt stock burden to a manageable level would improve their development prospects. This means rethinking the current debt relief strategy, which still leaves many countries with debt service requirements beyond their capacity to pay. The focus should be on reducing the stock of debt to sustainable levels, even if that means differences in treatment across countries.

Even with transformed policies, higher savings, and better investments, Africa will still require exceptional external assistance for at least another decade. But countries cannot expect an increased flow of foreign resources without undertaking the economic reforms necessary for growth and poverty reduction. And such economic reforms will probably not take place until the conditions for good governance are established.

■ ■ ■ ■

Adjustment is the necessary first step on the road to sustainable, poverty-reducing growth. But adjustment programs in Sub-Saharan Africa have been burdened with unrealistically high hopes, driven in part by awareness of the real poverty that economic growth can help alleviate. Some proponents of adjustment thought that it could quickly put African countries on a much higher growth path than before. Too often there has been little effort to determine whether Africa's disappointing economic performance in the aggregate represents a failure to adjust or a failure of adjustment. Opponents have wrongly cast and criticized adjustment as an alternative to measures supporting long-term development. The resulting confusion has sometimes led to sterile debate about the efficacy of adjustment policies. More important, it has risked creating undue pessimism among African countries and donors. That pessimism is unwarranted, for there has been progress. The turnaround in growth shows that adjustment—even incomplete adjustment—can put African countries back on the road to development.

Notes

1. See box 1.3 in chapter 1 for a listing of the countries included in the study sample.

2. Schadler and others (1993) examined similar issues for the group of countries benefiting from the International Monetary Fund's Enhanced Structural Adjustment Facility. They used a different methodology but reached broadly similar conclusions.

3. Complete macroeconomic data were available for only twenty-six countries.

4. Data on the value of privatizations come from Schwartz and Lopes (1993).

CHAPTER 1

Why Africa Had to Adjust

S
UB-SAHARAN AFRICA'S ECONOMIC GROWTH, NEVER
spectacular, has been the weakest among developing
regions (figure 1.1). The region most in need of growth to
reduce poverty has had the least. Between 1965 and 1985,
its GDP per capita increased less than 1 percent a year on
average. More worrisome, its economic performance actually began deteriorating in the mid 1970s. After growing an average of
2.6 percent a year between 1965 and 1974, GDP per capita stagnated
or turned down thereafter in most Sub-Saharan countries (figure 1.2).
By the early 1980s, few Sub-Saharan countries had kept their per capita
GDP growth in line with the rest of the world's, and many had a lower
GDP per capita than before independence some twenty years earlier.
The economic situation worsened in the first half of the 1980s, with
further deteriorations in the terms of trade and sharply reduced access
to international finance. For more than two-thirds of all Africans, real
incomes were lower in 1985 than in the mid-1970s.

Southeast Asia presents a startling contrast. In 1965 Indonesia's GDP
per capita was lower than Nigeria's, and Thailand's lower than Ghana's.
Indonesia relied on oil as much as Nigeria did. Thailand, much like
Ghana, was a poor agricultural country. Who could have predicted then
that in 1990 Indonesia's GDP would be three times that of Nigeria? Or
that Thailand would become one of the world's best performing
economies, while Ghana would be struggling to regain its former income level?

Few areas of economic activity were exempt from the stagnation and
decline. After healthy increases in exports in 1965–73, the growth
slowed—and then plunged to negative levels between 1981 and 1986
(figure 1.3). Exports of manufactures declined slightly between 1970

Figure 1.1 Average Annual GDP per Capita Growth, 1965–85

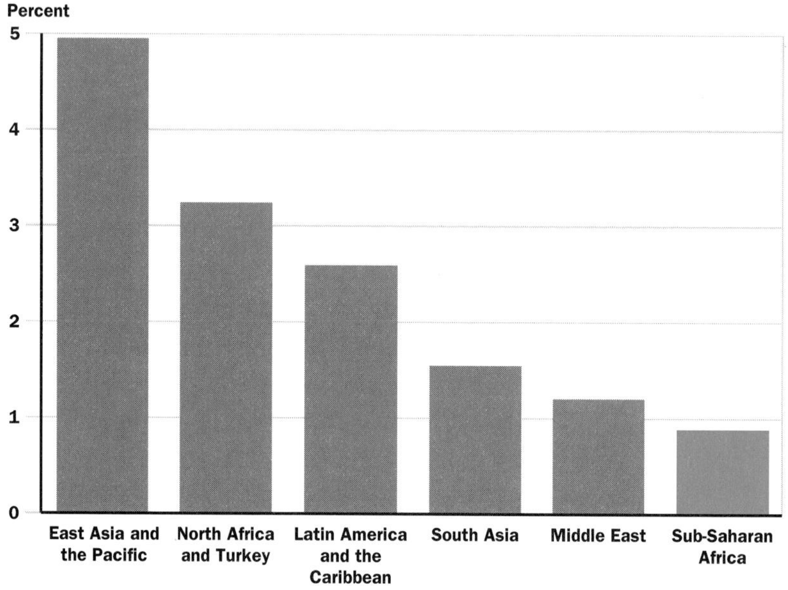

Long-term growth rates in Sub-Saharan Africa lagged behind those of other regions.

Note: Growth rates were calculated using the ordinary least-squares method.
Source: World Bank data.

and 1986, while increasing fivefold for Latin America, sixfold for the Middle East and North Africa, and thirteenfold for Asia's newly industrializing countries. Even agricultural exports slipped, as the region's share in developing-country exports of food and other agricultural products went from 17 percent in 1970 to 8 percent in the mid-1980s. The region also lost ground in its exports of ores and minerals. Only in oil did Africa improve its export share.

Most of the region's economies failed to diversify their export base and continued to rely on only one or two commodities. In the mid-1980s, primary products generated 80 percent of Africa's export revenue, roughly the same share as in the 1960s, and manufactured exports were significant in only a handful of countries. Meanwhile, exports of agricultural products became even more concentrated. Nine major commodities accounted for 76 percent of the region's agricultural exports in the 1980s—up from 70 percent in the 1960s (appendix table A.1). Countries elsewhere, by contrast, diversified their export base and increased their shares in world exports of primary commodities.

Figure 1.2 GDP per Capita

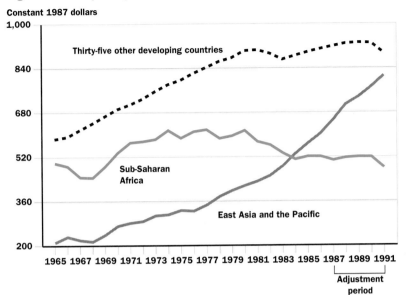

Constant 1987 dollars

African economies stagnated while others improved steadily.

Source: World Bank data.

Agriculture, particularly important for Africa's growth, did worse than other sectors. Between 1965 and 1980, agricultural growth rose only 2 percent a year—less than the rate of population growth—and between 1981 and 1985, it fell 0.6 percent a year. Compare that with agricultural growth of 3.2 percent a year in East Asia, 2.5 percent in South Asia, and 3.1 percent in Latin America.

By the mid 1980s, symptoms of the malaise were evident almost everywhere. The returns on World Bank investment projects were much lower in Africa than in other regions, and more than a quarter of those projects failed to generate a positive rate of return. It was (and still is) almost impossible to attract foreign private capital—either in investment or loans—and portfolio investment flows were negligible. The international prices for Africa's government debt in secondary markets were the lowest for developing countries, reflecting the markets' perception of African countries as uncreditworthy. The physical infrastructure, already poor, deteriorated from lack of maintenance, and the quality of government services suffered. Health and education indicators, though better than in the 1960s, were still a long way below those for other developing countries. Clearly, it was time for African economies to begin to adjust.

Figure 1.3 Average Annual Growth in Exports

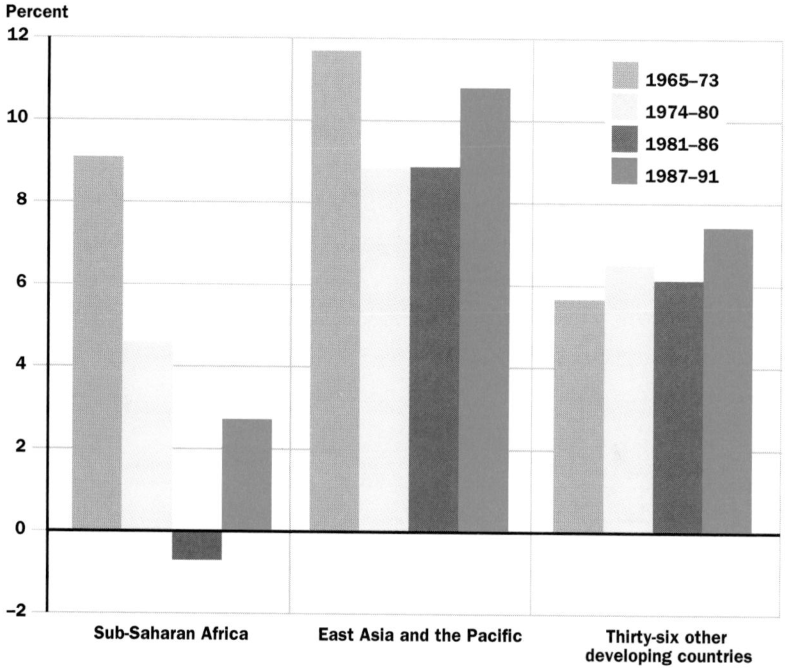

Percent

Legend:
- 1965–73
- 1974–80
- 1981–86
- 1987–91

X-axis categories: Sub-Saharan Africa, East Asia and the Pacific, Thirty-six other developing countries

Africa's exports took a sharp dive in the early 1980s.

Note: Exports valued in local currency, constant prices.
Source: World Bank data.

Understanding the Stagnation and Decline

THERE IS NO SINGLE EXPLANATION FOR AFRICA'S POOR PER-formance before the adjustment period. The main factors behind the stagnation and decline were poor policies—both macroeconomic and sectoral—emanating from a development paradigm that gave the state a prominent role in production and in regulating economic activity. Overvalued exchange rates and large and prolonged budget deficits undermined the macroeconomic stability needed for long-term growth. Protectionist trade policies and government monopolies reduced the competition so vital for increasing productivity. In addition, the state increased its presence in the 1970s, nationalizing enterprises and financial institutions and introducing a web of regulations and licenses for most economic activities. More important, the development strategy had a clear bias against exports, heavily taxing agricultural exports, one of the largest suppliers of foreign exchange.

The choice of poor policies may be understandable in light of conditions in Africa after independence. Because of the lack of domestic capital and entrepreneurs, the unwillingness to rely on foreign capital, and the underlying distrust of the market, almost all African countries chose (with the full support of aid donors) to rely on the state. They had the company of countries in Eastern Europe, Latin America, and South Asia—and the encouragement of many development economists.

Industrialization was believed to be the key to rapid growth, because of declining prices for primary commodities and because of the benefits of reducing reliance on imported manufactures. Agriculture, rather than being stoked as the engine of growth, was taxed to provide the resources to build a modern industrial sector. Governments drew up five-year plans, created public enterprises, and enacted regulations to control prices, restrict trade, and allocate foreign exchange in pursuit of social goals. At the same time, countries were struggling to establish themselves as nations and put new governmental structures in place. But governments became overextended, particularly relative to their weak institutional capacities, as they tried to build national unity and deliver on the promises of independence.

Factors outside Africa also contributed to the decline of the 1970s and 1980s, though their importance is too often exaggerated. Non–oil exporters suffered falls in the terms of trade, but the losses, which actually began in the 1960s, were no larger than those for other developing countries. But the volatility of export receipts—and thus of foreign exchange earnings and fiscal revenues—complicated macroeconomic management. Depending on the availability of foreign exchange, imports went through cycles of compression and decompression, as did growth. Investment budgets and public sector employment expanded rapidly in boom years, hampering adjustment in bust years. Poor policies failed to encourage export diversification and increase international reserves to smooth the impact of adverse shocks.

Domestic Factors: Poor Policies Largely to Blame

There is ample evidence that sound macroeconomic and sectoral policies are associated with higher growth (see box 1.1). Policies in Sub-Saharan Africa, however, have generally been worse than those elsewhere.

Overvalued exchange rates. The presence of unofficial, parallel markets for foreign exchange—in countries with flexible exchange rates—

Box 1.1 Policies Matter for Growth

RESEARCH ON THE DETERMINANTS OF LONG-term growth shows that better policies typically mean faster growth (Barro 1991; Easterly 1992; Killick 1992). The most successful economies maintained good macroeconomic policies, as measured by low inflation, prudent fiscal stances, and realistic exchange rates. Among the macroeconomic variables, the absence of a parallel market—an indication that the exchange rate is not overvalued—generally has the strongest explanatory power. Sectoral policies, such as those for finance and trade, also matter. Countries with larger and more developed financial markets generally grow faster. The same is true for countries with more open trade regimes.

Estimates of how changes in indicators of country policies would affect growth suggest that policies matter a great deal (box table 1.1). For example, a reform package that in the long run raised enrollment ratios by 10 percentage points, eliminated a parallel market premium of 20 percent, raised the ratio of equipment investment to GDP by 3 percentage points, and increased financial depth (the ratio of M2 to GDP) by 10 percentage points would likely raise the annual per capita growth rate by 2.6 percentage points. And if policy reforms were helped by an improvement in the terms of trade of 1 percentage point of GDP a year, annual GDP per capita would grow between 0.4 and 0.8 percentage points. All these improvements, added to the 0.9 percent annual growth that Africa experienced between 1965 and 1985, would bring Africa's long-run GDP per capita growth rate to about 4 percent a year—close to East Asia's.

Box Table 1.1 How Would Changes in Selected Variables Affect GDP per Capita Growth?

Variable	Increase in variable (percentage points)	Estimated change in growth (percentage points)
Ratio of investment to GDP	1	+0.1 to 0.2
Primary school enrollment ratio	10	+0.2 to 0.3
Secondary school enrollment ratio	10	+0.2 to 0.3
Parallel market exchange rate premium	10	−0.4
Ratio of M2 to GDP	10	+0.2 to 0.4
Ratio of average producer input price to world market price	10	−0.4
Ratio of government consumption to GDP	10	−1.2
Ratio of equipment investment to GDP	1	+0.3
Ratio of average change in terms of trade to GDP	1	+0.4 to 0.8

Source: Easterly (1992), table 1.

reveals overvaluation of the real effective exchange rate.[1] Africa's parallel market premiums have been by far the largest in the developing world, and they increased significantly until the adjustment period (figure 1.4). During the economic crisis in the first half of the 1980s, the average premium was almost 300 percent. Rough estimates indicate that a 10 percent premium is likely to reduce GDP growth by 0.4 percentage points a year (box 1.1). But the impact wanes as the premium goes up, and a 100 percent premium cuts GDP growth by 2 percentage points a year. For Ghana between 1974 and 1980, the parallel

Figure 1.4 Premium on the Parallel Market for Foreign Exchange

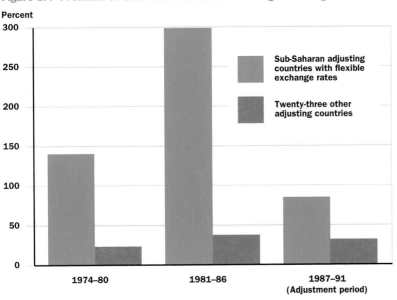

Note: The premium is calculated as the percentage difference between the parallel market exchange rate and the official exchange rate (in domestic currency at the end of the period).
Sources: International Currency Analysis, Inc. (various years); IMF data.

The parallel market premium has been dramatically higher in Africa than elsewhere.

market premium of more than 200 percent explains a slowdown in GDP growth of about 3 percentage points a year.

Heavy government spending. Among the more common indicators of good fiscal policy are a small budget deficit and a low ratio of government consumption (that is, current spending on goods and services) to GDP. Most Sub-Saharan countries had neither. However, while Africa's budget deficits were not much larger than those elsewhere, the ratio of government consumption to GDP was a different story. Consumption began to increase in the early 1960s and reached its peak—nearly 17 percent of GDP—in the early 1980s, exceeding the ratios of other regions by 5 to 6 percentage points (figure 1.5). That excess was important in deterring growth, for statistical analysis shows that over the typical range of government expenditure, each 10 percentage point increase in the ratio of government consumption to GDP typically reduces GDP per capita growth by 1.2 percentage points.

Inward-looking trade policy. Africa's trade policies have also been poor. Most Sub-Saharan economies followed an inward-oriented, import-substitution strategy, supplemented by widespread use of tariff and

Figure 1.5 Government Consumption as a Share of GDP

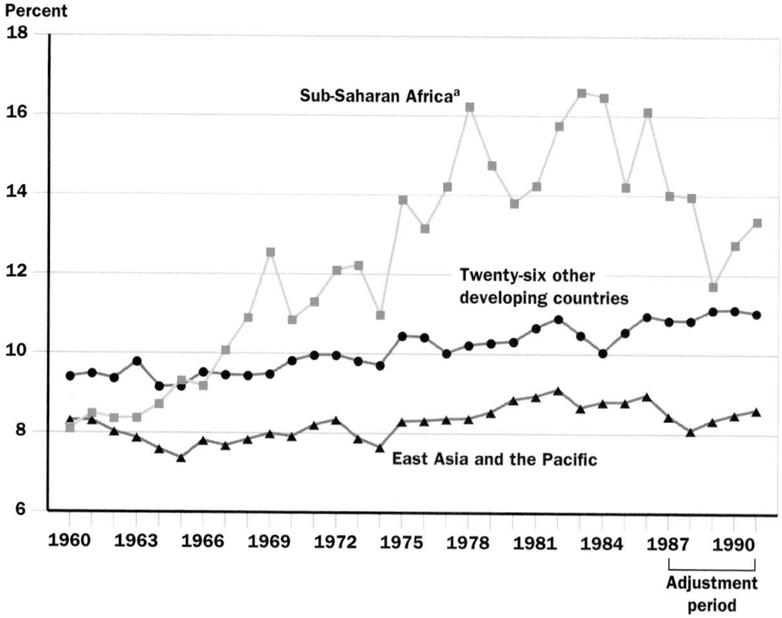

Percent

Note: Data are weighted by 1980 GDP in U.S. dollars.
a. Includes twenty-five countries only.
Source: World Bank data.

African governments outspent others on purchases of goods and services.

nontariff barriers to reduce external competition, mainly in manufacturing. Dollar's (1992) index of outward orientation showed Sub-Saharan African countries as the least outward-oriented—and Asia's high-performing economies as the most (figure 1.6).[2] Of the twenty countries with the highest nontariff barriers, eleven were in Sub-Saharan Africa (Pritchett 1991). This protectionism was another unfortunate policy choice, because competition increases productivity while trade restrictions increase input prices and the cost of capital, choking growth.

Political instability. Political and social stability also are usually associated with higher rates of growth (Barro 1991; Fosu 1992), and the instability in Sub-Saharan Africa partly explains its sluggish performance. More than half the region's countries have been rocked by civil war, uprisings against the government, and devastation from drought and famine, and their average per capita GDP growth was –0.5 percent a year for 1965–85. By contrast, the region's eleven stable countries had an average growth rate of 1.4 percent (Hodd 1991). But the strong

Figure 1.6 Outward Orientation of Selected Country Groups, 1965–85

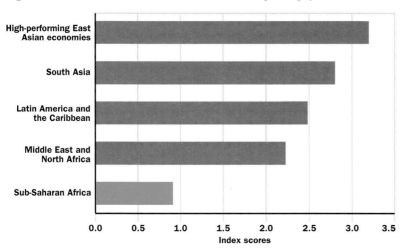

In openness to foreign trade, Africa trailed the world.

Note: A high score corresponds to more outward orientation.
Source: World Bank (1993a), figure 6.4.

association between stability and growth merely raises the question: which is the cause, and which the effect?

Other domestic factors. What about other domestic factors, such as human capital? Of all endowments, human capital probably does most to fuel long-term economic gains. Simply put, countries with skilled people grow faster. The fact that Sub-Saharan Africa trails other regions in social indicators can thus help to explain its slow growth. But how does one reconcile Africa's protracted decline with the fact that human capital, measured by several indicators, *improved* in Sub-Saharan Africa after independence? Primary school enrollments increased from 41 percent of the eligible population to 69 percent between 1965 and the mid-1980s, with girls accounting for much of the increase. Secondary school enrollments increased from 2 to 14 percent, with almost equal increases for boys and girls. Health and nutrition indicators also showed progress. Infant mortality was cut in half, the number of doctors and nurses per capita increased, and life expectancy at birth rose by eight years.

Financial strength is another important determinant of growth: countries with more developed financial sectors grow faster. And financial strength, measured by various indicators, improved in Africa. For instance, M2 as a share of GDP, a measure that indicates how well-developed the financial sector is, increased from about 15 percent in the early

1970s to 20 percent in the mid-1980s. So financial development, like human development, was stemming the decline, not causing it.

International Factors: Surmountable Obstacles

Changes in the terms of trade do have an impact on long-term growth. Easterly and others (1993) found that over the 1980s, for example, a negative terms-of-trade shock averaging 1 percentage point of GDP a year lowered growth by 0.8 percentage points a year. Like other regions, Africa suffered a fall in the terms of trade between the early 1970s and the mid-1980s. But on an annual basis, the terms-of-trade decline was small and thus not a major factor in Africa's poor growth record. Moreover, increased external transfers partially offset the falling terms of trade, limiting the downturn in growth.

Of course, external income from terms-of-trade shocks and external income from transfers (grants or loans) differ in their economic effects and fungibility.

■ External loans have to be repaid, while grants and export earnings do not.

■ The windfall of additional foreign exchange from higher commodity prices can be used freely, while many grants-in-kind, such as food and medicine, do not provide readily available foreign exchange. Even the financial resources provided under grants and loans are often partially tied.

■ Loans and grants primarily affect public income, while changes in the terms of trade have a larger impact on private income.

In practice, however, it is difficult to draw a sharp distinction between income from terms-of-trade gains and that from grants and loans. The reason: loans are often converted to grants or forgiven, and terms-of-trade changes affect the public sector because marketing boards and trade taxes have generally stabilized the real producer prices of exports. Because of the overlapping nature of these two sources of income, we examine their joint evolution.

Declining terms of trade. Most Sub-Saharan economies faced deteriorating terms of trade between 1970 and 1986 (figure 1.7). Oil exporters were the main exceptions, with improvements of more than 100 percent. Non–oil exporters suffered losses of about 30 percent, while mineral exporters were even harder hit, with losses of about 50 percent.

Figure 1.7 Barter Terms of Trade

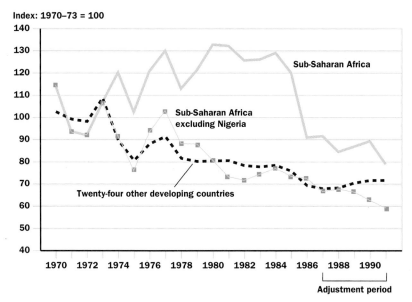

Index: 1970–73 = 100

Note: Data are means weighted by 1980 GDP in U.S. dollars.
Source: World Bank data.

Setting aside Nigeria, Africa's terms-of-trade losses resembled those in other developing countries.

For Sub-Saharan Africa as a whole (excluding Nigeria because of its oil and sheer size), the declining terms of trade meant a drop in external income equivalent to 5.4 percent of GDP between 1971–73 and 1981–86.[3] Though large, the loss was spread over twelve years, for an average annual loss of 0.4 percentage points. Adding Nigeria to the picture reduces the twelve-year loss to just 3.3 percent of GDP, or 0.3 percentage points a year. Again, the losses were biggest for mineral exporters (about 1.5 percentage points a year) and more moderate for the agricultural exporters (about 0.3 percentage points a year). Oil exporters gained from higher prices, increasing GDP about 0.3 percentage points a year.

Although the worsening terms of trade hindered growth, they were not decisive in Africa's stagnation and decline. If an annual income loss of 1 percentage point from declining terms of trade reduces the annual rate of growth by no more than 0.8 percentage points (Easterly and others 1993), then the falling terms of trade can account for no more than 10 percent of the reduction in growth rates between the early 1970s and the mid-1980s. Even for Zambia, probably the region's hardest-hit country, the terms-of-trade deterioration explains only 1 percentage point of the 3.4 percentage point reduction in annual GDP growth. Moreover, Sub-Saharan Africa was not alone. Most low-income countries elsewhere had similar deteriorations in their terms of trade—around 20 percent on average since the early 1970s—and yet they enjoyed faster growth as a result of better policies.

Higher external transfers. Net external transfers increased during the 1970s, in part to compensate for the income losses from the weakening terms of trade. Although the rise in net transfers did not fully offset those losses, it would have been difficult for external sources to have given Africa more assistance. Almost all indicators show that Sub-Saharan Africa already received more assistance than any other region (table 1.1). Net transfers to Sub-Saharan Africa (minus Nigeria) increased from 3.7 percent of GDP in the early 1970s to between 6 and 7 percent of GDP in the late 1970s and early 1980s. By contrast, they remained under 2.4 percent of GDP for the low- and lower-middle-income countries in other regions. Africa was receiving almost $20 per capita in net external transfers, four times the amount going to poor countries elsewhere.

The higher external transfers, however, did not always coincide with African countries' needs for foreign exchange. The transfers in the second half of the 1970s rose with commodity prices, and they fell when commodity prices retreated in the early 1980s. But the average annual

Table 1.1 External Capital Transfers for Low-Income Countries

Indicator	1971–73	1974–80	1981–86	Adjustment period, 1987–91
Net transfers (percentage of GDP)				
Sub-Saharan Africa	2.5	4.3	3.6	4.7
Excluding Nigeria	3.7	7.0	6.4	7.0
Selected other countries[a]	1.1	2.3	1.7	1.1
Net transfers per capita (U.S. dollars)				
Sub-Saharan Africa	5.14	19.18	18.23	16.30
Excluding Nigeria	6.63	22.92	23.11	24.65
Selected other countries[a]	1.59	5.37	5.70	4.01

Note: Net transfers equal net transfers on debt (loan disbursements minus amortization minus interest) plus grants (excluding technical assistance) plus IMF net transfers.

a. Twenty-seven non-African countries with up to $1,200 GNP per capita in 1990.

Source: World Bank data.

flow of net transfers in the late 1970s and early 1980s was about 3 percentage points higher than in the early 1970s, and the economic decline and stagnation started in the mid-1970s when external transfers were high—about 6 percent of GDP.

Moderate income losses overall. The external environment for Sub-Saharan Africa worsened only slightly between the early 1970s and the mid-1980s, because the increase in external transfers partly offset the income loss from deterioration in the terms of trade. If Nigeria is excluded, the decline in the terms of trade caused GDP to drop 5.4 percentage points between 1971–73 and 1981–86, but the increase in external transfers meant an increase in GDP of 2.7 percentage points (table 1.2). Adding these two effects, the total income loss between 1971–73 and 1981–86 was 2.7 percent of GDP, or 0.3 percentage points a year. From this perspective, the external environment was not much different in the mid-1980s from what it had been fifteen years before (and for the oil exporters, the external environment was better).

Meanwhile, Sub-Saharan Africa's GDP per capita growth rate sank 3.2 percentage points (from 2.5 to –0.7 percent). Only a small part of that decline, however, can be attributed to the reduced flows of external income (figure 1.8). Recall that an annual income loss of 1 percent of GDP is estimated to reduce GDP growth by 0.4 to 0.8 percentage points a year (box table 1.1). Between 1971–73 and 1981–86, the annual income

Table 1.2 Effects of Changes in External Income on GDP, 1971–73 to 1981–86

	Change in GDP (percentage points)		
Item	Due to changes in the terms of trade	Due to changes in net transfers[a]	Total
Sub-Saharan Africa			
Period average	–0.3	1.1	0.8
Annual average	–0.0	0.1	0.1
Sub-Saharan Africa excluding Nigeria			
Period average	–5.4	2.7	–2.7
Annual average	–0.5	0.2	–0.3

a. Net transfers equal net transfers on debt (loan disbursements minus amortization minus interest) plus grants (excluding technical assistance) plus IMF net transfers.
Source: World Bank estimates.

Figure 1.8 Changes in GDP per Capita Growth and External Income in Sub-Saharan Africa, Various Periods

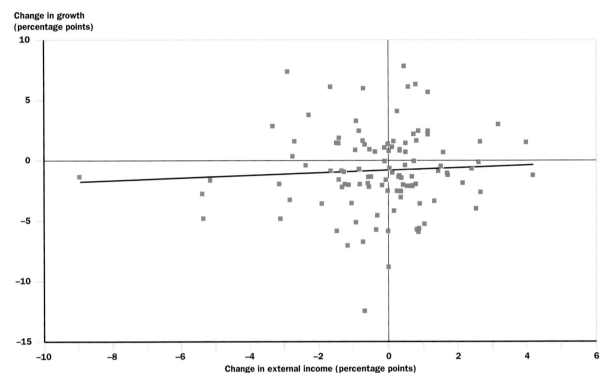

Note: This figure plots three changes (between 1965–73 and 1974–80, between 1974–80 and 1981–86, and between 1981–86 and 1987–91) for thirty-nine countries.

Source: World Bank estimates.

External income shocks had only a small effect on long-term GDP growth.

loss from changes in net transfers and the terms of trade was only 0.3 percent of GDP. The expected effect on GDP growth would thus be a decline of 0.1 to 0.2 percentage points a year—far less than the 3.2 percentage point drop Africa actually suffered.

Failures to capitalize on better terms of trade. Long-term trends in the external environment played only a secondary role in Africa's long-term decline in growth. They may have had a much larger indirect influence on growth, however, to the extent that they contributed to poor policy choices. African countries' limited capacity to manage terms-of-trade fluctuations often led them to adopt exchange rate, fiscal, and agricultural policies that undermined growth over the medium term. Paradoxically, positive terms-of-trade shocks were often as costly as negative ones. A handful of countries had faltering growth despite a better external environment. For example, GDP per capita stagnated in

Nigeria during its oil boom, when the country was flooded with foreign exchange from oil revenues and external loans (box 1.2). Why? The windfall financed wasteful current expenditure, ill-advised investment projects, and capital flight.

The main problem with a windfall is that governments increase spending as if the higher revenues were permanent. And once increased, government spending is difficult to reduce. Consider the coffee and cocoa booms in Côte d'Ivoire and Kenya during the late 1970s. Current and especially capital spending increased, leveraged by external borrowings. But once the booms were over, revenue could not continue to match the spending increases, and governments were left with large deficits. The high expectations generated by the boom made trimming the public sector politically painful. And increasing revenues to cover debt service obligations was difficult because export earnings were dropping. Many of Côte d'Ivoire's macroeconomic problems in the 1980s stemmed directly from expanding the public sector too much during the 1970s boom.

Explaining What Econometric Analyses Don't Explain

The evidence shows that poor policies clearly hurt Africa's long-term growth far more than a hostile external environment did. But neither policy choices nor external factors explain all of the low growth. Cross-country econometric analysis shows that Sub-Saharan Africa has grown more slowly than other regions even after differences in macroeconomic policies, endowments, political instability, and external shocks are taken into account (Easterly and Levine 1993). Other factors—the bias against agriculture, extensive government intervention in the economy, weak infrastructure, and the difficulties of the political and social transition following independence—have been suggested to account for the residual difference in growth performance.

Let us start with the bias against agriculture, perhaps the most important "omitted" variable in econometric analysis. Most Africans live in rural areas, and the region relies heavily on agriculture for foreign exchange. Yet agriculture has been heavily taxed, much more than in other regions (Schiff and Valdes 1992). Producers of agricultural exports—typically forced to sell their crops to marketing boards that monopolized exports—received real prices half those received by producers of similar crops in other countries (Akiyama and Larson 1989). This stifled the region's agricultural growth.

Box 1.2 Nigeria's Missed Opportunity

THE GOVERNMENTS OF INDONESIA AND NIGERIA collected sizable windfalls (about 20 percent of GDP) from the increases in oil prices between 1973 and 1981 (Gelb 1988). Spending judiciously, Indonesia grew steadily. Nigeria, however, saw its GDP per capita growth drop considerably after 1973, and by the end of the 1980s its real GDP per capita was below that in 1973 (box figure 1.1). Where did Nigeria go wrong?

- In Nigeria large budget surpluses from higher oil prices gave way to large budget deficits as expenditure (particularly capital expenditure) increased. In Indonesia, fiscal policy was much more conservative, due in part to a balanced-budget law that prohibits government spending from exceeding government revenues, including official foreign borrowing.

- In Nigeria, government consumption almost doubled between 1965–72 and 1981–86 and then declined sharply after oil prices plummeted in 1986 (box table 1.2). In Indonesia the

Box Table 1.2 Selected Economic Indicators for Indonesia and Nigeria

Indicator	1965–1972	1973–1980	1981–1986	1987–1990
Public consumption (percentage of GDP)				
Indonesia	7.3	9.5	10.9	9.2
Nigeria	8.4	12.4	15.6	11.6
Investment (percentage of GDP)				
Indonesia	12.8	23.3	28.1	33.9
Nigeria	16.6	26.5	16.5	15.4
Real effective exchange rate (index: 1972 = 1.0)				
Indonesia	1.0	0.8	0.9	1.3
Nigeria	1.2	0.8	0.5	1.3

Source: World Bank data.

Box Figure 1.1 Real GDP per Capita in Indonesia and Nigeria

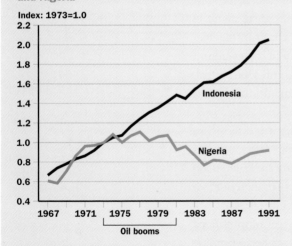

Index: 1973=1.0

Source: World Bank data.

increase and the subsequent decline in government consumption were not as dramatic.

- Nigeria directed its spending to the cities rather than the countryside. Most agricultural spending went to large-scale, capital-intensive projects with low rates of return. Nonagricultural projects, such as a new capital city and an integrated iron and steel industry, also had low returns. Indonesia, by contrast, balanced its investments among physical infrastructure projects, education, agricultural development, and capital-intensive industries (primarily fertilizer), directing a high proportion of its resources to rural areas.

- With the collapse of oil prices, Nigeria slashed investment dramatically, while Indonesia continued to devote a larger share of its GDP to investment. The low incremental capital-output ratios (ICORs) in Indonesia (4.1 for 1973–81) suggest that it was much more successful than Nigeria (with an ICOR of 30.2) at converting investment into sustained growth in current output.

■ Nigeria's real exchange rate had appreciated almost 50 percent by the end of the second oil price increase in 1981, and not until the big devaluations of 1986 and 1987 did it return to 1973 levels. Indonesia, by contrast, had greater real exchange rate appreciation than Nigeria after the first oil price shock in 1973–74, but it devalued its currency much sooner, with a big devaluation in 1978 that led to further depreciation of the exchange rate thereafter.

These different policy choices influenced the growth and structure of exports. Before the first oil price shock, oil made up more than 80 percent of Nigeria's exports, compared with 50 percent for Indonesia. Nigeria moved toward greater dependence on hydrocarbons, with oil exports rising to more than 90 percent of exports. Only after the big devaluations in the mid-1980s did Nigeria have any growth in its non-oil exports. Indonesia strengthened and diversified non-hydrocarbon exports during and after the oil price booms. With substantial growth in non-oil exports throughout the 1970s and 1980s, oil exports constituted only about 20 percent of Indonesia's total exports by the end of the 1980s.

Another reason why econometric analyses do not fully explain Africa's low growth may be that easily accessible policy indicators fail to capture the intricacies of policy intervention in the region. African governments took an active stance in setting prices, nationalizing banks, establishing price controls, rationing foreign exchange, creating public monopolies for agricultural exports, imposing licenses to restrict the activities the private sector could undertake, and creating many state enterprises and giving them special access to scarce credit and foreign exchange. None of these interventions nor their impact is easy to quantify, because the required data are generally either unavailable or unreliable.

Moreover, these interventions created a strong bias against the private sector, which also must have contributed to the economic decline. Administrative bottlenecks, rents from licensing requirements, and inefficient public services imposed high costs on private business. The gradual breakdown in judicial systems and the expropriation of private property in many countries in the 1970s left many private enterprises, particularly foreign ones, doubtful about the wisdom of continuing to invest. Some businesses continued only under special contracts or special trade restrictions that offset the high risks.

A third important factor is the extent and quality of infrastructure. Africa's slow growth may be attributable in part to its relatively inefficient transport system, telecommunications network, and public utilities. It is unlikely, however, that the infrastructure base actually deteriorated during the mid-1970s to early 1980s, which might have accounted for some of the decline in GDP growth, because investment in infrastructure burgeoned during this period.

A fourth possible factor that econometrics neglects is ideology, which has been important in setting the policy agenda in African countries. Classifying countries as African capitalists, African populist-socialists, and Afro-Marxists—according to the prevailing ideology—shows that the capitalists experienced the fastest growth (Young 1982). There were exceptions, of course. Some Afro-Marxist countries (especially Congo) did well thanks to the oil windfall, while some capitalist countries (such as Zaire) did not, because of political and social instability.

A fifth factor that should be considered is the widespread deterioration in governance in the 1970s and 1980s. As countries tried to meet the aspirations for rapid development that were unleashed at independence, and as they tried to consolidate their political base, they expanded the role of the state. Highly authoritarian and highly centralized governments were inimical to the development of local organizations and associations that might have demanded better governance. The costs associated with poor governance extend beyond what is usually captured in policy variables.

All these factors no doubt played some role in Africa's poor economic performance. But we can only speculate about their relevance, because they are difficult to quantify and test rigorously.

The Needed Switch in Policies

THE REFORM PROGRAMS THAT MANY AFRICAN COUNTRIES initiated in the mid-1980s—with the support of the International Monetary Fund, the World Bank, and other donors—reflected a new paradigm. The reforms attempted to reduce the state's role in production and in regulating private economic activity. They assigned more importance to exports, especially those from the much-neglected agricultural sector. And they placed more emphasis on maintaining macroeconomic stability and avoiding overvalued exchange rates. The process of revamping the policy framework in line with this new paradigm became known as structural adjustment.

One of the most fundamental shifts in the development strategy for Africa was to view agriculture not as a backward sector but as the engine of growth—an important source of export revenues and the primary means to reduce poverty. Improving the incentives and the infrastructure services for farmers is now a key element in adjustment programs. On the macroeconomic side, the focus is on keeping inflation low, exchange rates competitive, and budget deficits sustainable. Furthermore, to enable people to develop efficient and productive businesses, the state is pulling back from direct intervention in the economy and improving its capacity to provide basic services and a stable policy environment.

In the next three chapters, we assess the extent of structural adjustment reforms in Sub-Saharan Africa. We report on twenty-nine countries with adjustment programs in place during the latter part of the 1980s (see box 1.3). How far have those countries come in reforming their policies? And how much further do they have to go? Chapter 2 focuses on changes in macroeconomic policies, usually tackled early in the adjustment process to eliminate major distortions. Chapter 3 examines progress in trade and agricultural reforms, vital to making more efficient and productive use of economic resources. Chapter 4 examines reforms in the areas crucial to a reorientation of the role of the state: the financial sector, the public enterprise sector, and the public sector. These assessments provide a basis for examining the payoffs to the adjustment process, the subject of chapter 5. Chapter 6 reviews the evidence on the impact of adjustment on poverty and the environment. The book concludes with chapter 7, a look at the road ahead for African adjusting countries.

Will the shift in policies enable Africa to catch up? Standard growth theory predicts that low-income countries will grow faster than high-income countries, because they can borrow technologies from the rest of the world and increase the marginal productivity of capital more rapidly than advanced countries. But this requires actively taking advantage of the technology, knowledge, and experience of other nations. And in Africa, the commitment to an outward-oriented development strategy is not yet strong.

Even with good policies, catching up is not easy. So far, low-income countries have had less success than middle-income countries in growing quickly. Poor policies explain some of the lag, but poor endowments might also limit the potential for rapid growth in the short term, underlining the importance of investing in human capital and strengthening

Box 1.3 Country Coverage and Time Frame of the Study

THIS STUDY FOCUSES ON TWENTY-NINE COUNtries in Sub-Saharan Africa that were undergoing structural adjustment sometime between 1987 and 1991 (see box table 1.3). We excluded the very small economies, some of which had adjustment programs, because there is less information about them and because external aid disproportionately affects their macroeconomic performance. We also excluded countries that did not have adjustment programs between 1987 and 1991, either because they experienced great social unrest or civil war during most of those years or because—mainly in the case of countries in the South African Customs Union—they had a tradition of better policies and were less affected by the external problems of the early 1980s. Mauritius was also excluded because it "graduated" from adjustment in the mid-1980s.

The text refers to 1987–91 as "the adjustment period," although individual country experience does not always conform precisely to this definition. We used 1987 as the starting point because more than half the countries had initiated reform programs by then. We made 1991 the cutoff point because macroeconomic data for all countries were available only through that year. A few countries in the sample, such as Ghana, Kenya, and Malawi, actually launched their adjustment programs in the early 1980s and had already implemented some durable reforms by 1987. Other countries, including Côte d'Ivoire and Zambia, started adjustment in the early 1980s but later reversed important reforms; later still, they adopted new programs. Several other countries, such as Burkina Faso, Rwanda, Sierra Leone, and Zimbabwe, did not initiate reforms until very late in the adjustment period.

Box Table 1.3 Classification of Countries

Countries in the study sample (adjusters during 1987–91)		Countries not in the study		
		Small countries[a]	Countries with civil unrest	Other countries
Benin	Madagascar	Cape Verde	Angola	Botswana
Burkina Faso	Malawi	Comoros	Ethiopia[b]	Lesotho
Burundi	Mali	Djibouti	Liberia	Mauritius
Cameroon	Mauritania	Equatorial Guinea	Somalia	Namibia
Central African	Mozambique	São Tomé and	Sudan	Swaziland
Republic	Niger	Principe	Zaire	
Chad	Nigeria	Seychelles		
Congo	Rwanda			
Côte d'Ivoire	Senegal			
Gabon	Sierra Leone			
The Gambia	Tanzania			
Ghana	Togo			
Guinea	Uganda			
Guinea-Bissau	Zambia			
Kenya	Zimbabwe			

a. With populations under 500,000 in 1991.

b. Ethiopia recently ended its civil war and embarked on a wide-ranging reform program.

institutional capacity. Africa's high rate of population growth—over 3 percent a year—puts additional stress on the limited resources available for improving human capital. Adjustment programs can establish a framework that encourages sound investment and efficient resource use. They are no substitute, however, for the long-term development efforts needed to build the capabilities of Africa's people. (See box 1.4 for a discussion of the relationship between adjustment and development.)

What is encouraging is that in the 1960s, before their takeoffs, Indonesia, Malaysia, and Thailand had conditions similar to those in Africa in 1990 (table 1.3). GDP per capita was higher on average in Southeast Asia, but Indonesia's income was close to that in Ghana, Malawi, and Tanzania today, and Thailand's was comparable to that of

Box 1.4 Adjustment for Sustained Development

ECONOMIC AND SOCIAL DEVELOPMENT IS A process of achieving sustainable increases in health, education, material consumption, and environmental protection—in short, improving standards of living over the long term. Structural adjustment contributes to development by establishing the market-friendly incentives needed to put economies on sustainable, poverty-reducing growth paths. But adjusting the incentive framework to foster efficient production and private initiative will not alone bring about development. As *Sub-Saharan Africa: From Crisis to Sustainable Development* (World Bank 1989a) points out, development also depends on good governance, appropriate infrastructure and institutions, and better-trained people. Sound policies and a strong infrastructure create the conditions for economic growth, but growth will be raised and sustained only if human and institutional capabilities are built up. This requires investments in basic health and nutrition, education, and technical skills. It also requires that public and private institutions be restructured to create an environment in which capable people can work effectively, and that political leadership be committed to nurturing those institutions, not to politicizing them for narrow objectives.

Africa's structural adjustment programs, and those elsewhere, were almost always mounted in response to a crisis triggered by external shocks but engendered by poor policies. No economy can function well for long if it has rampant inflation, an overvalued exchange rate, excessive taxation of the agricultural sector, scarce supplies of needed imports, regulations on prices and production, deficient public services, and limited financial services. To shore up such economies, the first order of business should be fundamental policy reform—restoring macroeconomic balances and reducing the large distortions in the incentive framework. This sets the stage for the more efficient allocation of resources and capital accumulation needed for development to take place.

Often there is synergy between policy reform and a country's level of development. Greater technical and institutional capacity makes it easier to adjust policies to changing conditions, and stronger adjustment efforts increase the returns on investment and speed up the development process. Moving from a vicious circle of bad policies and a low level of development to a virtuous circle of good policies and a higher level of development is the challenge facing Africa.

Table 1.3 Sub-Saharan Africa in 1990 versus Southeast Asia in 1965: Means for Selected Indicators

Indicator	Sub-Saharan Africa, 1990[a]	Indonesia, Malaysia, and Thailand, 1965[b]
GDP per capita (constant 1985 international dollars)[c]	1,030.0	1,320.0
Agriculture share of GDP (percent)	32.0	37.0
Manufacturing share of GDP (percent)	11.0[d]	10.3
Savings share of GDP (percent)	16.0	17.0
Investment share of GDP (percent)	16.0	16.0
Export share of GDP (percent)[e]	29.0	21.0
M2 share of GDP (percent)	19.4	19.6[f]
Urban share of total population (percent)	29.0	18.3
Primary school enrollment (percentage of eligible population)	68.0	80.0
Secondary school enrollment (percentage of eligible population)	17.0	18.0
Adult illiteracy rate (percentage of population over age 15)[g]	50.0	35.3
Population per physician (thousands)[h]	23.5	15.0
Infant mortality (number of deaths before age 1 per 1,000 live births)	107.0	90.3
Life expectancy (years)	51.0	52.5
Population growth rate (percent)	3.1[i]	2.7[j]

a. Data are weighted means for selected countries.

b. Data are unweighted means.

c. Data are based on results of the United Nations International Comparisons Program (ICP). For details on the calculations, see World Bank (1992d), pp. 299–301.

d. Data are for 1989.

e. Exports of goods and nonfactor services.

f. Indonesia data are from 1969.

g. Illiteracy is defined here as the inability to read and write a short, simple statement on one's everyday life.

h. Physicians here include medical assistants who have less training than qualified physicians but who perform similar services, including operations.

i. Average annual growth rate from 1980 to 1990.

j. From 1964 to 1965.

Sources: World Bank (1992d and 1993d); World Bank data; IMF data.

middle-income African countries today. One major difference between Asia then and Africa now: Africa has lower primary school enrollment. This is not inconsequential; emphasis on universal primary education was a key to achieving rapid and equitable economic growth in the best-performing Asian economies (World Bank 1993a). And African countries with a higher percentage of children enrolled in primary school in 1960 grew more quickly over the next two decades than countries with lower enrollment rates (figure 1.9). Africa's runaway population growth also puts it at more of a disadvantage than Asia in the 1960s. With half the population under fifteen years old, Africans of working age face an enormous challenge—bringing about the high rate of economic growth needed to provide a better future for the next generation.

Figure 1.9 Education and GDP per Capita Growth

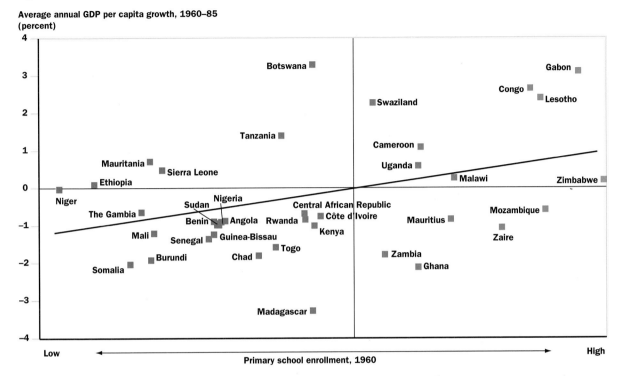

Average annual GDP per capita growth, 1960–85
(percent)

Note: This figure is a partial scattergram based on a regression of primary school enrollment and other factors on GDP per capita growth.
Source: Barro (1991).

Higher primary school enrollments pay off in higher growth.

The importance of reforms for Africa's economic future cannot be overstated. With today's poor policies, it will be forty years before the region returns to its per capita income of the mid-1970s. But a sound development strategy and a dose of good luck can change the picture. Ghana, for example, has the potential to become a middle-income country by the fiftieth anniversary of its independence, as box 1.5 shows. We should be mindful that the Asian countries that have been stunning the world with their strong GDP per capita growth since 1960 had almost no growth between 1930 and 1960 (Maddison 1989). This does not mean that success will come easily to Africa in the next three decades. It does mean that rapid growth is possible, and that Africa's poor record over the past twenty years is no reason for undue pessimism about its future.

Box 1.5 Moving from Adjustment to Development in Ghana

THE GHANAIAN ECONOMY STANDS AT A CROSS-roads. Its adjustment program is one of the most successful in Sub-Saharan Africa. Since 1983, a decade of stabilizing policies has yielded broad budget balance, strong export growth, a reasonable external position, and substantial structural reforms, including privatization or closure of some loss-making publicly owned companies. Even so, real growth has remained at only about 5 percent a year. And although per capita income rose about 2 percent a year, ending the 1980s at $390, Ghana is still among the world's poorest countries. At this growth rate, the average poor Ghanaian will not cross the poverty line for another fifty years.

What would it take for Ghana to become a middle-income country by the year 2007, the fiftieth anniversary of Ghanaian independence? What would ensure that the average poor Ghanaian would no longer live in poverty by then? In recent years, Ghana's policymakers have begun to refocus their attention from short-term adjustment issues to longer-term growth and development issues.

The recent dynamic growth in East Asia shows what can be achieved with pragmatic government policies and a disciplined, hard-working population that responds to the right incentives. Malaysia and Thailand, which were poorer than Ghana in the 1960s, managed to double per capita income and reduce poverty dramatically in about ten years. They have now eclipsed Ghana in other measures of development as well (box figure 1.2). Ghana can profit from East Asia's experience by emphasizing three areas: education and health, openness to international markets, and partnership between government and the private sector.

Human development. Most successful economies achieve near-universal literacy as a precondition for rapid growth. While Ghana's secondary and tertiary education systems compare favorably with those of the fast-growing Asian economies at the start of their economic ascent, the same is not true in primary

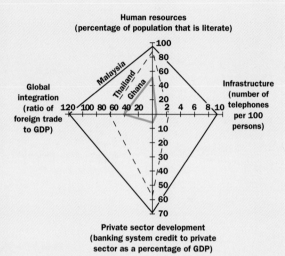

Box Figure 1.2 Development Diamonds for Ghana, Thailand, and Malaysia, 1989

Source: World Bank (1993b).

education. Ghana's literacy rate is about 55 percent, and its functional literacy rate about 35 to 40 percent—much lower than in many other African countries. Ghana needs to focus the bulk of its education spending on literacy programs and primary education, relying more heavily on private funding for secondary and tertiary education. In the area of health, Ghana must redirect resources from hospitals and curative care to equitable primary health care, preventative medicine, and nutrition programs.

Openness. Strong export performance has been an important factor in East Asia's rapid growth. If Ghana is to achieve similar success, it must export more aggressively, focusing especially on agriculture, agro-processed products, and light manufacturing. At 15 percent of GDP, Ghana's export ratio is low because noncocoa, nonmineral exports are small.

What can the government do to push export growth? It can continue its appropriate exchange rate policies, which provide nondiscriminatory export incentives. It can change production and trade regulations to facilitate the entry of foreign companies and improve tariff levels, export finance, and quality control. It can promote better export infrastructure (better telecommunications, warehousing, and refrigeration). And because labor costs are an important factor in determining the competitiveness of exports, Ghana can work to link wage bargaining more closely to labor productivity.

Working with business. Ideally, governments should have a clearly defined role and a complementary relationship with the private sector. East Asian governments have geared their spending to promoting and not competing with the private sector. Moreover, because of vigorous revenue mobilization, the public sector has been a net saver since the 1960s, rarely crowding out the private sector.

Ghana's spending has been less prudent, and, although fiscal policy is improving, there is scope to do far better. The public sector deficit could be reduced by cutting transfers to state enterprises; reducing unfunded liabilities, such as end-of-service benefits; reducing costly subsidies for water, electricity, and transport; and improving revenue mobilization through a value-added tax. At the same time, spending (in such areas as primary education and health, transport infrastructure, and research and extension) will have to increase considerably to accelerate growth. For this reason, Ghana must not only improve financial management of the public sector but also encourage private investment.

Private sector confidence and investment have been undermined by a web of old controls and regulations, a lack of transparency in enforcing those regulations, and continued government ownership of production activities, despite the government's stated intention of leaving those activities to the private sector. Ghana is, however, already making serious efforts to improve the climate for business—pushing for clearer business procedures, due process, and speedy divestiture.

Source: World Bank (1993b).

Notes

1. The countries of the CFA franc zone, which have fixed exchange rates pegged to the French franc, have no parallel markets for foreign exchange.

2. The index of outward orientation measures the extent to which the real exchange rate is distorted away from its free-trade level by the trade regime. The high-performing Asian economies are Hong Kong; Indonesia; Japan; the Republic of Korea; Malaysia; Singapore; Taiwan, China; and Thailand.

3. Estimating how changes in the barter terms of trade affect income is complex, and alternative methods may be applied. We calculated the average terms-of-trade index (using the barter terms-of-trade index) for the periods 1970–73 and 1981–86. The "income effect" of changes in the terms of trade between the two periods was then calculated by multiplying the ratio of exports of goods and nonfactor services to GDP in 1987 by the percentage change in the average terms-of-trade index between 1970–73 and 1981–86. The "income effect" thus is a measure of the share of GDP gained or lost as a result of terms-of-trade changes.

CHAPTER 2

Moving Toward Sound Macroeconomic Policies

THE MACROECONOMIC SITUATION IN SUB-SAHARAN Africa reached crisis proportions in the early 1980s. External imbalances mounted as real export revenues plummeted and imports remained unchanged. Currencies were wildly overvalued, with the parallel market premiums for foreign exchange exceeding 100 percent. Budget deficits soared to more than 7 percent of GDP, and because of the debt crisis, many countries lost their access to commercial lending.

African countries had to reestablish a balance between income and spending to improve the balance of payments. This required a tightening of fiscal and credit policies and a depreciation of the real exchange rate. Tight fiscal and credit policies cut overall spending in the economy, while depreciation expanded production in the tradable sector and eased the recessionary impact of the tighter demand policies. Macroeconomic packages of this type worked for Costa Rica, Indonesia, the Republic of Korea, and other developing countries facing similar imbalances during the early 1980s. In Africa, Ghana and Mauritius were among the first to take bold steps along these lines. But in the first half of the decade, other countries did not do enough to reduce their budget deficits, and they were reluctant to depreciate their currencies to restore competitiveness.

The failure to take drastic action early was coupled with a series of inappropriate responses that merely deepened the crisis. Most countries with flexible exchange rates failed to devalue and to contract demand. Instead, they imposed foreign exchange controls and intensified the use of import licenses to allocate their increasingly scarce foreign exchange.[1] The new restrictions deprived domestic firms of intermediate inputs and spare parts, strangling growth and worsening the allocation of resources. Such moves locked many of these economies in a vicious circle. Increases in the parallel market premium for foreign exchange led to further deteriorations in the recorded trade balance, forcing the authorities to impose even tighter import restrictions. Shrinking exports and worsening export prices (in domestic currencies) reduced official export earnings, further increasing the parallel market premium. Growth suffered along the way, as producers lost access to the imported inputs they needed to keep production going. GDP per capita in countries with flexible exchange rates declined at 1.5 percent a year in the first half of the 1980s, after stagnating in the second half of the 1970s. Forced to look for better alternatives, most of them started reform programs in the mid-1980s—programs that combined better macroeconomic and sectoral policies with large increases in external financing.

The macroeconomic crisis was different for countries with fixed exchange rates.[2] They suffered balance-of-payments and fiscal problems similar to those in the countries with flexible exchange rates, but they never restricted access to foreign exchange.[3] They continued to abide by the rules of the CFA franc zone and maintained fully convertible currencies. Their crises were less severe than those in other African countries because exporters benefited from the real depreciation of the French franc—the peg for their currencies—against the dollar in the first half of the 1980s. Nonetheless, the fixed exchange rate countries saw their GDP per capita growth plummet—about 3 percentage points between 1974–80 and 1981–86—and their real imports shrink by about 25 percent. Côte d'Ivoire's crisis was particularly severe, with GDP per capita growth collapsing from 3.5 percent a year in the late 1970s to –5 percent in the first half of the 1980s.

The adjusting Sub-Saharan countries generally improved their macroeconomic policies in the second half of the 1980s. Tighter fiscal and credit policies, accompanied by increased foreign financing, helped improve the balance of payments and move economies out of the import-compression phase of adjustment. The policy packages have been most effective when they controlled inflation and brought about the much-needed depreciation of the real exchange rate. Despite the improvements, none of the countries in the region has yet achieved a good macroeconomic stance. In what follows we analyze the three key components of macroeconomic adjustment programs—monetary, fiscal, and exchange rate policies—and we examine the overall policy packages.[4]

Fiscal Deficits Down—But Not Out

MOST AFRICAN COUNTRIES STARTED THE 1980S WITH large fiscal imbalances from high government spending—the legacy of commodity booms in the late 1970s—and declining trade tax revenues because of the collapse of commodity prices in the early 1980s. Budget deficits (including grants) in excess of 7 percent of GDP were the norm. Because high budget deficits usually mean rapid money growth, high inflation, and large current account deficits, this was hardly the basis for a sound macroeconomic climate (Easterly and Schmidt-Hebbel 1991; Kiguel and O'Connell 1993).

Budget Deficits

A low budget deficit is not a sufficient sign of good policy, but it is certainly a necessary component. More than half of the African adjusting countries reduced their overall budget deficits between 1981–86 and 1990–91. Other measures of fiscal health, such as the primary deficit, provide a similar picture.

The overall fiscal deficit including grants indicates how much the government would have to borrow to achieve fiscal balance. Because most countries have limited access to domestic and foreign financing, the overall deficit measures the potential risks of resorting to inflationary finance or financing deficits domestically in other distortionary ways (such as incurring arrears with government suppliers or taxing the financial sector). Based on this indicator, the adjusting countries in the region improved their fiscal performance, reducing the median overall deficit including grants from 6.4 percent of GDP in 1981–86 to 5.2 percent of GDP in 1990–91 (figure 2.1). But the median improvement disguises differences among country groups (appendix table A.2). Five of the six countries with the largest reductions (more than 5 percentage points)—Burundi, The Gambia, Malawi, Tanzania, and Zambia—are low-income, flexible exchange rate countries. In contrast, the middle-income countries, those with fixed exchange rates, and the oil exporters had their overall fiscal balances deteriorate, with Cameroon and Côte d'Ivoire having the largest increases in deficits.

Another measure of the fiscal balance is the primary deficit, calculated by deducting interest payments from total expenditure. Change in the primary deficit is considered a better indicator of fiscal performance

Figure 2.1 Fiscal Indicators for African Adjusting Countries
(medians)

Fiscal Deficit

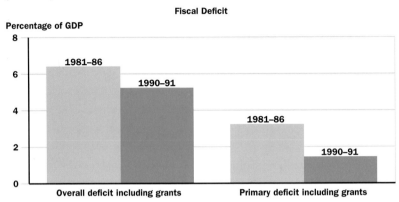

Total Revenue and Expenditure

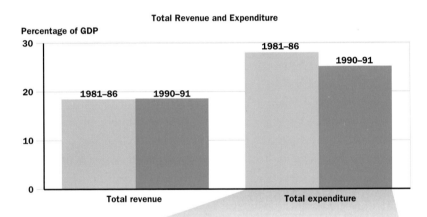

Composition of Total Expenditure

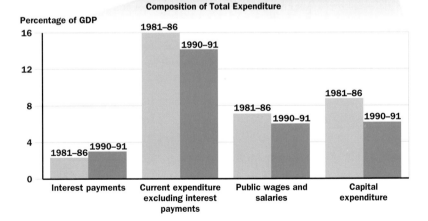

Deficit reductions were primarily due to lower expenditures.

Note: Chad, Guinea, and Guinea-Bissau are excluded because of insufficient data.
Sources: IMF staff estimates; Nashashibi and Bazzoni (1994).

than change in the overall deficit, because fluctuations in external interest payments are largely beyond government control in the short term. The primary fiscal deficit as a share of GDP improved in the adjusting countries, with a median decrease of almost 2 percentage points. This was more than the decrease in the overall fiscal deficit, because interest expenditures rose in most countries and partly offset efforts to reduce the overall deficit. Again, as with the overall fiscal balance, improvements in the primary fiscal balance were larger for the low-income countries and those with flexible exchange rates than for the middle-income countries and those with fixed exchange rates.

Despite the deficit reductions, the fiscal situation in Sub-Saharan Africa is still fragile. Most countries still rely heavily on grants to avoid fiscal imbalances, and the median deficit excluding grants has remained large—about 8 percent of GDP—since the 1980s. Indeed, the 1.3 percentage point increase in external grants between the early 1980s and 1990–91 contributed heavily to reducing the overall budget deficit during this period.

Expenditure Fell, But Revenue Increased Only Slightly

The reduction in budget deficits was helped by lower spending, with a median decline of 1 percentage point of GDP, despite an increase in interest payments of about 0.9 percentage points of GDP. Most of the cuts were in capital spending; the median fell from 8.7 percent of GDP in the early 1980s to 6.1 percent in 1990–91. This was unfortunate, because the level of capital spending was not excessive in most countries, although its composition needed improvement. The cuts were deeper for the middle-income and the fixed exchange rate countries, and deepest for the oil exporters—not surprising because they started with bloated public investment programs.

The overall public wage bill generally fell less than 1 percentage point, as inflation eroded public sector wages. But in the middle-income and oil-exporting countries, which expanded employment and kept real wages high, median spending on wages and salaries rose 3 to 4 percentage points. The five countries with the largest increases in the wage bill as a share of GDP (Cameroon, Congo, Côte d'Ivoire, Gabon, and Zimbabwe) are all middle-income countries, and three of them are oil exporters.[5]

Ideally, spending cuts by African governments would have been reinforced by revenue increases. But in more than half the countries, government revenue did not increase. For all the adjusting countries, the

Table 2.1 Fiscal Policy Stance, 1990–91

Good or adequate	
The Gambia	★★★★
Ghana	★★★★
Mauritania	★★★★
Senegal	★★★★
Tanzania	★★★★
Fair	
Burundi	★★★
Burkina Faso	★★★
Gabon	★★★
Malawi	★★★
Togo	★★★
Poor	
Benin	★★
Central African Rep.	★★
Kenya	★★
Madagascar	★★
Mali	★★
Nigeria	★★
Rwanda	★★
Uganda	★★
Very poor	
Cameroon	★
Congo	★
Côte d'Ivoire	★
Mozambique	★
Niger	★
Sierra Leone	★
Zambia	★
Zimbabwe	★

Note: A "good or adequate" rating indicates a budget surplus or an overall budget deficit (including grants) of less than 1.5 percent of GDP; "fair," a deficit of 1.5–3.5 percent; "poor," a deficit of 3.6–7.0 percent; and "very poor," a deficit of 7.1 percent or more. Chad, Guinea, and Guinea-Bissau are excluded because of insufficient data.

Source: Appendix table B.5.

median tax revenue as a share of GDP fell 0.5 percentage points. Revenue losses were particularly large—as much as 9.8 percent of GDP—in the oil-exporting countries with fixed exchange rates (Cameroon, Congo, and Gabon). The decline in oil prices and the appreciation of the real exchange rate reduced their revenue from trade taxes, and fixed exchange rate countries as a whole were hard-hit by deep recessions. Nigeria, the only oil exporter with a flexible exchange rate, avoided such revenue reductions by effecting a large real depreciation that more than offset the decline in oil prices. Low-income countries with flexible exchange rates did better as a group, because trade taxes increased and economic growth picked up. Ghana and Tanzania did particularly well, but Madagascar, Uganda, and Zambia suffered revenue declines largely because of the erosion in the real value of tax revenues associated with higher inflation.[6]

Fiscal Stance

The criterion for classifying countries by fiscal stance was the overall budget deficit (on an accrual basis including grants), which shows the amount of financing required.[7] Countries with high budget deficits after grants generally need to improve their fiscal accounts to avoid inflation or crowding out domestic investment. While high budget deficits are not necessarily inflationary in the short term—as they can be financed directly or indirectly, domestically or abroad—they are likely to be inflationary in the longer term if they are sustained.

Based on the size of the total fiscal deficit including grants, all countries still need more fiscal adjustment—and in some instances considerably more. Only five countries had a good or adequate fiscal stance in 1990–91 (table 2.1), and two of them—The Gambia and Tanzania—rely heavily on grants. This shows how fragile public finances are in Africa, and how quickly a fall in external assistance could destabilize them.

Monetary Policy Mostly on Track

THE MAIN GOALS OF MONETARY POLICY ARE TO MAINTAIN low rates of inflation and suitable levels of economic activity through adequate real interest rates. In Africa during the adjustment period, there was no clear trend in the evolution of monetary policy. Median inflation—generally low to begin with—fell a couple of percentage points, with wide variation across countries. There was also progress in reducing (or eliminating) the highly negative real interest rates that discourage savings. But in some countries, the choice of poor or inconsistent macroeconomic policies resulted in highly positive real interest rates, which are not conducive to growth.

We analyzed the monetary stance in African adjusting countries based on three indicators: the revenue from printing money (seigniorage), the rate of inflation, and the real interest rate. With few exceptions, monetary policies in 1990–91 were fair or better (table 2.2). Inflation was not a major problem in most of the economies, and seigniorage was low compared with other developing countries, but there was room for improvement in interest rate policy.

Seigniorage and Inflation

Governments, through their central banks, obtain revenue from their exclusive privilege of printing money. That revenue, expressed as a share of GDP, is called seigniorage.[8] The main advantage of using seigniorage as an indicator of monetary policy—as opposed to other common indicators, such as money growth—is that it tells whether central banks are printing money to finance budget deficits. The higher the seigniorage, the larger the resources that governments gain from printing money, and thus the more inflationary the monetary policy. But higher seigniorage does not always mean a higher inflation rate, especially in the short run. It is not inflationary if it accommodates an increase in the demand for money, if it is mainly transitory, or if there are lags in the transmission of increases in the money supply to prices. In the longer run, however, higher seigniorage means higher inflation. As a general rule, seigniorage of more than 2 percent of GDP is risky, because the economy will eventually have high inflation; seigniorage of more than 3 percent for several years indicates large macroeconomic imbalances.[9]

Most Sub-Saharan African countries have had low or moderate seigniorage, consistent with the fact that inflation has also been relatively low (appendix table A.3). The median rate of inflation was just 10.6 percent before the adjustment period, certainly lower than in Latin America and no higher than in other developing countries. By 1990–91,

Table 2.2 Monetary Policy Stance, 1990–91

Good or adequate	
Burkina Faso	★★★★
Burundi	★★★★
Central African Rep.	★★★★
Côte d'Ivoire	★★★★
Gabon	★★★★
Mali	★★★★
Fair	
Benin	★★★
Cameroon	★★★
Congo	★★★
The Gambia	★★★
Ghana	★★★
Kenya	★★★
Madagascar	★★★
Malawi	★★★
Mauritania	★★★
Niger	★★★
Nigeria	★★★
Rwanda	★★★
Senegal	★★★
Togo	★★★
Uganda	★★★
Zimbabwe	★★★
Poor	
Mozambique	★★
Tanzania	★★
Very poor	
Sierra Leone	★
Zambia	★

Note: Ratings range from "good or adequate," which generally means low seigniorage (less than 0.5 percent of GDP), low inflation (less than 10 percent), and reasonable interest rates (−3 to 3 percent), to "very poor," which means high seigniorage, inflation over 100 percent, and high or extremely negative interest rates. Chad, Guinea, and Guinea-Bissau are excluded because of insufficient data.

Source: Appendix table B.5.

it had dropped to 8 percent. Even among the flexible exchange rate countries, which have had the highest inflation rates in the region, the median has hovered around 20 percent—high by international standards, but not a sign of major macroeconomic imbalance.

The fixed exchange rate has been a useful discipline mechanism. Nine of the ten countries with seigniorage below 0.5 percent of GDP in 1990–91 had fixed exchange rates, and their median inflation was just 0.6 percent. Some countries with high seigniorage have not always had high inflation (though they might be headed in that direction if the high seigniorage persists).[10] Only three countries—Sierra Leone, Tanzania, and Zambia—had high seigniorage and high inflation in 1990–91, showing that their monetary policy was poor and improvement clearly needed.

Interest Rates

High real interest rates usually mean that monetary (or credit) policy is tight and that the monetary authorities are trying to cool off the economy. Low real interest rates, by contrast, generally indicate expansionary monetary policy. Real interest rates that for long periods remain high and negative—or high and positive—are a problem. The highly negative ones indicate that inflation is high and depositors heavily taxed, hurting domestic savings. The highly positive ones suggest that credit policies are too tight and that there is excess demand for credit—or that a high rate is needed to stem capital flight because people expect a depreciation. Highly positive rates are riskier for the financial soundness of banks; forced to lend at high real rates to remain profitable, they assume more risk than prudent financial practices would warrant.

Interest rates in Africa have limited value as an indicator of monetary policy because they are not market-determined—financial markets are thin and the government sets the rates. Interest rate liberalization and a decline in inflation have helped eliminate extremely negative real interest rates (appendix table A.4), though interest rates continue to be negative in a few countries, particularly Sierra Leone and Zimbabwe. In contrast, eleven countries—ten of them with fixed exchange rates—had high real interest rates in 1990–91 (above 3 percent). Those elevated rates were the result of tight monetary and credit policies needed to restrain aggregate demand, to support the fixed exchange rate, and to avoid capital outflows.

Mixed Progress in Exchange Rate Policy

MOST SUB-SAHARAN AFRICAN COUNTRIES REQUIRED A real depreciation to compensate for the worsening terms of trade in the 1980s. In addition, many countries started with large premiums in the parallel foreign exchange market and needed massive devaluations of the official exchange rate. Countries with flexible exchange rates—which either devalue from time to time or have a crawling peg or a managed float—can make real depreciations quickly. But countries with fixed exchange rates find rapid depreciations more difficult because prices are inflexible downward. By and large, countries with flexible exchange rates have made significant progress in increasing their international competitiveness, while those with fixed rates are still struggling to make the much-needed real depreciation—in part because fiscal policies were not supportive (box 2.1).

Different exchange rate regimes call for different methods of assessing exchange rate policy. For countries with flexible exchange rates and non-convertible currencies, the parallel market premium is a good indicator of exchange rate policy. For countries with fixed exchange rates and convertible currencies, by contrast, the parallel market premium is very small or nonexistent, even though the real exchange rate may be misaligned. We thus need other methods to assess the external competitiveness of these countries. Our strategy was to compare them with other countries that have similar exchange rate regimes and faced similar external shocks.

Flexible Exchange Rate Regimes: The Parallel Market Premium Fell and External Competitiveness Quickly Improved

Adjusting countries with flexible exchange rate regimes entered the adjustment period with markedly overvalued exchange rates and high parallel market premiums for foreign exchange. They defended their international reserves through foreign exchange rationing and trade restrictions. Reducing the high premiums, an important part of adjustment programs in these economies, reduces implicit taxation on exports, curbs rent-seeking activities, and lessens administrative discretion in the allocation of foreign exchange.[11]

Many African countries with flexible exchange rates traditionally had steeper premiums than other developing countries. Of the non-African adjusting countries covered in the World Bank's most recent report on

Box 2.1 Differences in Monetary and Fiscal Policies for Fixed and Flexible Exchange Rate Regimes

THE MACROECONOMIC ADJUSTMENT STRATEGY differs under fixed and flexible exchange rate regimes. Countries with fixed exchange rates need to rely on tighter credit and fiscal policies as a way of reducing domestic demand and improving the balance of payments (sometimes called the "internal adjustment" strategy). These policies also put downward pressure on domestic prices and real wages to bring about a real depreciation. The flexible exchange rate countries, by contrast, support tighter demand with devaluation.

While both strategies result in a tightening of demand, countries with fixed exchange rates need to do more, especially in reducing budget deficits. But while they adopted a policy of tight money, reflected in high real interest rates and low seigniorage (box figure 2.1), they did not do enough in fiscal policy. Their deficits in 1990–91 were higher than those in the flexible exchange rate countries in the region. They reduced government spending—but not enough to offset the falling revenues (box figure 2.2).

Countries with flexible exchange rates also tightened credit, but they generally followed looser monetary policies and had higher seigniorage and inflation. They also had better fiscal policies. Their median overall budget deficit including grants fell from 7.3 percent of GDP in 1981–86 to 4.5 percent of GDP in 1990–91, while the median deficit for the fixed exchange rate countries increased from 6.0 to 6.3 percent of GDP. Revenues explain much of the difference: median revenue rose from 18.4 to 19.7 percent of GDP in the flexible exchange rate countries; it dropped from 18.4 to 16.3 percent of GDP in the fixed exchange rate economies. Both groups managed to reduce total spending, but the fixed exchange rate countries used less desirable means to do so: they increased the wage bill slightly and cut capital spending, while the flexible exchange rate countries relied more heavily on cuts in the wage bill.

Box Figure 2.1 Monetary Policy Indicators: Comparing Means for Countries with Fixed and Flexible Exchange Rates

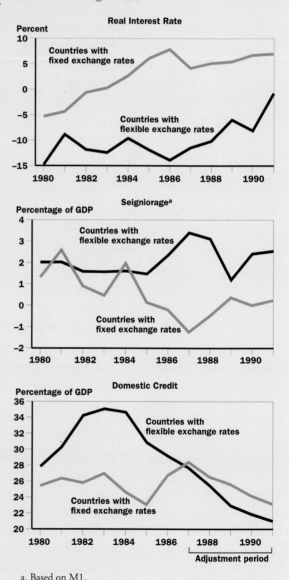

a. Based on M1.
Source: World Bank data.

Box Figure 2.2 Fiscal Indicators: Comparing Medians for Countries with Fixed and Flexible Exchange Rates

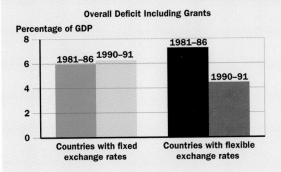

Overall Deficit Including Grants

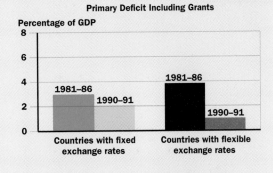

Primary Deficit Including Grants

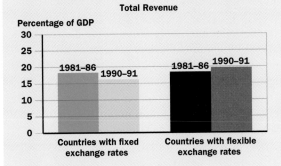

Total Revenue

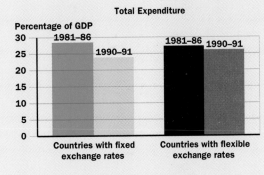

Total Expenditure

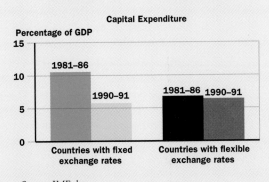

Capital Expenditure

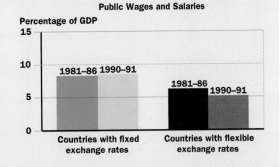

Public Wages and Salaries

Source: IMF data.

53

adjustment lending (World Bank 1992a), few had the three-digit pre-miums of African countries, and for those few, the episodes were shorter than in Africa.

After the mid-1980s, African adjusting countries made good progress in reducing the parallel market premium, and by 1990–91 none had the four-digit premiums of the early 1980s (appendix table A.5). Moreover, devaluations have not led to a permanent increase in inflation (box 2.2).

Box 2.2 Devaluations Need Not Be Inflationary

WHY HAVE DEVALUATIONS IN THE FLEXIBLE EXCHANGE RATE countries changed relative prices without causing inflation in the medium term? There are at least four reasons.

First, most countries needed a real depreciation to restore external balance, in part because they experienced a significant deterioration in the terms of trade. Under these circumstances, the devaluations helped move relative prices toward their equilibrium and so were not inflationary.

Second, real depreciations generally had a favorable impact on the budget in domestic currency terms, increasing revenue more than spending. This is partly because devaluation increases the domestic purchasing power of external grants, an important source of revenue. Another major source of government income, trade tax revenue, also rises as imports become more expensive in domestic currency terms. And there are often gains in export revenue, especially in countries that export mineral resources—such as Nigeria and Zambia—and where the state is in partnership with the mining companies or is able to tax the windfall gain from the real depreciation.

Third, much of the potential impact of a devaluation was absorbed early in the parallel market by the depreciation of the parallel ex-change rate. Prices of many tradable goods had increased as goods were smuggled in from neighboring countries. So, when the govern-ment finally devalued, domestic prices had already adjusted to the new "equilibrium" in the official exchange rate, and there were no further inflationary pressures.

Fourth, most countries in the region do not have a tradition of high inflation, so, unlike many Latin American countries, they do not have in place the wage-indexing mechanisms that set in motion the vicious inflation-devaluation cycle. This pattern might explain why devaluations increased inflation where inflation was high to start with (Sierra Leone and Zaire) but not where it was low.

Despite this progress, the median premium for African adjusting countries was about 25 percent in 1990–91, four times that for adjusting countries in other regions. Not surprisingly, countries that reduced the premium significantly also had large real depreciations. The average exchange rate premium fell from 300 percent in 1981–86 to 46 percent in 1990–91, with the median falling from 60 percent to 25 percent. Ghana and Mozambique made particularly impressive reductions (from 1,098 percent to 3 percent and from 2,111 percent to 63 percent, respectively), as did Guinea, Nigeria, Tanzania, and Uganda. However, because these countries had extremely high premiums in the first place, even these large reductions were not always enough to achieve good exchange rate policies.

There were exceptions to the general progress in exchange rate policy. Zambia had a reversal when poor macroeconomic policy decisions led to an increase in the premium—from about 45 percent in the mid-1980s to 600 percent in 1988.[12] The premiums also rose in Mauritania and Sierra Leone after the mid-1980s, as macroeconomic instability increased. In Burundi and Kenya, which had low or moderate premiums at the outset, the changes were not as dramatic because exchange rate policy remained fairly sound.

Reductions in the premium were accompanied by substantial increases in external competitiveness during the 1980s. The median real effective exchange rate depreciated by 78 percent between 1981–86 and 1990–91. Even countries that entered the adjustment period with lower premiums—such as Burundi, Kenya, and Madagascar—depreciated their real exchange rates (by around 60 percent on average).

Most countries with flexible exchange rates had low or moderate premiums in 1990–91, and thus fair to good exchange rate policies (table 2.3). This certainly is an improvement over the mid-1980s. But about a third of them still had a premium of more than 30 percent in 1990–91, indicating room to do better.[13]

Fixed Exchange Rate Regimes: No Improvement in External Competitiveness

In the second half of the 1980s, adjusting countries with fixed exchange rates became less competitive internationally as their terms of trade worsened. It is difficult to assess their policy stance because there is no parallel foreign exchange market to establish the misalignment of

Table 2.3 Exchange Rate Policy Stance for Countries with Flexible Exchange Rates, 1990–91

Good or adequate	
Ghana	★★★★
Guinea	★★★★
Guinea-Bissau	★★★★
Kenya	★★★★
Madagascar	★★★★
Fair	
Burundi	★★★
The Gambia	★★★
Malawi	★★★
Nigeria	★★★
Uganda	★★★
Zimbabwe	★★★
Poor	
Rwanda	★★
Very poor	
Mauritania	★
Mozambique	★
Sierra Leone	★
Tanzania	★
Zambia	★

Note: A "good or adequate" rating indicates a premium of 0–10 percent on the parallel market for foreign exchange; "fair," a premium of 11–30 percent; "poor," a premium of 31–50 percent; and "very poor," a premium of 51 percent or more.
Source: Appendix table B.5.

the real exchange rate. Looking at changes in the real exchange rate is no help without knowing what the new equilibrium rate would be, given changes in the terms of trade, the availability of external financing, and so on. Adjusting African countries with flexible exchange rates are not a useful benchmark, because they entered adjustment with grossly overvalued exchange rates.

Instead, we looked at the behavior of the real effective exchange rate in a reference group of developing countries outside Africa—countries that exported primary products but did not enter the 1980s with high parallel market premiums.[14] Their real exchange rates depreciated by 60 percent on average between 1980 and 1990, strongly suggesting that the African economies needed to depreciate by at least that much to remain competitive in international markets.[15] But the real depreciation in Africa's fixed exchange rate economies—just 5 percent on average between 1980 and 1990–91—fell well short of that mark (figure 2.2). A few countries even had a real appreciation (appendix table A.6).

The depreciation of the dollar against the French franc that started in 1985 was the wrong thing at the wrong time for countries in the CFA franc zone. The lower inflation in France also exacerbated the problem, because the only way the franc zone countries could achieve a real depreciation in a reasonable time without devaluing was by reducing domestic

Countries with fixed exchange rates achieved less real depreciation than other developing countries, despite similar falls in the terms of trade.

Figure 2.2 **Barter Terms of Trade and the Real Effective Exchange Rate**

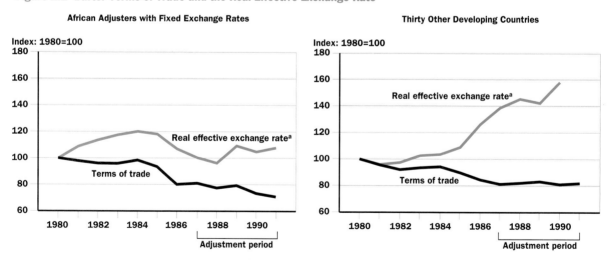

a. An increase in the real effective exchange rate constitutes a depreciation; a decrease constitutes an appreciation.
Source: World Bank data.

prices. Their failure to depreciate as much as other countries exporting similar products meant a loss of competitiveness. Ten of the twelve fixed exchange rate countries with data available entered the 1990s with poor or very poor stances on exchange rate policy (table 2.4).

Further Progress Needed in Macroeconomic Policies

HOW MUCH HAVE MACROECONOMIC POLICIES CHANGED overall? This is a difficult question to answer. There are clear problems in constructing a single measure of all the changes in fiscal, monetary, and exchange rate policies. Is a reduction in inflation more or less important than one in the parallel market premium? Are there significant gains in the overall policy environment if the premium falls to low levels but inflation remains high (say, close to three digits)? Are there net benefits to reducing inflation from 20 percent to 5 percent if this causes an appreciation of a grossly overvalued domestic currency? Does reducing the budget deficit by 3 percentage points have the same impact regardless of whether the initial deficit is 15 percent of GDP or 4 percent of GDP?

Although no method can address these complex questions satisfactorily, we created an aggregate index that, while imperfect, summarizes changes in fiscal, monetary, and exchange rate policy. Details about the construction of the index and alternative ways of calculating it are presented in appendix B.

By and large, the adjusting countries in Sub-Saharan Africa have improved their macroeconomic policies, increasing their international competitiveness and reducing inflation (figure 2.3). Of the twenty-six countries for which we could compute the index of change in overall macroeconomic policies, fifteen made advances. Ghana, Tanzania, and The Gambia improved the most, reflecting in part highly distorted initial conditions. But eleven countries suffered deteriorations, with Cameroon, Gabon, Côte d'Ivoire, and Congo having the largest. Macroeconomic policies worsened slightly in Benin, the Central African Republic, Rwanda, Sierra Leone, and Togo.

Even when different time periods or different policy variables are used to evaluate the change in macroeconomic policies, the evidence

Table 2.4 Exchange Rate Policy Stance for Countries with Fixed Exchange Rates, 1990–91

Good or adequate	
None	★★★★
Fair	
Niger	★★★
Poor	
Benin	★★
Burkina Faso	★★
Central African Rep.	★★
Gabon	★★
Mali	★★
Togo	★★
Very poor	
Cameroon	★
Congo	★
Côte d'Ivoire	★
Senegal	★

Note: A "good or adequate" rating indicates a depreciation in the real effective exchange rate of more than 40 percent between 1980 and 1990–91 (non-African countries averaged 60 percent). A "fair" rating indicates a depreciation of 21–40 percent; "poor," a depreciation of 6–20 percent; and "very poor," a depreciation of 0–5 percent or an appreciation. Chad is excluded because of insufficient data.

Source: Appendix table B.5.

More than half of the countries improved their macroeconomic policies.

Table 2.5 Countries Ranked by Overall Macroeconomic Policy Stance, 1990–91

Adequate
1	Ghana	★★★★

Fair
2	Burundi	★★★
3	The Gambia	★★★
4	Madagascar	★★★
5	Malawi	★★★
6	Burkina Faso	★★★
7	Kenya	★★★
8	Gabon	★★★
9	Mauritania	★★★
10	Nigeria	★★★
11	Senegal	★★★
12	Togo	★★★
13	Mali	★★★
14	Uganda	★★★

Poor
15	Central African Republic	★★
16	Niger	★★
17	Benin	★★
18	Rwanda	★★
19	Tanzania	★★
20	Zimbabwe	★★

Very poor
21	Côte d'Ivoire	★
22	Cameroon	★
23	Congo	★
24	Mozambique	★
25	Sierra Leone	★
26	Zambia	★

Note: Countries are ranked by the overall scores reported in appendix table B.5, which reflect their fiscal, monetary, and exchange rate policy stances. Chad, Guinea, and Guinea-Bissau are excluded because of insufficient data.

Source: Appendix table B.5.

Figure 2.3 Change in Macroeconomic Policies, 1981–86 to 1987–91

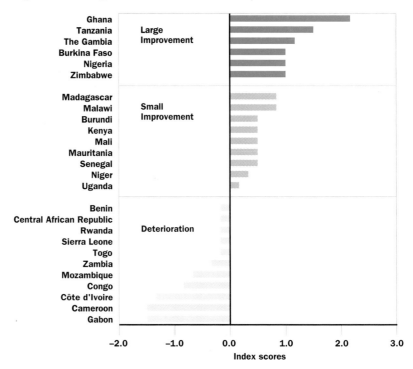

Note: Chad, Guinea, and Guinea-Bissau are excluded because of insufficient data.
Source: Appendix table B.1.

clearly points to progress in more than half of the adjusting countries (see appendix B). Burkina Faso, The Gambia, Ghana, Nigeria, Tanzania, and Zimbabwe consistently show large macroeconomic improvements, while Cameroon, Congo, Côte d'Ivoire, Gabon, and Togo always appear among the group with deterioration in policies. And although some countries shift groups, as should be expected, this does not alter the finding (presented in chapter 5) that better policies are associated with better outcomes.

None of the countries in the region, however, has yet achieved a *good* macroeconomic stance (table 2.5), with a four-star rating across the board in fiscal, monetary, and exchange rate policies. Improvements in policies have moved several countries closer to a "good" rating, but more reforms are still needed. Even in countries that have gone the furthest, the fiscal balance is fragile, inflation is above international levels, and the parallel market premium for foreign exchange has not been eliminated.

Ghana, which has the best macroeconomic policies in Africa, still had an unacceptable inflation rate of about 28 percent in 1990–91, while Burundi and The Gambia, which rank second and third, had parallel market premiums of about 20 percent. In other countries, even substantial steps forward leave them a long way from adequate policies. Tanzania, for example, cut the parallel market premium by two-thirds during the adjustment period, but it was still more than 70 percent in 1990–91. It is worrisome that even the best performers in Africa do not come close to matching the good macroeconomic policies typified by Chile, Malaysia, Mexico, and Thailand, where inflation is close to 10 percent per year, budget balances range from deficits of 2 percent of GDP to small surpluses, and currencies are fully convertible (at least for current account transactions).

Notes

1. See Rutihinda (1992) for a vivid description of Tanzania's response to the crisis.

2. The countries with fixed exchange rates are the thirteen members of the CFA franc zone. They are grouped into the West African Monetary Union (Benin, Burkina Faso, Côte d'Ivoire, Mali, Niger, Senegal, and Togo) and the Central African Monetary Area (Cameroon, the Central African Republic, Chad, Congo, Equatorial Guinea, and Gabon). Each area is served by an independent regional central bank, the Banque Centrale des Etats de l'Afrique de l'Ouest in West Africa and the Banque des Etats de l'Afrique Centrale in Central Africa. Both areas have broadly similar monetary and exchange rate arrangements. The key features are a fixed exchange rate, pegged to the French franc at 50:1 from 1948 until 1994; a fully convertible currency; open trading arrangements; and a relatively disciplined monetary policy.

3. Cameroon, Congo, and Gabon benefited from higher oil exports.

4. The section on fiscal policy is largely based on Nashashibi and Bazzoni (1994), which presents a detailed discussion of fiscal performance in Sub-Saharan Africa between 1980 and 1991. The classification of countries by fiscal indicators is ours, although it is based on data in that study measuring the size, quality, and sustainability of the fiscal adjustment.

5. The increase in Zimbabwe resulted from a shift of teachers' salaries to the central budget.

6. This is known as the Olivera-Tanzi effect (see, for example, Tanzi 1978).

7. Ideally, an evaluation of the fiscal policy stance would take into account such variables as the size of the current imbalance, the structure of government revenue, the patterns of government expenditure, and the dependence on external grants to close fiscal imbalances. But no single fiscal indicator adequately summarizes fiscal stance, and there are great difficulties in evaluating fiscal policy—especially its sustainability, an issue discussed in more detail in Tanzi (1991) and Blejer and Cheasty (1993).

8. Our definition of seigniorage is a version of Fischer (1982) and was calculated as $(M1_t - M1_{t-1})/GDP_t - g_t(M1/GDP)t$, where $M1_t$ is the stock of money at the end of period t, GDP_t is gross domestic product at time t, and g_t is real GDP growth. In other words, seigniorage measures the inflationary impact of money creation (that is, the increase in monetary growth in excess of what is

needed to satisfy the transactions demand for money). This concept of seigniorage corresponds to the so-called inflation tax only in the long run (when there are no changes in money demand). We use M1, as opposed to the monetary base, because most African countries implicitly or explicitly collect this revenue on all non-interest-bearing deposits (checking accounts), either because the banks are publicly owned or because they impose high reserve requirements on these deposits. Other measures of seigniorage (such as those based on the monetary base or those based on total revenue from money creation—the first term in the equation above) do not change our results in any significant way.

9. The relationship between seigniorage and inflation is discussed in Fischer (1982) and Dornbusch and Fischer (1993), among others. Seigniorage in countries with single-digit inflation rates generally is less than 1 percent of GDP (in the United States it is about 0.5 percent of GDP). In Argentina in the early 1980s it was about 6 percent of GDP, with inflation in the range of 600 percent a year. There are cases, however, in which moderate seigniorage (about 2 percent of GDP) is associated with high and accelerating rates of inflation (Brazil and Israel in the 1970s and 1980s).

10. It is difficult to understand why Benin fell into this group, because it has traditionally been a country with low seigniorage and low inflation, and it abides by the monetary rules of the CFA franc zone. High seigniorage in this period appears to be unusual and probably reflects a short-term increase in the money supply, following a couple of years in which the money supply declined.

11. A premium for foreign exchange in the parallel market indicates that the official exchange rate is inconsistent with domestic monetary and fiscal policies and that the central bank cannot satisfy the demand for foreign exchange at the official exchange rate. To the extent that the premium allows countries to keep the official exchange rate out of equilibrium, it measures overvaluation. And because overvaluations indirectly tax exports, the premium is also frequently used as an indicator of trade pol-icy. We view the parallel exchange rate premium primarily as a measure of overvaluation, but as an imperfect measure for at least two reasons. First, it indicates overvaluation only over the long term; in the short term it is driven by expectations and so should be viewed only as an indicator of the exchange rate that clears the market at a given time. Second, over the long term the premium reflects not only overvaluation but also the risks of transactions in the parallel market.

12. There were signs in 1992 and early 1993 that the premium was once again being reduced significantly.

13. Mozambique and Tanzania have recently made significant improvements.

14. The countries in the reference group faced a deterioration in the external environment similar to (though probably smaller than) that faced by the African fixed exchange rate economies between 1980 (the pre-crisis period) and 1990 (when most developing countries outside Africa had completed their adjustment of the real exchange rate). The reference group comprised thirty non-African adjusters discussed in the World Bank's third report on adjustment lending (World Bank 1992a). The underlying assumption was that because the African countries with fixed exchange rates experienced larger declines in the terms of trade than did countries in the reference group, they should have responded with roughly similar real depreciation. While changes in the terms of trade are usually the most important factor affecting the equilibrium real exchange rate, a more precise calculation would also take into account changes in productivity, capital flows, and so on. Readers interested in alternative methodologies should see Devarajan and de Melo (1991), Devarajan, Lewis, and Robinson (1993), and Elbadawi and Majd (1992).

15. We take 1980 as our starting point because in that year, according to most observers, the real exchange rate in the countries of the CFA franc zone was at an appropriate level to support internal and external balance under the then-favorable terms of trade.

CHAPTER 3

Unleashing Markets

SUSTAINED GROWTH REQUIRES MORE THAN A HIGH RATE
of investment. It requires unleashing markets so that competition can help improve the allocation of economic
resources. It also requires getting price signals right and
creating a climate that allows businesses to respond to
those signals in ways that increase the returns to investments (World Bank 1991c). Having the proper macroeconomic framework—the subject of chapter 2—provides the incentives needed for
new investment and productive use of resources. But trade, agricultural, and other regulatory reforms—the subject of this chapter—are
essential complements to reducing the government interventions that
distort prices and tie up markets.

In this chapter we assess the extent of reforms and come to the following conclusions. The African countries undergoing structural adjustment have moved a long way toward good trade policies. They have
reduced administrative rationing of foreign exchange and eliminated
many nontariff barriers. Yet they still have a long way to go. Much of the
progress in import liberalization still depends on large flows of external
assistance. Furthermore, adjusters have not done enough to reduce the
commercially oriented elements of protectionism—tariffs, nontariff
barriers, and industrial restrictions—that existed before the macroeconomic crisis of the early 1980s.

Reforms of agricultural pricing and marketing systems are under way
across the continent. Almost all countries have taken steps to ensure that
producer prices for Africa's major agricultural exports track world prices
more closely. In a few cases, they have done this by abolishing state marketing boards; more frequently, they have allowed the private sector to
compete with the marketing board, or they have adopted pricing for-

mulas with a clear link to world market prices. There has been a major retrenchment of government involvement in food crop marketing, particularly where the evasion of controls was previously widespread. But reform of the maize marketing boards in eastern and southern Africa is proceeding more slowly. And much remains to be done in both the export and food crop sectors to take advantage of entrepreneurial talent in agricultural marketing and input distribution and to create a level playing field for private traders.

African governments have also moved to deregulate prices and markets in other sectors. Widespread price controls are a thing of the past. There has been considerable progress in removing government monopolies, particularly in commerce. In many countries, rice, sugar, tea, and other principal commodities can now be imported freely by the private sector. But monopolies linger in such key sectors as petroleum, wheat, and fertilizer and in certain financial and infrastructure services. Overall, countries have a long way to go in creating a favorable business climate for the private sector.

Trade Reforms

THE COUNTRIES THAT ENTERED ADJUSTMENT WITH MASsively overvalued exchange rates and heavily rationed foreign exchange have made tremendous strides in liberalizing imports. The large depreciations of the exchange rate and the adoption of macroeconomic policies consistent with a sustainable balance of payments have done away with foreign exchange rationing, eliminating the import scarcity premiums reflected in parallel market prices. The large inflow of external funds to support liberalized import schemes has also played a major role in abolishing foreign exchange rationing. While this constitutes enormous progress from the policies imposed during the crisis of the early 1980s, for many countries it is simply a return to their policy stance before the crisis and is dependent on continuing external assistance.

Any discussion of Sub-Saharan trade reform, particularly import liberalization, must make two distinctions. First, import controls driven by short-run balance-of-payments problems—usually implemented through foreign exchange rationing—differ from the longer-term, protectionist import restrictions—usually implemented through tariff and nontariff barriers. Much of the liberalization so far has attacked the short-run controls. Second, the import situation recorded in national statistics under official exchange rates differs from the actual quantity of imports and their market prices because of widespread smuggling and the commonplace evasion of tariffs and import controls. Much import liberalization in Africa has merely rationalized the situation in parallel markets and reallocated the "rents" previously embodied in official controls.

These two distinctions—between short-run import controls and long-run commercial policy and between official statistics and real practice—must be taken into account when evaluating the impact of trade reform. Normally, a devaluation would make domestic producers of import substitutes better off by raising the prices of competing imports, while a reduction in import barriers would make them worse off by increasing competition from goods at lower prices. The major reduction in import barriers in Africa has come from the lifting of import controls, not from tariff reform per se. But the price changes facing individual firms and industries have varied enormously, depending on the access to rationed imports and foreign exchange before the reforms.

Many domestic manufacturers, particularly parastatals, had access to imported inputs and—perhaps more important—to external credit to finance capital goods at the artificially cheap official exchange rate. Their products generally were protected from competition or faced competition at the parallel market price. These firms, because they relied on foreign financing to produce heavily protected goods, were hit extremely hard by devaluation and by a reduction in import barriers. First, the devaluation increased the cost of servicing their external debt and the cost of their imported inputs. Second, the reduction in import barriers meant that they encountered more competition, which dampened the potential rise in the prices of importable outputs from a devaluation. How much their profitability suffered depended on how much they benefited from rationing before the reform and whether they continued to be protected by import monopolies or other trade barriers. This double shock to many large industrial parastatals is perhaps what lay behind their financial difficulties in some countries. Firms operating in the informal sector, which had less access to rationed inputs, were hit less hard—and many even benefited from increased access to vital inputs.

The reality is that actual import prices in many flexible exchange rate countries probably have not changed much on average, because they already reflected parallel market prices before the reform period. Liberalizations probably have not substantially expanded the quantities of goods available on the open market, except in the few cases where goods were tightly rationed. But the liberalizations have eliminated rents accruing to those who obtained rationed goods and enforced controls.

Trade reform in the fixed exchange rate countries obviously differs from the foregoing storyline. The reason: the convertibility arrangements for these countries enabled them to avoid foreign exchange rationing and many of the excesses of import restrictions. This partly explains their superior economic performance before the adjustment period. But imports by these countries have recently plunged, despite the continuing real appreciation of the CFA franc, especially after 1985. This plunge reflects a compression of domestic demand—not an increase in direct barriers to imports. Moreover, the combination of an appreciating real exchange rate and severe recession has made it very difficult for them to liberalize imports, as domestic producers of import substitutes already are under tremendous pressure from cheap foreign imports and declining domestic demand.

Box 3.1 What Is Trade Reform, and How Would We Know If There Has Been Some?

UNDER ANY SET OF TRADE POLICIES, THE ECONomy attaches a set of relative prices and profitabilities to various activities. These prices act as incentives to determine the structure of production and consumption of goods, which in turn determines the amount and composition of imports and exports. New trade policies change relative prices, either implicitly or explicitly, and thus affect production and consumption decisions. Import liberalization consists of moving toward market determination of prices and thus toward market determination of the level and composition of imports and domestically produced importables.

To evaluate the extent of import liberalization in Africa, we must analyze the effect of government policy instruments on relative prices. Four trade interventions are common: rationing foreign exchange, erecting nontariff barriers to imports, imposing tariffs, and using other domestic policies (such as re-

served monopolies, reference prices, and quality requirements) that do not intervene directly in trade flows but nevertheless affect trade. Assessing the distortions from each of these barriers is conceptually straightforward but practically impossible in Sub-Saharan Africa for three reasons.

First, in countries without fixed exchange rates and convertible currencies, the policy restrictions that have been most important in creating trade distortions are the foreign exchange allocations and licensing requirements for imports. The incidence of barriers can be measured—for example, one can calculate the fraction of all goods subject to import licensing requirements. But barriers generally are administered in a way that makes the distortionary impact far from transparent. In one country, all goods might require a license, but the licenses are freely granted. In another, only half the goods might

Liberalizing Imports

Because of overlapping, less-than-transparent trade restrictions in Sub-Saharan Africa, no single measure of trade distortion can be used unassailably to assess how much any country has liberalized imports or to make fine comparisons across countries (box 3.1). But Africa's trade regimes can be classified by the four phases of liberalization that Krueger (1978) described in her classic study: complete or nearly complete government control or rationing of imports, heavy use of nontariff barriers for protectionist purposes, mostly or exclusively tariff-based protection, and free trade (table 3.1). The range of policies within each category is large, but the overall framework is useful in tracking reform efforts.

There are two typical patterns of trade reform in Africa (figure 3.1):

- Most adjusting countries with flexible exchange rates have moved away from complete control over imports and foreign exchange and toward the use of extensive trade barriers, especially nontariff barriers—and in some cases toward modest, mostly tariff-based

require a license, but few receive them. The distortion is thus greater in the country with fewer license requirements. Moreover, the availability of foreign exchange can strongly determine the allocation of imports and the severity of distortions, even for the same incidence of trade barriers, because the administration of the system might change with the perceived constraints on foreign exchange availability.

Second, measuring price distortions requires knowledge of what domestic prices are and what they would have been without the barrier. Even using border prices as a proxy for the latter requires accurate measurement of the difference between the world price and the domestic price—extremely difficult for all but the most standard commodities. To compare the domestic price of, say, a man's shirt made in Kenya or Zambia with the "world" price of a man's shirt involves numerous complex and debatable ad-

justments for quality, durability, and fashion. These direct price comparisons are difficult and expensive and hence are rarely possible to obtain for an economy or even a sector (except in the case of commodities). And they are never available over time in a way that would allow the evolution of import distortions to be assessed.

Third, the effects of various barriers often overlap, so examining the reform of any single aspect of the import regime can mislead. The same import item might be subject to a tariff of 30 percent, an import license requirement, and general foreign exchange rationing. If tariffs on this good fall, have imports been liberalized? Maybe, maybe not. If the premium implicit in the licensing (the price increase due to the license) was higher than 30 percent, import flows are unaffected by a tariff reduction, so revenue is lost from the tariff reduction without any gain in import liberalization.

Table 3.1 Phases in Liberalizing Import Regimes

Phase	Comment	Examples outside Africa
Complete or nearly complete government control over imports	Usually the result of severe macroeconomic disequilibria	Peru (1987), Brazil (1966)
Extensive trade barriers, with widespread nontariff barriers	Typical of highly protectionist import-substituting regimes	Argentina (1970s), Brazil (1980s), India (1970s), Turkey (early 1980s)
Modest, mostly tariff-based protection	Typical of most industrialized countries	Republic of Korea (late 1980s)
Free trade or low, uniform tariffs	Rare	Hong Kong (ongoing), Chile (late 1980s), Argentina (early 1990s)

Source: World Bank staff.

protection. Some—Tanzania and Zambia, for example—have eliminated rationing but have not fully eliminated lists restricting allowable imports, or they have relied heavily on donor financing for systems of open general licenses (described later). But a few countries—notably Ghana—have begun to solidly commit themselves to making foreign exchange available through realistic exchange rates and to eliminating all but a few nontariff barriers. Even Ghana, however, lags behind Mauritius, which completed its adjustment program early on, including extensive trade reforms (box 3.2).

■ The second set of countries never resorted to widespread foreign exchange rationing and has moved slowly toward import liberalization. This group includes the flexible exchange rates countries that never experienced a severe macroeconomic crisis, such as Kenya and Zimbabwe, as well as the fixed exchange rate countries that maintained convertible currencies throughout the period. A few of the latter have made progress in eliminating nontariff barriers and in tariff reform.

To evaluate import liberalization in Africa, we look at four common interventions: foreign exchange rationing, nontariff barriers to imports, tariffs, and regulatory barriers that indirectly affect trade.

Eliminating foreign exchange rationing. Devaluing extremely overvalued currencies and reducing the rationing of foreign exchange for imports are among adjustment's biggest achievements in the 1980s in flexible exchange rate economies. Some countries (Ghana and Uganda) have depreciated the exchange rate enough to eliminate rationing. Other

Figure 3.1 Evolution of Trade Policy in Selected Countries during the Adjustment Period

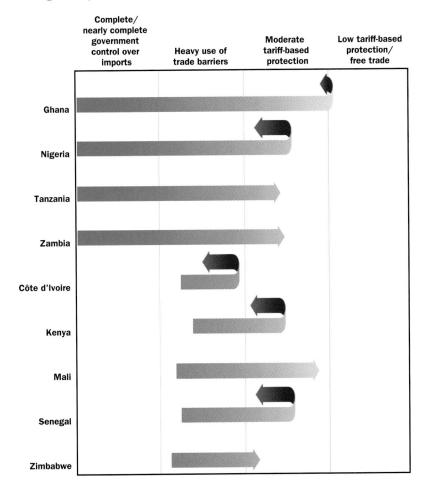

Source: World Bank staff.

Despite much progress, many countries have not firmly committed to low or moderate tariffs.

countries (Tanzania and Zambia) have undertaken substantial reforms, but the reforms have been halting and incomplete. Still others (Madagascar and Nigeria) launched substantial reforms now threatened with reversals. A fourth group (Kenya and Zimbabwe) has avoided an overvalued currency but retains import controls. Our assessment of progress in eliminating foreign exchange rationing is based on three indicators: nonmarket foreign exchange allocation mechanisms, parallel market premiums for foreign exchange, and the rationing of imports (appendix table A.7).

Box 3.2 Trade Reform: Mauritius and Ghana

SOME TWENTY-FIVE YEARS AGO, BRITISH ECONO-
mist James Meade pointed to Mauritius as an example
of a country where the "outlook for peaceful development is poor" (Meade 1967). Instead of fulfilling
Meade's bleak prognosis, Mauritius went on to become the brightest star in the somewhat dim firma-
ment of Sub-Saharan African economies in the 1980s.
Unemployment dropped from a high of 22 percent in
1983 to about 3 percent in recent years, and per capita
income increased by more than half between 1983 and
1990. Mauritius's success has been attributed to many
factors, particularly a propitious external environment,
but surely much of its good fortune (including its ability to take advantage of external events) was due to its
trade and macroeconomic policies.

Disciplined exchange rate management and sound
macroeconomic management overall have kept the
real exchange rate remarkably stable. Throughout the
1970s and early 1980s, it did not change from year to
year by more than a few percentage points. About
1982 (the exact year depends on the data series used),
the real exchange rate did begin to appreciate in the
wake of macroeconomic and structural imbalances.
Even in the early 1980s, however, the appreciation
was not severe (between 3 and 28 percent, again depending on the series) and was soon reversed by depreciation to a level below that of the 1970s.

During the 1970s, administrative controls over
foreign exchange allocation and imports were not
generally used to correct balance-of-payments problems, as they commonly were in other countries.
Mauritius was not plagued by the distortions caused
by large-scale parallel markets in foreign exchange and
multiple exchange rates. This changed to some extent
in the late 1970s, and by 1981, quotas covered 65
percent of imports. Elimination of these quotas was
one of the first steps in the country's structural adjustment program. At the same time, tariffs on some of
these products were increased, though overall protection clearly declined. The most protected sectors were
a relatively small part of the manufacturing sector, so
the potential for damage was limited. The adjustment
program later reduced and rationalized tariffs, though
not to the low levels of Latin America or East Asia.

As is well known, Mauritius's success was reflected
in the phenomenal growth of its export processing
zones and (to a lesser extent) tourism. The foundation
for this growth was laid by the policies mentioned
above, in conjunction with unusually good ancillary
policies. Unlike many other countries, traditional exports were not heavily taxed. And most productive activity was in private hands (state-owned enterprises accounted for only 8.7 percent of GDP). This put the
private sector in a good position to take advantage of the

Although nearly every country had almost universal discretionary
control over imports in the crisis period, many had moved to nondis-
cretionary access for imports by late 1992. In several countries, however,
including Kenya, Nigeria, and Madagascar, renewed balance-of-payments pressures have threatened, or resulted in, reversals. Despite massive exchange rate reforms, no flexible exchange rate country has established complete convertibility of its current accounts. Even so, a large
number permit untrammeled access to foreign exchange for imports, either through a foreign exchange auction or through less restrictive licensing. In several countries, mechanisms other than eliminating or reducing foreign exchange licensing have helped to relax the foreign

export processing zone incentives, and indeed most of the early investment came from domestic sources.

Ghana's advances in trade policy have been more recent and more fragile. They began slowly in 1983, following a period in which per capita income had fallen 30 percent since 1970. The most radical and important reform was the overhaul of the foreign exchange system, from one of grossly overvalued exchange rates and administrative allocation to one relying on an auction and interbank market. The result has been the virtual elimination of a parallel market premium that reached 2,100 percent in the early 1980s, along with the corruption and rent-seeking caused by distortions of such magnitude. The exchange market is still not exactly free, since the auction is "Dutch"—meaning that different purchasers pay different prices for the same commodity—and exporters still do not have full rights to retain their foreign exchange earnings. Further reforms are needed, but the progress since the pre-adjustment period has been substantial.

Other trade reforms have been significant, though not as dramatic as in the exchange market. Tariff reform early in Ghana's adjustment program was impressive (with the tariff rate structure now ranging from 10 to 30 percent), but it preceded the elimination of quantitative controls. Thus, when these were eliminated in 1987 and tariffs became the binding constraint on imports, protection fell precipitously. Producers howled, and high surcharges were subsequently imposed. These have since been reduced somewhat.

Nontraditional exporters have benefited from improvements in the duty drawback system and from increased foreign exchange retention rights. In the very important cocoa sector, incentives to producers have improved; producers' share of the free-on-board price increased from 35 percent to 54 percent between 1984 and 1990. While domestic marketing has been demonopolized, exports still are the exclusive domain of the state marketing agency, and privatization of state-owned plantations has gone slowly.

The adjustment program, though far from complete, arguably qualifies Ghana as the most advanced trade policy reformer in Sub-Saharan Africa after Mauritius. And the reforms have begun to show results. Since the program's inception, GDP has grown about 4 or 5 percent a year, compared with 0.1 percent annually between 1960 and 1983. Cocoa production has shot up 77 percent. In spite of cocoa's growth, nontraditional exports have grown fast enough to increase their share of total exports to 4.6 percent. Manufactured exports grew by 52 percent (though from a small base) between 1985 and 1990.

exchange constraint. One, called own-funds imports, allows anybody possessing foreign exchange to use it for imports, either choosing from a specified list of allowed imports or freely importing any item (box 3.3). Another mechanism is an export proceeds retention scheme, which permits exporters to retain a part of their foreign exchange earnings.

The parallel market exchange rate premium, the second indicator of the extent of foreign exchange rationing, has declined substantially since the initiation of reforms. This tells us that the value of a unit of foreign exchange is nearer the official price, and that rationing has lessened.

A third useful indicator is the gap between predicted (notional) imports and actual imports. This gap, attributable to an array of unob-

Box 3.3 Own-Funds Importing

ALLOWING OWN-FUNDS IMPORTS ELIMINATES the penalties associated with foreign exchange transactions and makes importing less risky. At the same time, it increases the demand for foreign exchange and gives exporters an incentive to meet that demand by smuggling more goods out of the country (or, where they are permitted to retain a certain percentage of their foreign exchange earnings, by increasing legal exports). Analytically, these own-funds schemes are equivalent to establishing multiple exchange rates, because they implicitly allow those with foreign exchange to sell it at the more attractive parallel market rate to those who want to import goods. The net impact on trade liberalization depends on the ease of smuggling imports and exports. If borders are porous, liberalization will have no impact. If exports are very difficult to smuggle out, the supply of foreign exchange will not increase, and the effect will

again be small. But if exports are price-responsive and easy to smuggle, allowing own-funds imports gives exporters an incentive to expand exports in order to supply imports that are in demand. This aids trade liberalization, increasing imports and (unofficial) exports.

Because own-funds imports are semiofficial flows, their magnitude is difficult to assess. For Tanzania in 1988, licenses for own-funds imports were *half* the total of non-donor-financed licenses—exceeding the amount of foreign exchange the government allocated directly. In Zambia own-funds imports were $100 million until an attempt at regulation reduced the recorded total to $7 million. Although own-funds imports can quickly bring a large liberalization, they are best seen as a short-term measure to facilitate a devaluation by establishing a (semilegal) parallel market for moving toward a liberalized official economy.

served impediments to imports, is measured by the index of implied import restrictiveness (Narasimhan and Prichett 1993). A high index number—the result of notional demand for imports being much higher than actual imports—indicates that imports face substantial restrictions, among them foreign exchange rationing.[1] When a currency is overvalued, imports are cheap at the official exchange rate, and notional demand is accordingly high. As overvaluation increases and the foreign exchange available to purchase imports dwindles, imports often fall—sometimes dramatically. In Ghana before its devaluation in 1983, the demand for imports far exceeded the actual level (figure 3.2). After devaluation, the actual level of imports approached the predicted level of demand.[2] Nigeria and Tanzania share a similar pattern. But some countries, like Kenya, appear to have tightened reductions on imports by raising nontariff barriers rather than by rationing foreign exchange.

Eliminating nontariff barriers. The second strand of evidence on import liberalization is progress in eliminating nontariff barriers (NTBs). Such barriers in Sub-Saharan Africa are predominantly government licenses or approvals for imports. Import licenses are usually connected to foreign exchange allocations, in the sense that a valid import license is

Figure 3.2 Evolution of Import Restrictiveness in Ghana

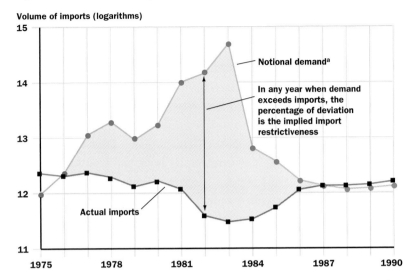

Volume of imports (logarithms)

Notional demand[a]

In any year when demand exceeds imports, the percentage of deviation is the implied import restrictiveness

Actual imports

In Ghana, depreciation and trade reform brought imports in line with demand.

a. Notional import demand is defined as $\alpha + \beta GDP + \gamma REER$, where α is a constant calculated to equalize actual and notional imports in the 1970s, β is an income elasticity equal to 1.25, γ is an exchange rate elasticity equal to 1, and REER is the real effective exchange rate.
Source: Narasimhan and Pritchett (1993).

needed to obtain foreign exchange. But these licenses have the additional function of protecting domestic producers from foreign competition. NTBs are a particularly virulent form of protection because they are not transparent in the price distortions they create. Furthermore, because the licenses are often specific to a firm, individual, or end-use, they not only limit the quantity of imports but often reduce their economic benefit, because those imports do not flow to those who need them most.

Progress has been made in reducing the number of goods requiring prior approval for import (appendix table A.8). Whereas many countries routinely required licenses for all goods, they now increasingly use a "negative list"—allowing what is not forbidden. Open general license (OGL) schemes have been one mechanism for liberalizing imports in this way. With an OGL scheme, a limited number of goods are placed on a list to be automatically approved for import and for the allocation of foreign exchange. The list is gradually expanded until the allowable items are so numerous that it becomes more efficient to move to a smaller, negative list. Many countries have an OGL scheme, and in some it covers a substantial proportion of imports.

The OGL schemes have helped phase in import liberalization. The expansion of unlicensed goods can move in step with the expansion of available foreign exchange, so as not to jeopardize the overall trade reform. The OGL goods are not rationed according to user and end-use (as with foreign exchange and NTB licensing), and they are available with little delay, so they can at least reach the users who most need them. This alone reduces much of the distortion caused by NTBs in the efficiency of resource allocation.

However useful they have been in reducing nontariff barriers, Africa's open general license schemes typically are neither open nor general. The schemes have enabled countries to move from a system of highly rationed imports to a more liberalized regime—but without committing to currency convertibility or an overall liberalization that might place central bank reserves at risk. Using an OGL scheme to liberalize nontariff barriers would not, then, constitute a rapid and complete opening of trade. The fraction of goods eligible for licenses often starts out small and increases gradually. In Zambia the scheme began in 1989 with only 10 percent of imports eligible, but 95 percent (excluding petroleum and fertilizer) were covered by September 1992. Similarly, Tanzania established an OGL scheme in 1987 but did not move to a negative list until 1991; in April 1992, a fifth of non-oil items still were not eligible for import.

There are two problems with open general licensing. First, in the early stages the move to an OGL scheme can increase, rather than decrease, the protection of domestic production. The first goods placed on an OGL list are those that are not produced domestically (so no one lobbies against them), but that are required as inputs for domestic production (so producers who use them lobby for them). By placing the input—but not the final product—on the list of goods that can be imported, the OGL scheme liberalizes the import of the input and lowers its price, but does not alter the price of the final product. Thus, it raises effective protection (the protection of the value added in a given activity). For example, under an OGL scheme covering industrial equipment but not shoes, a domestic manufacturer of footwear could import its capital goods more cheaply while maintaining its established price for shoes, thereby reaping higher profits.

A second problem with OGL schemes is that they often rely heavily on donor funds and are often linked rigidly to the official exchange rate set by the government. But the level of the official exchange rate, the goods eligible for import, and the funds committed to an OGL scheme may not be mutually consistent. There may, for example, be excess demand for OGL funds at the official exchange rate. In such instances, OGL imports are being subsidized at the same time that there is a substantial premium for foreign exchange in the parallel or own-funds market. Because the transition from an OGL scheme to liberalized imports is difficult, the recent history of OGLs has been rocky in many countries (such as Tanzania and Zambia).

Finally, caution is needed in using the number of goods that require licenses as an indicator of NTBs. A very few products sometimes account for a large part of domestic production. If an African economy has only, say, seven items under NTBs, but those seven items are maize, fertilizer, sugar, beer, soft drinks, cement, and steel products, this small list could easily cover half or more of all domestic value added in tradable items (excluding services and nontraded agriculture and industry). Nearly every country, not just those in Sub-Saharan Africa, retains a core group of commodities that it is reluctant to subject to import pressures, even with high tariffs.

Reforming tariffs. Tariff reform typically encompasses three steps. The first, already taken by many African governments, is rationalization: reducing the number of tariff rates, ad hoc exceptions, and separate levies and then assigning rates to products according to systematic criteria. The second step, often undertaken simultaneously with rationalization and currently under way in much of Africa, is to reduce the dispersion of tariffs, generally by raising the minimum tariff and lowering the maximum. Lowering the maximum is typically symbolic, since in practice the highest rates are avoided or evaded. The third and final step is to lower the overall level of tariffs to reduce the average level of domestic protection. This becomes important only after all other binding restrictions on imports have been eliminated—a point that most Sub-Saharan African countries have not yet reached.

Progress in rationalizing tariff codes—often to increase revenue collections—has been substantial. Pre-reform tariff codes were enormously complex (involving more than 2,500 separate items) and were often determined by ad hoc (and increasingly arbitrary) tax levies, rates, exemptions, and conditions. This led to tariffs that were irrational—in the sense that no government, whatever its objectives, would have chosen them. Typically the tariff codes were so cumbersome, so complex, and so riddled with exemptions that much revenue was sacrificed. Most

African countries are still remedying these problems—reducing the number of tariff rates, rationalizing those that remain, and improving administration and collection. Burkina Faso, Ghana, Mali, Senegal, and Togo are among those that have reduced the number of rates, oftentimes to only four or five. Many countries have also taken the second step in tariff reform, by lowering the maximum rates—Kenya from 170 percent to 60 percent, Rwanda from 270 percent to 100 percent, Tanzania from 120 percent to 40 percent.[3]

Because of the importance of tariffs for government tax revenue (Sub-Saharan countries rely on import duties for more than 20 percent of all tax revenue) as well as the exigencies of fiscal austerity, few countries have moved to the third step of reducing average tariff rates substantially. Indeed, for many adjusting countries, the ratio of tariff collections to import value (the average collected rate) has increased, perhaps a beneficial start. Average collected rates increased in Madagascar, Malawi, and Uganda and did not fall much even in countries that significantly reduced rates. In Kenya the trade-weighted average tariff dropped only from 40 percent to 20 percent during the course of reform, while collected rates fell from 18 percent to 14 percent.

Among the countries with fixed exchange rates, those in West Africa have made more progress in liberalizing trade than those in Central Africa. Five of the seven West African countries undertook important tariff reforms, although Côte d'Ivoire and, to lesser extent, Senegal later reversed their actions because of the combined pressure of the recession and import competition. Change has been slower in the Central African countries because of the need for a common approach (mandated by their participation in the Central African Customs Union), but a major reform effort is now under way. The Customs Union has announced plans for unionwide reform that will rationalize the tariff code by reducing the number of rates, minimizing dispersion, and lowering the average tariff—thus accomplishing most of the goals of tariff reform in one step.

Regulatory barriers. Another barrier to imports—seldom considered a barrier because it does not operate directly on trade—arises when a firm or set of firms is granted monopoly privileges over all sales of a good, whether it is produced domestically or imported. If these monopolists are not private firms, they are likely to choose the level of imports needed to protect domestic production. Many key industries (cement, sugar, fertilizer, petroleum) were—and still are—subject to such parastatal monopolies. Limiting the power of these monopolies is a politically difficult but necessary step to increase competition and reduce consumer prices.

Import liberalization also involves giving the private sector more freedom to import. Burundi, for example, had very restrictive licensing procedures for importers, limiting the number of importers. It has since relaxed these restrictions, allowing more competitive pressure.

Promoting Exports

During adjustment, the need to increase exports was clear—to improve both growth and the balance of payments. An overvalued currency has been the primary obstacle to exports, with devaluation a major part of the cure. But exports, especially traditional agricultural commodities, have also been often hurt by three other mechanisms:

- Export licensing and controls over export activity have been widespread.
- Export taxes have traditionally been high and an important source of government revenue. Although many countries have lowered them as part of adjustment programs, they linger in other countries because of fiscal concerns.
- Marketing boards, with monopoly control over the sale of exports and over domestic purchases from farmers, have reduced the profitability of exporting in many countries by offering export producers low prices. In some cases, devaluation led to huge improvements in border prices, but output did not jump dramatically because the marketing boards, in an effort to boost profits or cut losses, did not pass all of the increase back to producers.

For nontraditional exports as well, the major policy change has been the depreciation of the real exchange rate. Combined with reduced import protection, the devaluation increased the profitability of exports relative to the production of import substitutes or goods not traded. As an intermediate step, many countries (such as Nigeria, Tanzania, and Uganda) have given nontraditional exporters access to a more depreciated exchange rate through export proceeds retention schemes. Many countries are also doing more to promote nontraditional exports, using a variety of approaches:

- Most countries have some legal provision for duty drawbacks—rebating taxes paid on imported inputs used in export production. However, rebates are slow, documentation requirements onerous, and the programs administratively complex. Malawi, Senegal, Tanzania, Uganda, and Zambia have tried to simplify their duty drawback schemes, but when fiscal constraints are tight, the treasury tends to hold up customs tax rebates.

- Export processing zones (EPZs) allow exporters access to inputs at world prices without cumbersome duty drawback schemes. Successful in Asia, the zones vary from large fenced areas with their own extensive infrastructure to bonded warehouses and factories where export inputs are processed duty-free. In Africa, Mauritius has the most successful EPZ, and Madagascar has made a promising start with one. Kenya, Nigeria, Togo, and Zambia are also establishing EPZs or in-bond production arrangements.

- The relaxation of foreign investment codes, though not aimed explicitly at export-oriented investments, has been another important policy shift.

- Governments have also aided nontraditional exporters by streamlining reporting and licensing requirements and strengthening infrastructure.

Agricultural Reforms

AFRICAN FARMERS HAVE FACED THE WORLD'S HEAVIEST rates of agricultural taxation, perhaps partly because agriculture has been such a crucial source of revenue for African governments. African farmers were taxed explicitly through producer-price fixing, export taxes, and taxes on agricultural inputs. They were also taxed implicitly through overvalued exchange rates, which reduced the prices they obtained for their exports, and through high levels of industrial protection, which raised consumer prices. A study covering eighteen countries across the world showed that three broadly representative Sub-Saharan countries (Côte d'Ivoire, Ghana, and Zambia) taxed their farmers 70 percent more than the average for developing countries (Schiff and Valdes 1992). The high rates of taxation contributed to Sub-Saharan Africa's alarming decline in the average annual rate of agricultural growth—from 2.2 percent in 1965–73 to 1.0 percent in 1974–80 to 0.6 percent in 1981–85 (Cleaver 1993).

Reducing the taxation of the African farmer has been a top priority in agricultural reform. And agricultural reform is high on the adjustment agenda because agriculture accounts for roughly 35 percent of Africa's GDP, 40 percent of exports, and about 70 percent of employment. To meet food needs, raise incomes, and provide foreign exchange, the rate of growth in agricultural production over the next thirty years needs to be twice that of the past thirty years. Much of the increase will have to come from raising production in ways that conserve natural resources and thus ensure sustainable growth. Moreover, growth in the production of nontradable food staples is needed to enable production to keep pace with demand, limit the rise in consumer food prices, and help keep real wages competitive (Delgado 1992; Seckler 1993).

Some Export Producers Are Better Off, Despite Declining World Prices

Price trends for primary commodities over the past decade have been tough on African producers of agricultural exports. The real international prices of Africa's two major export crops—cocoa and coffee—dropped almost 70 percent between 1980 and 1990, and the real price of cotton, the third major export crop, 28 percent. Only two of the adjusting countries, Benin and Chad, registered an increase in the border price for their major agricultural exports—most likely a statistical anomaly. In the remaining countries, border prices (in foreign currency) fell. Given these declines, African governments have found it very difficult to improve real prices for producers of agricultural exports. But as figure 3.3 shows, ten of twenty-seven countries managed to do so by 1989–91, in part because they had substantial scope for adopting better policies.[4] Some gave producers a larger share of the border price at the official exchange rate (as measured by the nominal protection coefficient) by lowering export taxes, raising administered producer prices, reducing marketing costs, or liberalizing marketing. Others depreciated the real exchange rate and passed part of the higher local currency earnings back to producers. (Appendix C explains how policy and external factors interact in determining the real producer price.)

The remaining seventeen countries did not manage to offset the decline in world prices. In nine of these countries, governments nonetheless took measures to help their farmers. Either they raised producer

Figure 3.3 Change in the Real Producer Price of Agricultural Exports, 1981–83 to 1989–91

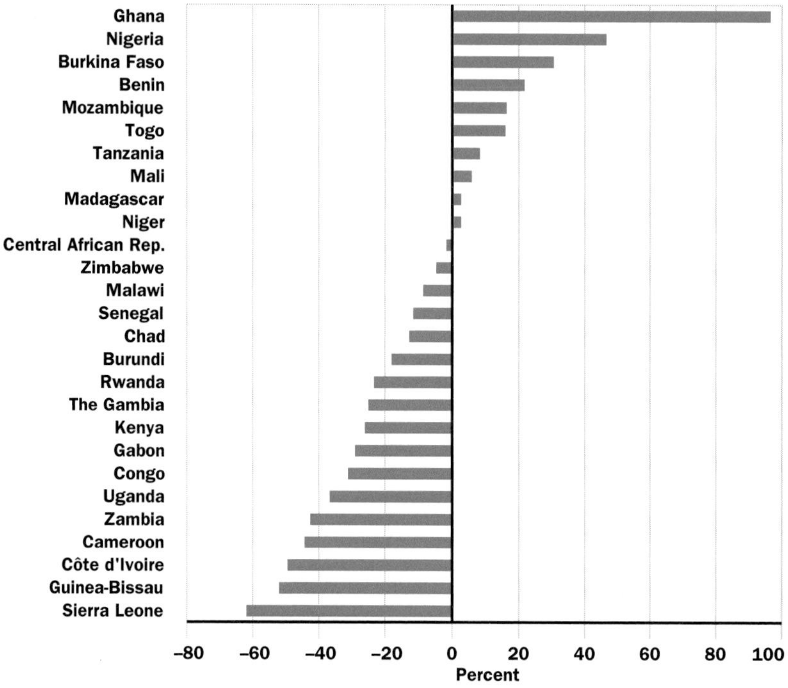

Real producer prices of export crops went up for ten countries, down for seventeen.

Note: Data for each country are based on the percentage change in producer price for each major crop, weighted by that crop's share in the total value of agricultural exports in 1985. Data on real prices were not available for Guinea. Mauritania was excluded because it has no major export crops.

Source: Appendix table A.18.

prices more than enough to offset the effects of an appreciating exchange rate, or they passed on to the producers part of the increase in the local currency proceeds from a depreciation. Although not enough to compensate entirely for the drop in world prices, these measures at least offset part of it. In the other eight countries, the combined effect of macroeconomic and agricultural policies worked against farmers and compounded the decline in world export prices.[5]

About two-thirds of the countries reduced the overall tax burden on agriculture during the 1980s (figure 3.4).[6] Did countries reduce both explicit taxation (from low producer prices) and implicit taxation (from overvalued exchange rates)? In general, no. Most countries reduced one but not the other (figure 3.5). Ghana, Nigeria, and Uganda significantly reduced the implicit taxation from the overvalued exchange rate through massive devaluations, but they taxed away some of the benefits by not passing all of the border price increase back to farmers. In contrast, Cameroon, Côte d'Ivoire, and Senegal took steps to give farmers a larger share of the border price as the real exchange rate became increasingly overvalued. Meanwhile, some countries did reduce levels of both explicit and implicit taxation: Guinea, Madagascar, Malawi, and, to a lesser extent, Burundi. But a few others increased both explicit and implicit taxation, notably Zambia and Guinea-Bissau.

Countries whose currencies became more overvalued in real terms tried to offset the loss in competitiveness with a decrease in explicit taxation—by reducing export taxes, squeezing marketing board profits,

Seventeen adjusting countries reduced overall taxation of agriculture.

Figure 3.4 Change in Overall Taxation of the Agricultural Sector, 1981–83 to 1989–91

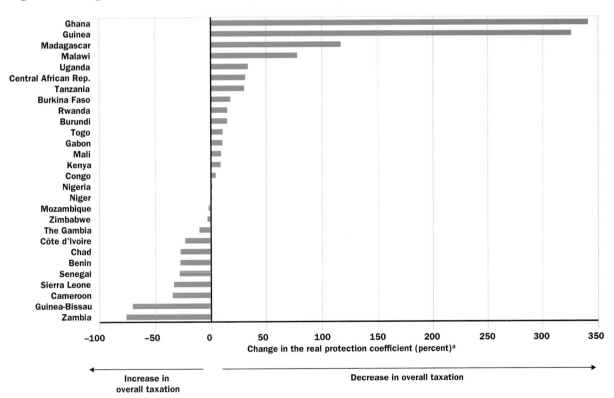

Note: Mauritania was excluded because it has no major export crops.

a. See appendix C for further discussion of the real protection coefficient as a measure of overall taxation.

Source: Appendix table A.19.

79

Figure 3.5 Changes in Explicit and Implicit Taxation of the Agricultural Sector, 1981–83 to 1989–91

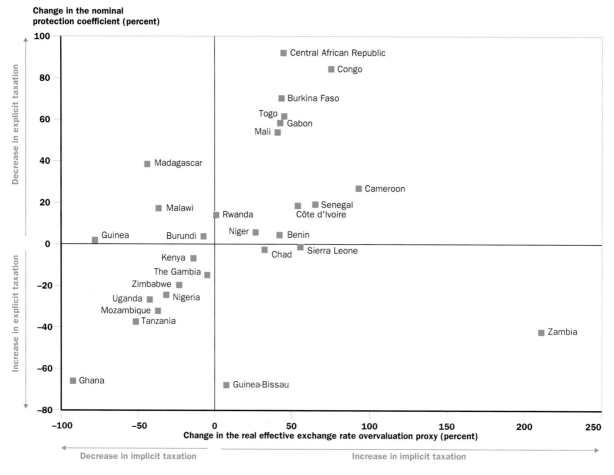

Note: Mauritania was excluded because it has no major export crops.
Source: World Bank estimates.

Few countries reduced both explicit and implicit taxation.

and subsidizing producer prices by borrowing from the banking sector and not repaying. But in about half these countries, the increase in overvaluation more than offset the reduction in explicit taxation, leading to an overall rise in taxation. In contrast, countries that devalued their real exchange rates, such as Ghana and Tanzania, were more successful in reducing the overall burden of taxation, even though they did not pass the full benefit of the devaluation back to producers. Only in Zimbabwe did the increase in explicit taxation offset the reduction in overvaluation. Evidently, for countries whose real exchange rates became more overvalued, it was difficult to reduce explicit taxation enough to counter the effects of the real exchange rate overvaluation. But in countries whose real exchange rates were devalued, it was easier for the government to reduce the overall tax burden on export producers even while appropriating some of the benefits of the real devaluation.

Some Progress in Liberalizing Export Crop Marketing

Reform efforts for export crop marketing fall into three categories: eliminating marketing boards, linking producer prices to world market prices while reforming marketing boards to reduce costs, and allowing the private sector to compete with marketing boards in crop purchasing and exporting. Most countries have undertaken at least some reform of their export crop pricing/marketing systems, though few have abolished marketing boards (appendix table A.9). Eliminating marketing boards is generally the best option from an economic standpoint, but it is often politically difficult. Nigeria eliminated all its marketing boards in one step in 1986, with good results once the initial difficulties were resolved. Other countries have eliminated marketing boards for some but not all of their export crops—coffee in Madagascar, for example, and groundnuts and cowpeas in Niger.

Several adjusting countries are experimenting with efforts to link producer prices to world prices. West and Central African cotton-exporting countries, where many parastatals for cotton production and marketing are jointly managed by foreign shareholders, are trying a two-payment system: a fixed sum at the time of crop purchase and a variable payment based on the unit prices and marketing board profits. In theory, if world prices are higher than expected at the time of export, these parastatals pass the windfall back to the producer in a second payment. It is not yet clear whether such systems will work. Their success depends on efficient administration and on passing on the benefits of world prices as promised. In Kenya, coffee producers sometimes do not receive the appropriate second payments, or they receive them only after long delays. In Malawi, shortcomings in a similar effort to link world prices to producer prices for smallholder producers of tobacco have led to a more liberalized system. Some smallholders now have the right to grow the lucrative burley tobacco and sell their crop on the auction floor.

The third type of reform—maintaining the marketing board but allowing private traders to compete—is meant to foster the benefits of competition and gradually demonopolize the marketing board or transform it into a completely private operator. Burundi is trying this approach with coffee; Tanzania, with cashew nuts.

Most of these reforms are too new to evaluate, though some appear to be succeeding (box 3.4). But the barriers to private competition can remain formidable. Often, marketing boards retain a de facto monopoly through control over processing facilities or privileged access to bank financing. Similarly, boards can squeeze out private agents by setting unprofitably low price margins and relying on the government or state banks to subsidize their losses. This can happen even when processing and marketing boards are ostensibly privatized if there are substantial barriers to entry. In Tanzania, ownership of coffee processing facilities has recently been transferred to cooperatives that were formerly state entities but are now—in principle at least—private. Other private agents, however, lacking the means to invest in costly processing facilities and facing other restrictions, find it very difficult to compete.

Box 3.4 Reversing Tanzania's Cashew Decline

IN THE EARLY 1970S, TANZANIA HAD ONE OF THE world's largest cashew nut industries, with marketed production of 145,000 tons (about 30 percent of world production). Despite a buoyant international market, Tanzania's production fell to less than 17,000 tons in the late 1980s. Several factors contributed to the downward spin: a cashew nut blight, the country's program of village development, a sharp and continuous decline in real producer prices, and major inefficiencies in the processing and marketing.

With the industry on the brink of collapse, the Tanzanian government announced in 1991 that the cashew nut market would be liberalized, with private traders allowed to purchase the crop and export it. The reforms have been gradual.

In the first season of reform in 1991–92, the government issued only vague guidelines through the media and sent no official instructions to the local authorities responsible for the policy changes. Private traders were given access only to certain buying areas (to protect the cooperatives) and were restricted to official buying prices. Private traders purchased only 17 percent of the marketed crop. Even so, producers got a higher share of the export price than they had earlier.

The second season in 1992–93 featured some improvements, but some barriers to private sector entry lingered. Even so, private traders purchased 43 percent of the crop and reestablished links to the trading firms operating in the 1950s and 1960s. They also expressed some interest in leasing long-dormant processing factories.

Under the new system, farmers are having their crop collected early and are being paid promptly, leading them to harvest rather than neglect their cashews. Production rebounded from 29,000 tons in 1990–91 to 41,000 tons in 1992–93, and farmers are beginning to rehabilitate their cashew farms and plant new trees.

A variant of the third type of marketing system is to allow full competition in domestic purchasing but to maintain government control over exporting, as Côte d'Ivoire is doing with cocoa and coffee. In such cases, producer prices would still be effectively linked to the export price set by the government, in contrast to other systems where private traders are allowed to export freely.

Assessing the Current Export Policy Stance

To compare countries' policy stances toward exporters today, the most appropriate method would be to compare the level of taxation across countries, corrected for reasonable transport and processing costs from the farmgate to the border. This is difficult to do with any accuracy. Instead, we used proxies for explicit and implicit taxation. As a proxy for explicit taxation, countries were ranked according to how much control the marketing boards or parastatals had over prices and marketing costs, taking into account significant overvaluation of the real exchange rate. Some marketing boards are more inefficient than others, of course, so the degree of control is not always a good indication of the degree of taxation. As a proxy of implicit taxation, the exchange rate policy stance developed in chapter 2 was used. The results are presented in table 3.2. The conclusion: no country has good macroeconomic policies *and* good agricultural policies. Most have exchange rate distortions (or did at the end of 1991) and government intervention in marketing.

More Liberal Food Crop Marketing

There has been good progress in liberalizing the marketing of the major staple food crops that were subject to extensive government control before the reforms. In countries that once intervened heavily, the disastrous financial position of many food crop marketing boards was a strong impetus for rapid reform. Of the fifteen countries with highly interventionist policies before adjustment, only two still intervene in a major way (table 3.3). In countries with less intervention initially, governments controlled only a small part of the marketed surplus, and there was widespread evasion through parallel markets. Many of the marketing reforms legitimized the existing situation, thus reducing barriers to private sector entry.

Table 3.2 Countries Classified by Agricultural Policy Environment

Real exchange rate policy, 1990–91	Marketing policy, late 1992		
	Most favorable[a]	Mixed[b]	Least favorable[c]
Good			
Adequate		Kenya	Ghana Madagascar
Fair	Nigeria	Burundi The Gambia Malawi Niger Uganda Zimbabwe	None
Poor or very poor	Mozambique	Benin Burkina Faso Cameroon Côte d'Ivoire Mali Rwanda Sierra Leone Zambia	Central African Republic Congo Gabon Senegal Tanzania
Unclassified	Guinea Guinea-Bissau	Chad	

a. Parastatal marketing board eliminated for major export crops.
b. Some government intervention in major export crops, but producer prices linked to world market prices.
c. Extensive government control (de facto or de jure) over collecting and exporting major export crops; producer prices not directly linked to world market prices.
Source: World Bank staff.

There was only limited interference in roots and tuber crops in the forest zone before adjustment. For example, much of the domestic produce sold through the government marketing boards in Congo and Guinea was grown on state farms that have since closed or been privatized. And although governments were involved in marketing coarse grains in many Sub-Saharan countries, they generally played a limited role. Government intervention was more widespread in domestic rice production and imports of rice and wheat, the major food staples of the urban sector. Almost all the countries that had public sector monopolies on rice imports have decontrolled these monopolies, though many still have monopolies on wheat.

Government intervention was the strongest in maize marketing in eastern and southern Africa. Reforms to create efficient, private maize

Table 3.3 Government Intervention in Marketing Major Food Crops

Country	Crop	Before reforms	Late 1992
Benin	Tubers	●	○
Burkina Faso	Millet; sorghum	●	○
Burundi	Beans	○	○
Cameroon	Cassava	◐	○
Central African Rep.	Cassava	●	○
Chad	Millet; sorghum	○	○
Congo	Cassava	◐	○
Côte d'Ivoire	Tubers	○	○
Gabon	Cassava	○	○
The Gambia	Sorghum; millet	●	○
Ghana	Tubers	○	○
Guinea	Rice	●	○
Guinea-Bissau	Rice	●	○
Kenya	Maize	●	●
Madagascar	Rice	●	○
Malawi	Maize	●	◐
Mali	Millet; sorghum	●	○
Mauritania	Millet	◐	◐
Mozambique	Maize	●	○
Niger	Millet	●	○
Nigeria	Yams	○	○
Rwanda	Sorghum	○	○
Senegal	Millet; sorghum	◐	○
Sierra Leone	Millet; rice	○	○
Tanzania	Maize	●	○
Togo	Maize	◐	○
Zambia	Maize	●	◐
Zimbabwe	Maize	●	●

● Major restrictions on purchases and sales.
◐ Limited intervention by government buying agency.
○ No intervention except in food security stocks.
Source: World Bank staff.

marketing have typically taken a long time to implement in these countries and have in some cases been reversed (box 3.5). The common package of reforms includes (a) moving farmer prices toward export or import prices, (b) announcing administered prices before planting times, (c) speeding payments to farmers and eventually liberalizing prices altogether, (d) relaxing maize movement controls and other restrictions on trade, and (e) restructuring parastatal maize marketing companies. The last of these has typically involved reducing the parastatals' commercial operations to convert them into buyers and sellers of last resort or

Box 3.5 Maize Marketing Reform

COUNTRIES IN EASTERN AND SOUTHERN AFRICA have reduced the scope of maize marketing boards, but they have had difficulty fully liberalizing the maize markets.

Kenya. Reform of Kenya's National Cereals and Produce Board began in 1982. The plan was to improve farmer incentives by moving to import parity pricing, having the treasury compensate the board for its market development activities, and relaxing maize movement controls and trading restrictions. On at least two occasions, the government wrote off the board's accumulated debts, which at one point had mounted to 5 percent of GDP.

After a decade of slow progress on the reforms, the government reversed several of them by reintroducing maize movement controls, halting the efforts to liberalize prices and restructure the board, approving an inadequate performance contract, and raising the maize reserves rather than lowering them—thus falling short of making the board a buyer and seller of last resort. Kenya has, however, substantially reduced the board's

activities in both the grain and the milling markets.

Tanzania. Since 1984, when some crop movement restrictions were lifted, Tanzania has progressively liberalized the marketing of food crops. Beginning in 1987, private traders could purchase grain from cooperatives in competition with the National Milling Corporation, although marketing outlets for farmers were still confined to the primary cooperative societies. In 1988 the grain trade was fully liberalized, and in 1990 the remaining restrictions on private grain purchase at the farm level were removed. The corporation effectively died in the 1991 season, when its access to crop finance ended. But the continuing use of the strategic grain reserve as a mechanism for price support raises fears that it may evolve into another maize board.

Private traders still face many informal administrative barriers and regulations. Local charges and levies are unevenly applied, and regional authorities continue to impose restrictions on private traders that raise the costs of marketing. In addition, the poor

guardians of food security stocks. The easiest measures to implement have been moving producer prices toward export or import parity; the hardest have been restructuring parastatals and negotiating their withdrawal from a mainstream commercial role. Despite almost universal agreement (among donors at least) that a parastatal marketing agency should act only as a buyer and seller of last resort, it has proved difficult thus far to limit parastatals to food security functions, in light of concerns about protecting producers' access to markets in remote areas.

Removing Fertilizer Subsidies and Liberalizing Distribution

Fertilizer use is extremely low in Sub-Saharan Africa—9 kilograms of plant nutrients per hectare of arable land in 1990. This is substantially below the 69 kilograms used in South Asia and the 262 kilograms in China. The paucity of irrigated land in Africa is not the reason; India is estimated to use at least three times more fertilizer on rainfed land than condition of feeder, regional, and trunk roads means high transport costs. Besides being hampered by legal restrictions, private traders have been unable to obtain credit, which is still confined to cooperative societies for grain purchases. Despite the obstacles, private traders have, in the context of partial liberalization, provided a market for farmers in accessible locales, improved food supplies, and stabilized food prices in urban areas. The increased competition so far, though still restricted, has already reduced profit margins in private trading.

Malawi. The government of Malawi undertook a series of agricultural marketing reforms in 1986 to address the financial crisis of the produce marketing agency, increase the efficiency of agricultural marketing, and allow prices to reflect more accurately the regional and seasonal demand for and supply of agricultural commodities. Achievements so far include a significant expansion of private maize trade, with more traders operating outside their home areas; the closure of some of the marketing

agency's buying centers (though fewer than agreed); and some increase in the difference between retail prices in private markets and the agency's prices.

Private traders, who are heavily concentrated geographically, confine themselves to short-haul consolidation of loads for the agency. Regulatory and other barriers keep them shut out of private export trade. They face severe transportation problems and limited access to credit. And they are still subject to official inspections on the roads, often requiring unofficial side payments that increase their cost of doing business. The marketing agency, by contrast, continues to operate a network of buying points only slightly less dense than before 1986. It cross-subsidizes its functions from lucrative export activities, to the detriment of private traders, and it is still far from being a buyer and seller of last resort. Despite these barriers, liberalization measures appear to be taking hold. In the 1992 season, private traders took a considerable share of the market and paid producers substantially more than the marketing agency did.

Sub-Saharan Africa does. More important deterrents to fertilizer use have been supply shortages and inefficient distribution systems, outcomes of extensive government intervention.

Fertilizers are generally expensive in Africa because of small procurement lots, inefficient marketing by public agencies, and high shipping, handling, and domestic transport costs. Under such conditions, fertilizer subsidies have had strong political appeal. Proponents argue that fertilizer subsidies can speed the adoption of agricultural innovations. Opponents contend that large subsidies reduce fertilizer use, because with limited funds available to finance the subsidies, only a limited amount of fertilizer is available. Moreover, subsidies disproportionately benefit well-off farmers able to secure rationed supplies. They also argue that public funds would be better spent on activities that improve the returns to agriculture, such as rural infrastructure and research and extension to develop and disseminate more fertilizer-responsive crop technologies.

...ntrols and Subsidies for Fertilizer

Country	Before reforms	Late 1992
Benin	●	✪
Burkina Faso	●	○
Burundi	●	○
Cameroon	●	⊗
Central African Republic	●	✪
Chad	●	○
Congo	—	—
Côte d'Ivoire	✪	○
Gabon	—	—
The Gambia	●	○
Ghana	●	○
Guinea	●	○
Guinea-Bissau	○	○
Kenya	●	○
Madagascar	●	○
Malawi	●	●
Mali	●	○
Mauritania	●	○
Mozambique	—	○
Niger	●	○
Nigeria	●	●
Rwanda	⊗	⊗
Senegal	●	○
Sierra Leone	●	⊗
Tanzania	●	⊗
Togo	●	○
Uganda	●	⊗
Zambia	●	○
Zimbabwe	⊗	⊗

● Marketing controlled and prices subsidized.

✪ Marketing controlled, but at world prices.

⊗ Marketing liberalized, but some fertilizers sold at below-market prices or prices controlled.

○ No controls on prices or marketing.

— Data not available.

Source: World Bank staff.

Efforts to eliminate subsidies have proceeded more slowly than expected, and progress has frequently come only after extended negotiations between governments and donors. Despite the problems, about half of the adjusting countries have completely removed fertilizer subsidies and liberalized their distribution systems (table 3.4). Subsidies have sometimes been lifted abruptly, usually when a devaluation suddenly eliminated indirect subsidies of imported fertilizer, and sometimes gradually, as with the easing of price controls or the phased removal of specific subventions. With subsidies reduced or eliminated, and most parastatal or cooperative fertilizer credit programs having abysmal loan repayment records and being shut down, governments have allowed the private sector to take a greater role in importing and distributing fertilizer.

Fears that removing fertilizer subsidies would reduce fertilizer use and lower crop production have proved to be unfounded (box 3.6). Such fears are often based on analysis that overlooks the potential for private marketing to develop and for marketing efficiency to be enhanced. Often, the more widely available supply (as the rationing of subsidized fertilizer is reduced) and the better price incentives for output counter the disincentives of removing the subsidy. Furthermore, because subsidies do not affect the marginal cost of production where fertilizer is rationed, removing the subsidies tends to have little effect on production, at least in the short term.

Letting Other Markets Work

BEFORE STARTING TO ADJUST, AFRICAN COUNTRIES HAD extensive systems of price controls and other controls on goods, labor, and interest rates. Evidence is scarce, but widespread parallel markets and rampant evasion suggest that controls on goods generally did not keep prices substantially below market levels. Indeed, some controls, maintained by according monopoly privileges to importing or producing parastatals, kept prices substantially above import prices (as with cement and wheat in Congo, for example). In many cases, controls provided rents and benefits for privileged elites instead of protecting consumers.

Reform programs have also included other regulatory and legal measures to promote private activity, such as reforms of company and bank-

Box 3.6 What Removing Fertilizer Subsidies Would Mean

THOSE WHO SUPPORT FERTILIZER SUBSIDIES argue that cutting them would reduce fertilizer use and undermine food production. Others charge that subsidies result in widespread shortages and poor distribution. What does the evidence show? Tanzania and Malawi are finding that removing large subsidies can ease supply constraints and result in greater fertilizer use, despite higher prices. In Nigeria, meanwhile, heavy subsidies have led to supply shortages that are choking agricultural growth.

Tanzania. The government of Tanzania aims to eliminate fertilizer subsidies by 1995. Already it has reduced subsidies from about 80 percent of the farmgate price in 1989 to about 40 percent in 1993. Critics of the subsidy cut have worried that it would undermine efforts to increase maize production in Tanzania's Southern Highlands, an area that receives a substantial portion of the subsidized fertilizer. So far, fertilizer use has not fallen, since supply previously was limited because of insufficient funds to cover the subsidy. Although the market for fertilizer supply has been liberalized in theory, the government agency that subsidizes fertilizer has effectively become the sole supplier. Anecdotal field evidence suggests that farmers have recently paid prices about 30 to 40 percent higher than those recommended. Because of the large excess demand at current subsidized prices, removing the subsidy and getting the government out of the market is projected to increase fertilizer use.

Malawi. In Malawi in 1983, the government committed to phasing out fertilizer subsidies completely by the 1989 season. The average subsidy fell from 30 percent in 1983–84 to 20 percent in 1987–88. But when rising transport costs and devaluation of the exchange rate led to substantial increases in imported fertilizer prices, the attempt to reduce the subsidy was abandoned, and it returned immediately to 30 percent.

The government has since renewed its pledge to phase out subsidies, this time by 1994–95. Fertilizer sales have continued to rise, even in the face of substantial increases in their official prices and stagnating producer prices for smallholders. Between 1980 and 1991, fertilizer sales to smallholders more than doubled, from 49,000 to 107,000 tons. This meant a quadrupling of plant nutrients, as the government encouraged the use of higher-analysis fertilizers. It also reflected an easing of supply, due in part to aid and probably some leakage of fertilizer from the smallholder sector to estates.

Nigeria. Nigeria briefly reduced fertilizer subsidies—from 85 percent in 1983 to 28 percent in 1986. However, when the currency was steeply devalued, the government failed to adjust fertilizer prices. Subsidies rocketed to about 90 percent of the price, and by 1989 fertilizer subsidies were consuming more than 70 percent of the central government's entire agricultural budget. The public sector could not meet demand at the subsidized prices. Fertilizer supplies became inadequate and unpredictable, and a large parallel market developed in which small farmers paid four times the official price. The fertilizer shortages—the result of massive subsidies—now constrain agricultural growth.

---

ruptcy laws and investment codes. Many countries have attempted to simplify investment procedures through one-stop investment shops, but numerous institutional problems remain to be ironed out. Several countries (notably Côte d'Ivoire) have set up antitrust regulatory bodies, and other legal and judicial reforms are under way. But it is too early to assess how successful these reforms are and what impact they will have on private activity. Of even greater importance than these piecemeal reforms may be the overall business climate, which in many countries remains hostile to private business (box 3.7).

Price Controls Largely Eliminated

Most countries have removed almost all price controls, keeping them for only a few strategic goods (table 3.5). Nine countries have lifted price controls on all goods except refined petroleum. The countries retaining substantial price controls include Burkina Faso, Cameroon, Côte d'Ivoire, Kenya, Madagascar, and Mozambique, but even these have sharply reduced the number of goods subject to control. In

---

Box 3.7 Africa's Harsh Climate for Business

AFRICAN GOVERNMENTS SOMETIMES SHOOT THEMSELVES IN the foot by tacitly or openly encouraging the harassment of successful entrepreneurs—harassment that often stems from public antagonism toward the business class. Some businesspeople clearly do engage in corrupt acts harmful to the state and society, and campaigns to prosecute tax evaders and others who violate corruption statutes are probably necessary, particularly if such prosecution recaptures revenue due the state. But the advantages must be weighed carefully, for overzealous administrative procedures can ruin profitable businesses and destroy the incentive to invest.

In the worst instances, unbridled harassment of entrepreneurs is sanctioned by law. In Ghana, where it is illegal to carry out "any act with intent to sabotage the economy," the law has on occasion been applied to the government's political adversaries or anyone enjoying economic gains. Those accused of economic sabotage are subject to imprisonment without trial and the freezing of their assets. Cases are heard outside the regular judicial system, and proceedings are not published. Those found guilty may be executed; there is no external appeal mechanism.

Large foreign companies, with ample capital and the option of going elsewhere, often have the economic clout to protect themselves from regulatory harassment. But local firms and smaller expatriate firms usually lack such leverage, making them the main victims. If the environment does not change, many will find a way to pull up stakes—depriving African countries of the capital, business acumen, and technical expertise essential for development.

Mozambique the proportion of GDP subject to price controls has dropped from 70 percent to 10 percent since 1986, although controls are still extensive.

Because most controls were ineffective, their removal probably had little impact on market prices, although there is not much evidence on this. But they were probably still a source of rent, and removing them should have reduced transaction costs and facilitated new entry, thus stimulating growth and greater competition. The largest benefits have been the increased incentives to agricultural production and the greater availability of a few key imports for which controls had been more effective, resulting in import rationing.

The one sector where prices have not been fully decontrolled is petroleum, and government intervention in that sector is very costly. Adjustment programs have attempted to improve procurement, eliminate panterritorial pricing, and reform pricing practices so that ex-depot prices and pump prices are quickly adjusted to reflect changing international price and exchange rates. Although procurement practices have improved in several countries, further improvements in procurement could bring significant savings (box 3.8), exceeding annual disbursements of World Bank adjustment loans to Africa. Furthermore, although many countries have reformed their pricing structure to reflect international prices, panterritorial pricing and fixed pump prices remain the norm. The benefit of a system in which pump price changes are set automatically according to some pre-agreed formula is that it prevents the government from collecting windfall revenues when import prices drop. It also makes it easier to pass along price increases when import prices rise. Only Mali has moved to eliminate all price controls on petroleum products. Rwanda, Uganda, and more recently Madagascar have automatic procedures for adjusting petroleum prices. Several other countries—Burundi, Malawi, Mozambique, Niger, and Togo—regularly update their ex-depot prices even though they do not have automatic procedures in place.

Reform is lagging in countries that refine imported or domestic crude petroleum. In most, the ex-refinery price to wholesalers is not set according to an import parity formula but rather on a cost-plus basis. Consumers thus pay for the inefficiencies of refineries (or the state pays in forgone tax revenue). Distributors are required to buy all or part of their refined products from government parastatals, often paying more than they would otherwise. In Kenya, for example, the five privately

Table 3.5 P

Country			
Benin			
Burkina Faso		●	
Burundi	●	○	
Cameroon	●	✪	
Central African Republic	●	⊗	
Chad	⊗	⊗	
Congo	●	⊗	
Côte d'Ivoire	●	✪	
Gabon	●	⊗	
The Gambia	✪	○	
Ghana	●	○	
Guinea	●	⊗	
Guinea-Bissau	●	○	
Kenya	●	✪	
Madagascar	●	✪	
Malawi	✪	⊗	
Mali	●	○	
Mauritania	●	○	
Mozambique	●	●	
Niger	●	⊗	
Nigeria	●	⊗	
Rwanda	●	⊗	
Senegal	●	⊗	
Sierra Leone	●	○	
Tanzania	●	⊗	
Togo	●	⊗	
Uganda	●	○	
Zambia	●	○	
Zimbabwe	●	⊗	

● Extensive controls (on twenty-six goods or more).

✪ Limited controls (on ten to twenty-five goods).

⊗ Few controls (on fewer than ten goods).

○ No controls.

Note: Price controls on refined petroleum products were excluded from consideration.

Source: World Bank staff.

Box 3.8 Getting More Mileage Out of Petroleum Reform

LARGE INEFFICIENCIES IN THE PROCUREMENT, refining, and distribution of petroleum products in many Sub-Saharan countries make reform of the petroleum sector urgent—and potentially fruitful. Except for Angola, Cameroon, Congo, Gabon, and Nigeria, the region's countries depend heavily on imported crude and refined petroleum products. Petroleum imports absorb 20 to 35 percent of export earnings, while domestic wholesale and retail sales generate about 40 percent of government revenue (Schloss 1993). For many African countries, petroleum imports are the single largest item in the balance of payments, and taxes on domestic petroleum sales are the biggest source of revenue. For the region as a whole, a rational system of oil procurement and distribution could save about $1.4 billion a year (at 1989–90 prices)—more than the World Bank's annual disbursements of adjustment policy loans to Sub-Saharan Africa.

Almost half the savings would come from improvements in procurement. African countries typically pay too much for their imported petroleum because of their limited foreign exchange, poor credit standing, and inappropriate bidding procedures symptomatic of monopoly control and government interference. The inefficiencies in procurement are greatest in the countries where governments are most heavily involved in importing petroleum (box figure 3.1).

Another 40 percent of the savings would come from improvements in refining. Refineries are poorly maintained and underused, the refined yields are insufficient to satisfy domestic demand, and the product mix is unsuitable for local markets. Locally refined products thus are not competitive with imported products.

The rest of the cost savings would come from better distribution. Poor storage, dilapidated infrastructure, inadequate market competition, and the extensive use of road transport all mean inefficiency.

About two-thirds of the total savings would be achieved through new operating procedures, better institutional arrangements, and the closing or retooling of inefficient refineries. The rest would require new investment in infrastructure.

---

owned petroleum distributors are required to procure 30 percent of the crude to be refined domestically from the National Oil Company.

Relaxing Labor Controls

The rigidities in hiring and firing workers and the practices for setting wages in some countries have raised production costs, reduced productivity, and stifled investment and job creation. Labor regulations protect the small minority of workers fortunate enough to work in the formal sector. The excessive cost of formal sector jobs limits job growth in that sector and compels the remainder of the rapidly growing labor force to seek employment in the informal sector. To enhance competitiveness and increase growth, adjustment programs have aimed at increasing the flexibility in labor markets. There has been little systematic study of labor market regulations in Africa or of their impact on economic activity, so it is difficult to evaluate the costs of various restric-

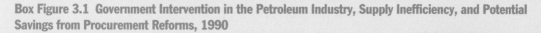

Box Figure 3.1 Government Intervention in the Petroleum Industry, Supply Inefficiency, and Potential Savings from Procurement Reforms, 1990

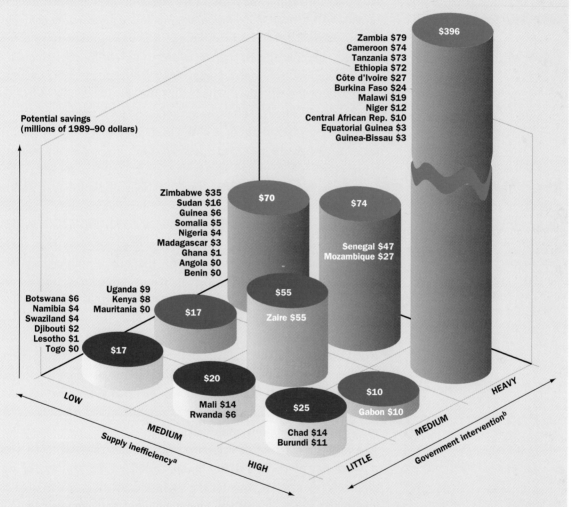

a. Supply inefficiency refers to procurement costs beyond those incurred in world markets under competitive conditions. Low inefficiency is defined as excess costs of $0–40 per ton; medium, $41–100 per ton; and high, more than $100 per ton.

b. Little government intervention is defined as 0–25 percent of crude oil and/or finished petroleum products imported by government agencies; medium intervention, 26–75 percent; and heavy intervention, more than 75 percent.

Source: Schloss (1993).

tions and the benefits of the reforms. Most of the regulations are believed to be more of an implicit tax than an absolute barrier. Firms usually find ways—sometimes costly—of getting around regulations.

The fixed exchange rate countries generally had more restrictive labor laws than the flexible exchange rate countries. This hampered their internal adjustment strategy, which was predicated on reducing real wages through nominal wage declines. Programs to remove restrictions on hiring and collective layoffs and to reform wage-setting procedures met with varying success. Mali adopted a new labor code in 1992, substantially liberalizing the labor market. In Côte d'Ivoire and Senegal, new labor codes were drafted after a long process of government consultation with employers' associations and the labor unions on labor market reform. Although the new codes have still not been officially adopted, both countries have already changed some provisions of the old codes.

Removing restrictions on hiring. In 1987 Senegal abolished a government employment agency that had a legal monopoly over placement and hiring; Côte d'Ivoire did likewise in 1992. Previously in Côte d'Ivoire, daily or seasonal workers who worked for more than ninety days continuously or intermittently for the same employer had to be offered full-time positions. Under the reform program, seasonal workers are exempt from this provision, and the obligation to regularize daily workers now comes into effect only after they have worked for one year. Daily workers receive a small salary premium prorated to equal the benefits that full-time workers would receive. In Senegal, restrictions on renewing temporary labor contracts were progressively lifted, and temporary contracts can now be extended for five years. For firms in the industrial free zone and those benefiting from the investment code, the period is unlimited.

Removing restrictions on collective layoffs. Collective layoffs in Côte d'Ivoire are subject to priority authorization by the Ministry of Employment. A new law was drawn up to change this, but it has been challenged by the unions. In Senegal the drafted labor code has substantially liberalized firing practices for small and medium-sized enterprises, with prior government authorization no longer needed. In Mali the right of an employer to lay off workers for economic causes is liberally defined to include economic distress, restructuring of the work process, and technological change.

Reforming wage-setting practices. The draft labor code in Senegal calls for (a) delinking different industry-specific wage scales from the minimum wage so that there is no automatic adjustment of the minimum wage increase, and (b) encouraging collective bargaining at the firm level. Côte d'Ivoire has not yet tackled wage-setting practices. The Mali labor code sets minimum wages for different vocational categories. It is not clear whether these minimums are binding, however, and thus what their impact is on wage rigidity and employment growth.

Demonopolization Proceeding Apace

Before reform, the private sector was prohibited—either by law or by practice—from competing with public enterprises in many key sectors (appendix table A.10). Many of these state monopolies have since been eliminated (appendix table A.11), either through the abolition of parastatals or through the liberalization of production or imports of key goods, both of which greatly increased the scope for private sector activity. Reform has been particularly noteworthy in the import and distribution of fertilizer, the import of key consumer goods, the liberalization of labor hiring, and commercial banking services. In addition:

- More than two-thirds of the countries with monopolies on rice imports and a third of those with monopolies on wheat imports have eliminated them.
- Eleven of twenty-seven countries have eliminated the monopoly on export crops, and half the countries have ended the monopolies on the distribution of petroleum.
- Telecommunications remains a public monopoly in almost all countries, although several have allowed private cellular phone services.

Establishing a Sound Incentive Framework: Mixed Results

ASSESSING GOVERNMENT INTERVENTION IN PRICES AND marketing is difficult because there is no standard indicator. We constructed a broad index to measure interventionist policies based on three factors: (a) the government's interference in setting producer prices for the major agricultural export commodity, (b) the degree of competition in five major sectors (petroleum imports and wholesale supply, retail distribution of refined petroleum products, fertilizer imports and/or distribution, wheat and/or rice imports, and the domestic marketing and distribution of the major food staple), and (c) the extent of price controls. Appendix tables A.12 and A.13 present the classification in more detail. Twenty-five countries were rated as having heavy intervention in the pre-reform period. By late 1992, however, only four were in that category; most of those previously rated "heavy" had moved into the "medium" category (table 3.6). Almost all adjusting countries have more to do, however, to provide a stable set of incentives for private sector–led development.

To evaluate the overall incentive framework in Sub-Saharan Africa, it is useful to consider market intervention policies in conjunction with

Table 3.6 Government Intervention in Selected Sectors

Country	Before reforms	Late 1992	Country	Before reforms	Late 1992
Benin	●	◐	Madagascar	●	●
Burkina Faso	●	●	Malawi	●	◐
Burundi	●	◐	Mali	●	◐
Cameroon	●	◐	Mauritania	●	◐
Central African Republic	●	●	Mozambique	●	◐
			Niger	●	◐
Chad	◐	○	Nigeria	●	○
Congo	●	●	Rwanda	◐	◐
Côte d'Ivoire	●	◐	Senegal	●	◐
Gabon	●	◐	Sierra Leone	●	○
The Gambia	●	○	Tanzania	●	◐
Ghana	●	◐	Togo	●	◐
Guinea	●	○	Uganda	◐	○
Guinea-Bissau	●	○	Zambia	●	◐
Kenya	●	◐	Zimbabwe	◐	◐

● Heavy intervention (government control over producer prices of agricultural exports, private sector competition restricted in key sectors, and fairly extensive price controls).

◐ Medium intervention (some government involvement in producer price setting, government monopolies in one or more key sectors, and some price controls).

○ Little intervention (no government involvement in producer price setting, private sector competition allowed in key sectors, and liberalized pricing of all goods other than petroleum products).

Note: Sectors include petroleum importing and wholesale supply, retail distribution of refined petroleum products, fertilizer importing and/or distribution, wheat and/or rice importing, and domestic food-crop marketing.

Sources: Appendix tables A.12 and A.13.

macroeconomic policies (fiscal, monetary, and exchange rate policies).[7] As table 3.7 shows, no country in the region has both little market intervention *and* a good or even adequate macroeconomic framework (if one assesses the framework according to the criteria developed in chapter 2). Most countries are still clustered in the groups with medium intervention and fair, poor, or very poor macroeconomic policies.

Still, it is encouraging to realize that if such a table had been constructed in 1985, almost all the countries would have been classified as having heavy government controls. As for the macroeconomic framework, all the countries outside the CFA franc zone would have been judged as having unsound policies. Most of the countries in the franc zone would have garnered better macroeconomic ratings, but even in 1985 there were indications that some had an unsustainable fiscal situa-

Table 3.7 Countries Classified by Macroeconomic and Market Intervention Policies

Macroeconomic policy stance, 1990–91	Government intervention in markets, late 1992		
	Limited	*Medium*	*Heavy*
Good			
Adequate		Ghana	
Fair	The Gambia Nigeria Uganda	Burundi Gabon Kenya Mali Malawi Mauritania Senegal Togo	Burkina Faso Madagascar
Poor or very poor	Sierra Leone	Benin Cameroon Côte d'Ivoire Mozambique Niger Rwanda Tanzania Zambia Zimbabwe	Central African Republic Congo
Unclassified	Chad Guinea Guinea-Bissau		

Sources: Table 2.5 and appendix table A.13.

tion. Thus the majority of countries would have occupied spots near the bottom right of the table. That a number of countries have moved up and left testifies to their progress in creating a policy environment more conducive to growth and poverty reduction.

Some countries' macroeconomic situations have also changed since 1990–91, the latest years for which standardized data are available. In Madagascar, for example, policies deteriorated significantly in 1992–93. In Sierra Leone, by contrast, the developments have been positive: inflation has plummeted, capital and social spending have increased, and real interest rates have been positive since mid-1992. No country appears to have reached the "good" macroeconomic classification, however. This underscores the fragility of the policy reform efforts.

Notes

1. The estimates of notional demand are based on a country's GDP level and import prices at official exchange rates. See note "a" in figure 3.2 for more details.

2. Interestingly, the predicted level was less than the actual level after 1987, an indication that the method for estimating notional demand is imperfect.

3. Burkina Faso, Mali, Mozambique, Senegal, and Zambia have also reduced their maximum tariff rates significantly.

4. Because of the difficulty of establishing the price that producers actually received for their crops, the data in figure 3.3 are indicative only of broad trends. The crops used to calculate price data for each country were as follows: Benin—cotton; Burkina Faso—cotton; Burundi—coffee, cotton, and tea; Cameroon—cocoa, coffee (arabica and robusta), and cotton; the Central African Republic—coffee and cotton; Chad—cotton; Congo—cocoa and coffee; Côte d'Ivoire—cocoa and coffee; Gabon—cocoa and coffee; The Gambia—cotton and groundnuts; Ghana—cocoa; Guinea-Bissau—cashew nuts, groundnuts, and palm kernels; Kenya—coffee and tea; Madagascar—cloves, coffee, and vanilla; Malawi—tea and tobacco; Mali—cotton; Mozambique—cashew

nuts, cotton, and tea; Niger—cotton and cowpeas; Nigeria—cocoa; Rwanda—coffee and tea; Senegal—cotton and groundnuts; Sierra Leone—cocoa, coffee, and palm kernels; Tanzania—coffee, cotton, and tea; Togo—cocoa, coffee, and cotton; Uganda—coffee and cotton; Zambia—cotton and tobacco; and Zimbabwe—cotton, sugar, and tobacco. The periods compared were 1981–83 and 1989–91. The intervening years were avoided because the mini-booms in coffee, cocoa, and tea in 1984 and 1986 would have skewed the results.

5. The nine countries that took measures to benefit farmers were Burundi, the Central African Republic, Congo, Gabon, Kenya, Malawi, Sierra Leone, Uganda, and Zimbabwe. The other eight countries whose policies worked against farmers were Cameroon, Chad, Côte d'Ivoire, The Gambia, Guinea-Bissau, Rwanda, Senegal, and Zambia.

6. For a discussion of the measure of overall taxation, see appendix C.

7. Because the index of macroeconomic policy stance is based in part on the parallel market exchange rate premium, it also captures certain elements of trade policy stance.

CHAPTER 4

Reforming the Public Sector

THE PUBLIC SECTOR LIES AT THE CORE OF THE STAG-
nation and decline in growth in Africa. By the mid-
1980s, the public sectors in most Sub-Saharan
countries had taken on too much. They were intervening—with poor results—in activities where markets work reasonably well, such as allocating foreign
exchange and directing credit. They were also doing a poor job of
providing such essential services as roads and primary schools.

Several factors account for the overextension and poor performance
of the public sector. The economic crisis of the early 1980s strained
Africa's already-limited technical and institutional capacities. Declining
growth reduced the tax base, depriving governments of the resources to
pay competent staff, improve infrastructure, and deliver social services.
The economic and political conditions prevailing when African governments gained power also played a part. The indigenous private sector
was very weak in Africa, and nonindigenous elites and foreigners relatively dominant. Given those circumstances, it was understandable that
governments took an interventionist stance. The then-dominant development paradigm supported this: the prevalent view was that developing countries could grow faster by taking an active role in production
and by directing the allocation of resources to bring about faster
industrialization.

The failures of this strategy are manifest everywhere, but conditions
have not changed radically. Public sector institutions remain weak, perhaps even weaker now that the economic crisis has taken its toll. The indigenous private sector continues to be economically weaker than other,
more established private sector groups. And reform has become even
more difficult, as the rents and other side-benefits of interventionist

policies have created powerful public sector constituencies with a strong interest in their perpetuation. Now more than ever, fundamental reform of the public sector is needed to reverse the economic decline, yet it has become more difficult to achieve.

World Development Report 1991 (World Bank 1991c) discussed the emerging consensus on the need for a market-friendly approach to development. That approach calls for governments to do less where markets work reasonably well and to do more where they don't. Four types of government action are especially vital: investing in human capital, providing a competitive climate for enterprises, opening markets to international trade, and ensuring stable macroeconomic management.

Chapters 2 and 3 assessed the progress of countries in undertaking the policy reforms needed to provide a stable macroeconomic foundation, unleash markets, and participate more fully in international trade. This chapter continues the analysis of reform efforts by examining the closely linked public enterprise and financial sectors, where reform is important for ensuring macroeconomic stability and for spurring private sector–led growth. We also look at efforts to generate and reallocate the resources needed for the state to carry out its essential functions. We do not, however, discuss building institutional capacity within the public sector—a long-term development challenge beyond the scope of adjustment programs.[1]

Reform efforts generally have not been too successful in the areas where the state has intervened most heavily. Privatizing and reforming state-owned enterprises and creating sound financial systems have proved to be among the most difficult of adjustment reforms. Public enterprise reforms have not yet leveled the playing field for the private sector because they have not significantly curtailed the public enterprises' privileged access to the budget, to the credit system, to tariff and nontariff protection, to special tax status, and to regulatory protection. With financial reforms, there has been movement toward reasonable interest rates and the restructuring and privatization of banks. Nonetheless, large fiscal deficits, poorly performing public enterprises, and continuing political interference still threaten to undermine development of the financial system.

Some countries have made progress rationalizing public expenditure, trimming the wage bill, and increasing resource mobilization. But there is little evidence that the allocation of resources within sectors or between sectors has improved substantially in favor of basic services. The long-run development tasks of creating the control structures and operating procedures to manage a modern and efficient civil service have barely begun. A precondition for this may be strengthening the institutions of civil society to create demand for better governance.

Public Enterprise Reform: Little Evidence of Significant Progress

THE PUBLIC ENTERPRISE SECTOR PLAYS TOO BIG A ROLE IN economic activity and employment in all twenty-nine of the adjusting countries in our study. In the 1970s, as African governments tried to accelerate development, the number of public sector firms mushroomed, and parastatal enterprises came to dominate many key areas of the economy. Statistics on the number of public firms, their share of formal sector employment, and their share of value added are limited and unreliable, but they provide some insights into the public enterprise sector before the reform period.

At least fifteen of the adjusting countries had seventy-five or more public enterprises by the early 1980s.[2] Ghana, Mozambique, Nigeria, and Tanzania had more than 300. The public enterprises accounted for over 20 percent of formal sector wage employment in a number of countries.[3] In Congo, Côte d'Ivoire, Guinea, Kenya, Mozambique, Nigeria, Tanzania, and Zambia, and possibly other countries as well, public enterprises accounted for more than 10 percent of GDP. They also accounted for a large share of public investment, domestic credit, and external loans.

Quantifying these shares is difficult. First, domestic credit statistics for many countries include net domestic credit to public enterprises as part of private sector credit, making it impossible to distinguish the share of credit to the public enterprise sector. In Burundi, Chad, Ghana, Guinea-Bissau, and Zimbabwe (about half the countries for which disaggregated data were available), the stock of credit to the public enterprises was as big as or bigger than credit to the private sector.[4] In Tanzania in 1988, fewer than twenty public enterprises held more than three-quarters of the government-owned National Bank of Commerce's portfolio of loans over $100,000. Second, external debt statistics underestimate the share of lending to public enterprises, because many governments on-lent external funds to the public enterprises. Third, public enterprise investment is extremely difficult to estimate, because it has not been systematically monitored and is financed from a variety of sources.

Public enterprises have been a major drag on the fiscal budget, the banking sector, and other quasi-fiscal sources of revenue (stabilization funds and social security funds). The returns on public capital invested in these enterprises were very low, and in many cases probably negative. Lacking proper accounting systems, most countries had little idea of the poor returns, although the opportunity cost of subsidies and equity contributions to public enterprises was frequently enormous. Financial support for public enterprises reduced the funds available for basic social services, crowded out private sector borrowing, and required higher tax rates, undermining the profitability of the private sector. Moreover, to improve the profits of public enterprises, governments adopted high trade tariffs, imposed nontariff trade barriers, and gave public enterprises preferential access to foreign exchange, special tax exemptions, and other regulatory advantages (such as monopolies over domestic production and imports). All in all, the special advantages accorded to public enterprises produced an environment unfriendly to private enterprises and made it difficult for them to compete.

Most African governments began public enterprise reform primarily to ease the fiscal burden and, usually secondarily, to increase efficiency. The first step in the reform process, difficult in itself, was to establish an inventory of public shareholdings. Countries then classified enterprises as strategic or nonstrategic, and the nonstrategic ones as commercially viable or nonviable. The viable nonstrategic enterprises were slated for privatization; those judged nonviable, for liquidation. Strategic firms—generally utilities, telecommunications, major transport parastatals, heavy industries, and agricultural marketing boards—were exempt from divestiture because of their economic importance. This was unfortunate, because they were the major cause of losses and economic distortions. Many governments commissioned studies of the strategic enterprises to identify ways of improving their efficiency and profitability. A number signed performance contracts with key enterprises. Countries also adopted institutional reforms to clarify their regulatory and legal frameworks and increase enterprise autonomy. And some adjustment programs tried to limit fiscal transfers and reduce public enterprise borrowing.

Assessing Public Enterprise Reform

The available data on the public enterprise sector are sparse and disappointing, showing no significant reduction in the number of enterprises, little improvement in their financial performance, unacceptable returns on government investment, and inability to meet the demand for cost-effective, efficient provision of public utilities. Divestiture is proceeding slowly among small and medium-sized firms and scarcely at all among large enterprises—not surprising since most big enterprises were classified as strategic. Spotty evidence suggests that financial flows from governments to public enterprises remain high, and there is some danger that direct fiscal transfers are being replaced by less obvious subsidies, such as bank financing. With a few notable exceptions, performance contracts and other attempts to boost the efficiency of enterprises remaining under state ownership have failed. Parastatal accounts, particularly those of the strategic enterprises, are rarely audited by independent accountants, and in most countries there is a long lag in producing any accounts at all (table 4.1). In Ghana in 1990, information was available for only 70 of some 300 public enterprises. Few countries monitor credit to the public enterprise sector. Often there is no systematic accounting of external funds on-lent to the public enterprise sector, nor any systematic tracking of repayments and arrears. And public enterprises continue to enjoy advantages provided by a regulating framework that protects them from competition.

The limited progress thus far suggests that there is an urgent need to rethink the approach to reforming the public enterprise sector in Africa, particularly the major enterprises. Opposition to more far-reaching divestiture programs appears to be subsiding, and more ambitious programs are on the drawing board, but the changes are too recent to have yielded concrete results.

Slow progress in reducing the size of the public sector. At first glance, privatization efforts appear to have been moderately successful. Almost all countries have managed to halt the increase in public enterprises, and several have begun to reduce the number. Throughout the region, reform has led to the privatization of hundreds of public enterprises, mostly small and medium-sized but also a few large ones. Among the twenty-nine adjusting countries, governments have divested themselves of about 550 firms—less than one-fifth of the total number of public enterprises—either by selling their holdings or by liquidating nonvi-

Table 4.1 Financial Auditing of Major Public Enterprises, Late 1992

Country	Timeliness of audits
Benin	◐
Burkina Faso	○
Burundi	●
Cameroon	◐
Central African Rep.	○
Chad	◐
Congo	○
Côte d'Ivoire	◐
Gabon	◐
The Gambia	●
Ghana	○
Guinea	○
Guinea-Bissau	○
Kenya	◐
Madagascar	○
Malawi	●
Mali	○
Mauritania	○
Mozambique	○
Niger	◐
Nigeria	◐
Rwanda	○
Senegal	◐
Sierra Leone	◐
Tanzania	○
Togo	○
Uganda	○
Zambia	○
Zimbabwe	●

○ No regular annual audits.
◐ Some firms audited annually.
● Many firms audited annually.
Source: World Bank staff.

able enterprises, with slightly more privatizations than liquidations (Shaikh, Kikeri, and Swanson 1993).

But progress has been uneven (table 4.2). Six countries—Benin, Ghana, Guinea, Mozambique, Nigeria, and Senegal—account for two-thirds of the divestitures. Only a handful of countries have divested more than 40 percent of their enterprises. And half the countries have been extremely slow to privatize any enterprises. In Kenya there have been almost no sales in ten years. A few countries have even expanded their public enterprise sectors. In Burundi the public enterprise sector grew during the adjustment period, with five firms divested but twelve new ones created. In Côte d'Ivoire the number of public enterprises rose from 113 in 1977 to 140 in 1990, despite the privatization of some 30 enterprises in the mid-1980s.

More important, the number of divestitures overstates the extent of privatization. Large enterprises with the bulk of public assets—airlines, railroads, mining, and utilities—have generally not been privatized. This is beginning to change, however. Ghana has recently privatized

Table 4.2 Divestitures of Public Enterprises, 1986–92

Percentage of enterprises divested	Number of enterprises before divestiture			
	0–50	51–100	101–200	More than 200
0–10	The Gambia Mauritania Rwanda Sierra Leone Zimbabwe	Burkina Faso Congo Uganda Zambia	Cameroon Côte d'Ivoire[a] Malawi[b]	Kenya Tanzania
11–25	Chad	Burundi Central African Republic	Madagascar	Ghana Mozambique
26–40	Niger		Guinea Nigeria	
41–60	Guinea-Bissau	Benin Mali Senegal Togo		

Note: Divestitures include partial sales, but not management contracts or leases.
a. Data are for 1989–92. Some thirty transactions in the 1980s are excluded.
b. Total number of enterprises includes 121 statutory bodies and 18 commercial parastatals.
Sources: Shaikh, Kikeri, and Swanson (1993); World Bank staff estimates.

gold and diamond mines, a brewery, and several medium-sized manufacturing units, and Nigeria has sold several hotels and a gasoline distribution company to private investors. In most countries, including most of those where the government has sold many firms, the focus on small and medium-sized enterprises means that the size of the public enterprise sector has hardly changed. The four public enterprises sold in Côte d'Ivoire in 1991 accounted for a mere 0.1 percent of the government's holdings. Possible exceptions are Benin, Guinea, and Nigeria, where some 5 to 15 percent of government shareholdings have reportedly been privatized (Shaikh, Kikeri, and Swanson 1993).

Further complicating the picture are problems with the data, as Berg (1993) documents. Sometimes enterprises are reported as sold when they are merely up for sale. Sometimes sales are recorded when the privatization agency and a buyer reach a preliminary agreement, even though the deal later falls apart. Of twenty-one enterprises listed as privatized in the Ghana divestiture agency's 1991 report, eleven returned to the state's portfolio in 1992. Another problem is that government data do not make much distinction between various types of transactions. The sale of a 3 percent government holding in a company largely under private ownership is treated just like the full privatization of a company that was completely government-owned. Moreover, a sale might turn out to involve the transfer of assets from one state enterprise to another. Such transactions include Mali's sale of a publicly owned vegetable oil mill to another state-owned enterprise, and Ghana's purported privatization of a brewery when in fact 45 percent of the equity was transferred from the government to publicly owned banks and insurance companies. Some liquidations are mere fiction, in that the firms had long before ceased to operate.

It is no surprise, then, that such limited privatization has had little impact on efficiency and economic growth. Berg (1993) cites several reasons. In some cases, a government has continued to hold a major share—and to intervene—in a partly privatized firm. In other cases, severance benefits to dismissed employees were so large that governments had to siphon public resources away from productive uses. Many privatizations did not lead to greater efficiency because the new owners received favors—tax benefits, duty-free imports, tariff protection, and priority access to credit and other scarce inputs—that reduced the social benefits. Where governments allowed buyers to defer payments, speculative buyers unqualified to run the enterprises sometimes bought them, hoping to resell for a quick profit. Pressure on governments to sell may also have led to ill-considered transactions. And cronyism and corruption have undercut the benefits of privatization. Transactions in Guinea and Nigeria, for example, have been criticized for their lack of transparency.

High financial flows to public enterprises. Many countries have improved the financial profitability of some key enterprises, but placing this progress in a broader context is difficult. Data are scarce, and there has been no systematic analysis of changes in financial flows to public enterprises, whether in loans directly on-lent or guaranteed by the government, in equity contributions from the government or other sources, or even in indirect grant assistance from donors. Nor are there estimates of revenue forgone from unpaid taxes, dividends, debt service payments, and tax exemptions. But a preliminary assessment based on scattered evidence suggests that financial flows to public enterprises remain substantial, and that the public enterprises remain a large drag on the government budget and financial system.

In some countries, the relatively low direct budgetary subsidies may not be indicative of the real fiscal cost of public enterprises. For example, an examination of financial flows between the Burundi government and fourteen core public enterprises during 1987–90 reveals large implicit subsidies. The government accumulated payment arrears to the public enterprises, primarily because of underbudgeting, but the enterprises themselves had considerable tax and debt service arrears to the government (table 4.3). The net outflow from the government to the public enterprises in 1989 was an estimated 19 percent of government expenditure. It is also instructive to examine the gross flows as costs to the government, under the assumption that the public enterprises, if privatized and operated like other commercial enterprises, would have received no government subsidies and would have paid taxes and dividends on their earnings. On this basis, public enterprises cost Burundi (in transfers and forgone revenue) an amount equal to 25 percent of total expenditure in 1989, or 1.5 times the education budget.

Burundi is probably not atypical. Ghana's public enterprises are thought to command a similar share of total expenditure, though reliable data are not available. In Tanzania, direct support (grants, subsidies, and transfers) was 7.3 percent of total expenditures in 1989. In addition to direct support, the central government engaged in short-term lending to public enterprises, which by 1991 had grown enormously. During

Table 4.3 Financial Flows between the Government and Public Enterprises in Burundi

(millions of FBu, current prices)

Item	1987	1989	1990 (estimated)
A. Flows from government to public enterprises	3,441	8,947	9,613
Budgeted subsidies	2,342	5,974	7,545[a]
Public enterprise debt service paid by government			
(net of reimbursement)	433	2,400	1,500[b]
Customs exemptions	666	573	568
B. Flows from public enterprises to government	1,142	2,425	3,241
Profit taxes	594	940	1,860
Dividends	548	1,485	1,381
C. Net flows from government (line A − line B)	2,299	6,522	6,372
D. Net arrears owed to (owed by) government	(735)	2,824	1,575
Owed to government by public enterprises	563	3,436[c]	2,011[d]
Owed by government to public enterprises	(1,298)	(612)	(436)
E. Total net outflow from government to public enterprises			
(line C + line D)	1,564	9,346	7,947
As a share of total government expenditure	3.7 percent	19.2 percent	14.8 percent

a. Includes taxes due and arrears.
b. Includes FBu 1,292 million to the coffee sector to offset losses caused by price declines.
c. Net debt service includes interest plus amortization.
d. Includes FBu 1,011 million for debt service and an estimated FBu 1,000 million for tax arrears.
Source: World Bank estimates.

the first six months of 1991 alone, the treasury lent—at about half the prevailing commercial interest rate—an amount equal to more than 9 percent of the previous year's development expenditure and net lending. Furthermore, the government allocated foreign exchange to public enterprises without requiring payment of the local currency counterpart— an implicit subsidy of about 3 percent of total government revenue in 1991. But the drain on public finances is not high for all countries: for Kenya, it was only about 1 percent of total expenditure in 1991, not counting implicit subsidies due to tax and other exemptions.

No clear trend in quasi-fiscal transfers. In some countries, a decline in direct fiscal subsidies can mask a shift to quasi-fiscal sources of financing, such as bank loans, and to other extrabudgetary sources of revenue. In Senegal, while direct operational subsidies from the budget declined between 1985–86 and 1988–89, there was a large rise in public expenditure overdrafts—a shift particularly difficult to evaluate. The International Monetary Fund's *International Financial Statistics* distinguishes the claims on nonfinancial public enterprises from the total claims on the private sector for only eleven of the twenty-nine adjusting countries. For those eleven countries, the picture is mixed, with about half showing a decline in the stock of credit to the public enterprise sector. Moreover, data on other sources of quasi-fiscal funding, such as social security funds, are particularly obscure, so there is no way of knowing whether the public enterprise sector has reduced its claim on the financial resources of the entire system.

Ineffective reform of nonprivatized enterprises. Performance contracts—also called contract plans—have frequently been used to improve the performance of public enterprises not slated for privatization. Spelling out the rights and duties of the enterprise and the government, they were devised to attack vague objectives, insufficient autonomy, and weak incentives. Senegal was the first Sub-Saharan country to implement performance contracts in the early 1980s. By 1988, fourteen countries either had signed or were drafting twenty-eight contracts, absorbing millions of dollars worth of technical assistance from donors.

Although contracts can be useful in identifying problems facing an enterprise, they generally have not been effective in improving the performance of key enterprises (Nellis 1990; Sherif 1993). A few countries report some success. In Mauritania and The Gambia, the governments agreed to make appropriate budget allocations for water and electricity, helping to put ailing utilities on their feet. More frequently, however, contracts have not produced results. In Cameroon, where the government signed contracts with major utilities, neither the government nor the utilities have lived up to their obligations and the contracts have had little impact. In Ghana only four of the eleven firms with performance contracts reached the negotiated targets, because of the lack of financial discipline and performance accountability (Sherif 1993).

Making a performance contract work may require conditions that seldom exist. Both parties must be committed. Some recapitalization is usually part of a restructuring program. And there must be enforceable targets, incentives for success, and censure or financial punishments for failure. Lacking these essentials, governments and enterprises have often disregarded carefully negotiated contract provisions. Governments have failed to make necessary management changes in the enterprises and to deliver promised financial resources. Enterprises have avoided difficult financial and personnel restructuring measures. So the considerable time, effort, and resources spent developing performance contracts have achieved relatively little. Perhaps more disturbing, attention may have been diverted from more fundamental reforms, such as divestiture.

It is difficult—in the absence of financial audits, information on quasi-fiscal transfers and tax exemptions, and productivity indexes—to judge whether the performance of public enterprises remaining under state ownership has improved. The general assessment, despite a few encouraging stories (box 4.1), is that the efforts at reform have been disappointing overall. Few "rehabilitated" public enterprises have made significant and lasting improvements, and many are being rehabilitated for a second and third time. Another worrisome trend is the ongoing, large annual investment in these public enterprises (often financed in part by donor funds), even though they are generating low or negative returns. Most public enterprise accounts are deficient, and where performance seems to be better, there is little evidence to suggest that sustainable improvements in management are responsible. Instead, the better financial performance could be the result of inflation, major tariff increases to accommodate inefficient management, or the government's assumption of public enterprise debts.

Box 4.1 Restructuring Public Enterprises: Zimbabwe's Encouraging Results

IN ZIMBABWE, RESTRUCTURING IS AT WORK AND HAS PRODUCED particularly encouraging results in the national railways. After independence in the 1980s, the National Railways of Zimbabwe grew into a major loss-maker, operating in a noncompetitive environment and supported by ever-increasing subsidies. The National Railways' deficit grew from $8 million in 1982 to $230 million in 1990, at which time the government attempted reform. As part of the country's adjustment plan, management of the railway was restructured, tariffs were increased by 50 percent over a year and a half to reflect economic costs, and the work force was cut about 3 percent. Other measures taken to improve efficiency included tightening staff supervision, improving management information systems, filling critical job vacancies, and increasing security to decrease theft. With higher tariffs and relatively stable traffic, the company increased revenue by 75 percent in the first year of adjustment and cut its deficit by half. The National Railways of Zimbabwe is being called a model to be applied to other public enterprises.

To the extent that observed improvements in financial performance are due to these factors, there is little reason to think that they reflect a sustainable improvement in the enterprise's productivity.

A few countries have experimented with nonasset divestiture for public utilities (leasing and concessions), with more success. Under leasing arrangements, a private contractor pays the public owner for exclusive rights to operate facilities and assumes full commercial risks. Concessions are similar to a lease, but the contractor has additional responsibility for certain investments. Côte d'Ivoire and Guinea have had generally favorable experience with lease contracts and concessions in the water supply and power sectors (box 4.2).

Financial Reforms: Limited Signs of Sustainable Progress

ESTABLISHING A SOUND, EFFICIENT FINANCIAL SYSTEM IS important to sustained economic growth, as a growing body of literature demonstrates.[5] King and Levine (1992) show that financial development is correlated with growth, because of higher investment and greater efficiency. A country's financial sector should perform several critical functions: operating the payment mechanism, mobilizing savings, allocating financial resources, offering a means of diversifying risk, and providing services to facilitate trade.

Financial systems in Sub-Saharan Africa have traditionally been characterized by weak resource mobilization, high credit losses, high intermediation costs, and excessive political interference. So Africa's financial depth is shallower than that in other developing regions. Bank deposits are just 15 percent of GDP. Furthermore, financial systems have not grown in real terms during the past decade. The low rate of financial savings in African countries is related to negative real interest rates, lack of confidence in the banking system, and political and macroeconomic instability, leading people to maintain savings in more tangible assets or to send their capital abroad. Part of the difficulty stems from structural, long-term problems: limited human resources and undiversified, small-scale economies. But government policy—reflected in ownership, interest rates, directed credit, and heavy taxation—has also weakened the financial systems.

Box 4.2 Lease Contracts and Concessions in Public Utilities

Water in Guinea. IN 1989, OWNERSHIP OF Guinea's urban water supply authority and responsibility for sector planning and investment were transferred to a new autonomous water authority, the Société Nationale des Eaux de Guinée (SONEG). A new company, the Société d'Exploitation des Eaux de Guinée (SEEG), was created to operate and maintain the facilities as a joint venture, with the government owning a 49 percent share and 51 percent owned by a private, foreign consortium. The strength of the Guinean arrangement lies in the clarity of responsibilities and incentives. Under the ten-year lease contract with SONEG, SEEG operates and maintains the system at its own risk, with its remuneration based on user charges actually collected and on fees for new connections. SEEG benefits if it improves collections and reduces operating costs and unaccounted-for water. SONEG has incentives to seek adequate tariffs and to invest prudently, based on realistic demand forecasts, because it has responsibility for capital financing. So far the collection ratio has increased dramatically, from 20 percent to 70 percent, and technical efficiency and coverage have improved. Tariffs are up sevenfold and are expected to reach the full cost-recovery level by 1998. In the interim, donor assistance is financing the foreign exchange costs of the operation, and the government has assumed debt service. The arrangement has been hampered by delays in equipment procurement by SONEG, which has affected SEEG's ability to improve the quality of service and its financial performance.

Power in Côte d'Ivoire. The performance of the Enterprise d'Electricité de Côte d'Ivoire (EECI), the parastatal responsible for the electric power sector in Côte d'Ivoire, deteriorated during the 1980s. In 1990 a major restructuring transferred responsibility for plant operation and maintenance to the Compagnie Ivoirienne d'Electricité (CIE), a new joint venture owned by a consortium of two French companies (with a 51 percent share), and by Ivoirian and other investors (with a 49 percent share). CIE has a leasing arrangement to generate, transmit, and distribute power, and it receives considerable technical assistance from its foreign owners. The government, through EECI, continues to own the facilities and bears responsibility for investments, sector policy, and planning. In the first eighteen months of the new arrangement, efficiency and service improved markedly. CIE raised the collection ratio from 60 to 90 percent, increased maintenance, reduced power outages, computerized business operations, and eliminated operating subsidies. An important reason for CIE's success was its status as a newly created operating entity rather than a holdover from the past, even though it retained some of the staff of EECI.

Water in Côte d'Ivoire. A concession for water supply services in Cote d'Ivoire was arranged in 1987, following twenty-five years of a lease contract. The lease had improved the service and internal efficiency of the operating company, the Société des Eaux de Côte d'Ivoire (SODECI), a mixed French and Ivoirian enterprise. However, financial troubles mounted in the 1980s because of policies enforced by the government regarding investment and tariffs, for which it retained responsibility. Under the new concession arrangement, SODECI became both operator and investor, with responsibility for all new urban water supply investments in the country. The company receives no operating subsidies, and all new investments are self-financed. Although the concession contract was not subject to competition, SODECI's operating fees were reduced substantially during the negotiations. The company's operating costs are now comparable to those of many water utilities in West Africa, while the quality of its service is far better than most. Private Ivoirians own a majority of SODECI's shares, and the company has succeeded in reducing expatriate staff while expanding operations.

Source: Kessides (1993).

With so many problems, Sub-Saharan Africa's financial systems were ill-prepared to cope with the economic crisis that came to a head in the early 1980s. The overall worsening of the economy further weakened the financial soundness of borrowers, especially the central governments and the parastatals. Agricultural parastatals and cooperatives often accounted for a large share of unpaid loans. Despite the general absence of competition, bank profits were generally low, and margins were inadequate to offset the growing deterioration of the portfolios. Problem loans mounted, and many private and public institutions became technically insolvent. Loan-loss ratios regionwide approached 40 to 60 percent, with banks in some countries showing bad loans for more than 90 percent of their portfolios. Overstaffing and branch expansion under government pressures further reduced bank profitability. Large and negative real interest rates and significant uncertainty about future policies led to capital flight, reduced financial intermediation, and problems with bank solvency and liquidity.

Many countries in Africa are undertaking financial reform programs focused largely on banking (table 4.4). The first objective is to reduce fi-

Table 4.4 Financial Sector Reforms Undertaken during the Adjustment Period

Liberalization and/or rationalization of interest rates	Restructuring of banks	Privatization of banks	Liquidation of banks
Benin	Cameroon	Cameroon	Benin
Burundi	Côte d'Ivoire	Côte d'Ivoire	Côte d'Ivoire
Congo	Ghana	Guinea-Bissau	Guinea
Côte d'Ivoire	Guinea	Madagascar	Niger
The Gambia	Kenya	Mauritania	Rwanda
Ghana	Madagascar	Senegal	Senegal
Kenya	Mali		
Madagascar	Mauritania		
Malawi	Rwanda		
Mauritania	Senegal		
Mozambique	Tanzania		
Rwanda	Uganda		
Tanzania			

Note: This table is not intended to be a comprehensive list of all the financial sector reforms undertaken.
Source: World Bank staff.

nancial repression—by aligning interest rates toward market equilibrium levels and reducing directed credit programs. The second is to restore solvency and improve the incentives under which banks operate. This involves restructuring and recapitalizing distressed banks, liquidating some development credit institutions and some other specialized entities, and privatizing banks. The third objective is to improve the financial infrastructure, strengthening supervision, auditing, and accounting practices and providing more training and development opportunities for staff. Improving the legal framework, though initiated with other adjustment reforms, is part of the longer-term development agenda for financial sector reform.

The reforms have had only limited success. Financial systems continue to finance the deficits of the central government and the overextended public enterprise sector. Continuing heavy regulation in the real sector discourages the emergence of profit-making private sector borrowers. A weak legal framework and an inability or unwillingness to enforce financial discipline further compromise efforts to improve bank portfolios. Although bad loans have been stripped from the balance sheets of many banks, apparently improving bank performance, there are new signs of balance-sheet problems. More encouraging, however, are the progress in reducing financial repression and the move to privatize more financial institutions.

African financial systems continue to be an extension of the fiscal system, in part because of heavy government ownership. Additionally, both central banks and commercial banks are often major lenders to the government. The public sector has a large share of total domestic credit in many African countries, crowding out the private sector. The monetization of budget deficits also undermines or prevents the development of interbank and money markets, and high taxation reduces the financial sector's profitability.[6]

In addition, there is significant public interference in the management of both public and private banks, eroding the quality of their portfolios. Credit allocation procedures are poor, as the public banks generally allocate credit following directives from the government (Tenconi 1992). Loans to parastatals are seldom evaluated, because they have the implicit or explicit backing of the government, and loans to the private sector are not systematically scrutinized. Government inspection and supervision of banks is grossly inadequate. Indeed, supervision is essentially nonexistent in countries where the banking system has been nationalized. Even in countries with nominally private banks, there may be a conflict of interest because members of the supervisory agencies often sit on the boards of the banking institutions. In most instances, prudential ratios have been ineffective in preventing the degradation of loan portfolios. The ratios sometimes were poorly designed, and banks sometimes lacked rules for classifying credit according to risk and for defining and handling delinquent loans. Not surprisingly, adjustment under such conditions has generally been slow and difficult.

Some Progress in Reducing Financial Repression

The rationalization and liberalization of interest rates, among the most common features of adjustment programs, have been somewhat successful in easing financial repression. Interest rates were fully liberalized in Burundi, The Gambia, Ghana, Kenya, Madagascar, Malawi, Mauritania, and Zambia (table 4.5). Rwanda followed a slightly different approach, with a program that set a floor for deposit rates and a ceiling for lending rates. The central banks in the CFA franc zone raised interest rates and eliminated preferential rates to maintain competitiveness with France.

These reforms have not always succeeded in reducing financial repression in countries with highly negative real interest rates. Although several countries had moved from significantly negative to acceptable real interest rates by the end of the adjustment period, Rwanda, Sierra Leone, and Zimbabwe had average rates ranging from –10 to –31 percent during 1990–91 (appendix table A.4). At the other end of the spectrum, in another problematic group, were eleven countries with highly positive real interest rates. Ten of these—all with convertible currencies and overvalued real exchange rates—had average real deposit rates above 5 percent during 1990–91. The limited success in achieving reasonable real interest rates, despite considerable attention to interest rate reforms, is not surprising given limited competition and continuing intervention in Africa's financial systems. Because most countries have few banks, and because most of those banks have significant public ownership, there is little scope for "true" market-determination of interest rates.

Burundi, Kenya, Rwanda, and Zaire have moved toward the use of treasury bill auctions to establish a benchmark rate for a market-determined interest rate structure. But too much reliance on this mechanism as a "true" market rate could be deceptive, particularly if the gov-

Table 4.5 Government Intervention in the Financial Market

Country	Interest rate for deposits		Interest rate for loans	
	Before reforms	Late 1992	Before reforms	Late 1992
Benin	●	⊗	●	◉
Burkina Faso	⊗	⊗	●	◉
Burundi	●	○	●	○
Cameroon	●	⊗	●	◉
Central African Rep.	●	⊗	●	◉
Chad	●	⊗	●	◉
Congo	●	⊗	●	◉
Côte d'Ivoire	●	⊗	●	◉
Gabon	●	⊗	●	◉
The Gambia	●	○	●	○
Ghana	●	○	●	○
Guinea	●	—	—	—
Guinea-Bissau	●	●	●	●
Kenya	●	○	●	○
Madagascar	●	○	●	○
Malawi	●	○	●	○
Mali	●	⊗	●	◉
Mauritania	●	○	●	○
Mozambique	●	●	●	●
Niger	●	⊗	●	◉
Nigeria	●	◉	●	◉
Rwanda	●	⊗	●	⊗
Senegal	●	⊗	●	◉
Sierra Leone	●	●	●	○
Tanzania	●	○	●	⊗
Togo	●	⊗	●	◉
Uganda	●	●	●	●
Zambia	●	○	●	○
Zimbabwe	●	◉	●	◉

● Rate set.
◉ Spread regulated.
⊗ Minimum deposit rate / maximum lending rate set.
○ No government control.
— No data available.
Source: World Bank staff.

ernment dominates the market. Transparent, fair auctions and trading in government securities may be more useful for fostering a trading culture in these countries, but they have not proved to be a reliable proxy for market-determined interest rates in the short and medium term.

Reducing Directed Credit

Countries have apparently had some success reducing directed credit. Many countries are scaling back their efforts to target credit to specific sectors, especially to unsound public enterprises or other quasi-public agencies. Several development finance institutions heavily involved in providing directed credit have been closed. For example, the 1989 reforms of the crop marketing system in the West African Monetary Union significantly reduced preferential credit programs.

Such reforms can be difficult to sustain, however. In Tanzania about two-thirds of all bank lending at the end of 1987 was to cover the operating deficits of the crop marketing parastatals. During 1988 the government officially took over 40 percent of these liabilities, but the crop marketing parastatals were more indebted to the banking system at the end of the year than at the beginning of 1987. While many countries have nominally eliminated directed credit policies or institutions, informal pressure to lend to the politically well connected may remain. No systematic analysis has been undertaken to determine if the elimination of formal directed credit programs has resulted in sounder portfolios.

Restructuring Balance Sheets, Recapitalizing, and Privatizing

Restructuring and recapitalizing insolvent or undercapitalized banks has been another important part of adjustment programs. The objective is to restore the viability of these banks and improve the quality of financial intermediation. In a typical restructuring operation, a newly created government agency absorbs the nonperforming loans of the banks, taking them off the bank's balance sheet, and the government and the shareholders infuse banks with new capital to enable them to restart normal operations under a revised incentive structure. For example, in Ghana in 1990, the government recapitalized ten state-owned commercial and development banks through a central bank bond issue and transferred the related bad loans and assets to a recovery trust for nonperforming assets. The internal restructuring of banks—including downsizing, changing incentives for managers (and changing the managers themselves), and insulating management from political interference—is essential for avoiding past mistakes but difficult to achieve.

Bank recapitalizations in Africa—without corresponding changes in the real sector, such as restructuring the parastatals—have generally failed. In the Central African Republic, one bank has been restructured three times. In Mauritania, five major state-owned banks were recapitalized at a cost of nearly 15 percent of GDP in 1988, but they are again suffering large losses of up to 50 or 60 percent of total loans. In Kenya in 1989, eight failed institutions were merged into a "turnaround" bank, Consolidated Bank Limited, now in difficulty.

The recapitalization operations have also been expensive. The fiscal cost in some cases was between 1 and 2 percent of GDP—1.5 percent of GDP in Ghana, 2.0 percent in Guinea, and 1.5 percent in Madagascar; in other cases, it was much larger. In Senegal the cost came to about 15 percent of GDP, mainly because the restructuring program covered nearly all losses for the distressed banks, rather than stripping out a portion of the bad debts. In Tanzania the cost of a partial restructuring is estimated at roughly 40 percent of GDP. Moreover, recovery of bad debts has generally been disappointing. Tenconi (1992) reports that the amounts Guinea recovered in the first five years after closing all government-owned banks amounted to about 3 percent of the portfolio. In Cameroon the total recovery rate for banks being liquidated was less than 5 percent by 1990, and liquidation costs, including severance pay, absorbed more than half the recovered amounts. In a few cases, the terms and conditions of the first restructuring operations involving foreign shareholders were overly generous to these shareholders and set a costly precedent for restructuring other banks.

Guinea-Bissau, Madagascar, and Senegal privatized all or at least a few of the restructured banks. Ghana and Tanzania kept the restructured banks in the public sector. In the very few cases in which restructuring was accompanied by privatization or by the creation of private banks—or both—there is no evidence that banks are generally performing well. Guinea-Bissau found that the banks rapidly accumulated bad debts without an appropriate interest rate structure. Privatization without attention to the underlying policy framework and to restructuring the real sector is thus unlikely to improve the performance and efficiency of the banking sector.

In many countries, the public sector dominates the banking system. For the region's adjusting countries, the government has equity in approximately half of the banks and is the majority owner of more than a third. In 1992 the government was the majority holder of all banks in Congo and Tanzania. In four other countries—Burkina Faso, Burundi, Chad, and Rwanda—the public sector holds at least a minority stake in all banks (Tenconi 1992). Most countries have fewer than ten banks (most of them government-owned). And only Côte d'Ivoire, Kenya, Nigeria, and Zambia have six or more *private* banks, facilitating some competition and independence from public interference. In the few countries with substantial private capital participation, the domestic shareholders are usually closely linked to the political authorities.

Despite these difficulties, more banks are being privatized, and new private financial institutions are entering the markets—a welcome trend that reverses the nationalization of financial institutions in the 1960s and 1970s. In the twenty-nine countries examined in this report, the number of banks in which the government holds a controlling interest was reduced from 106 to 76 as a result of liquidation and privatization between 1982 and 1992 (table 4.6). The government-owned banking systems of Benin and Guinea were closed and replaced by privately owned banks (some with government participation in Guinea).[7] While the total number of commercial banks increased by 15 percent between 1982 and 1992, the number with no government participation almost doubled. Nigeria had twenty-four fully private banks in 1992, compared with just nine in 1982. These are clear signs of a more open attitude toward private ownership, but the public sector still dominates the financial system, and further progress is needed in reducing its role.

Improving Financial Infrastructure and Regulatory Capabilities

Financial markets in Africa are particularly lacking in skilled professionals—a result of relatively low education levels and relatively short periods of independence in these countries. Although things are now changing, foreign banks continued to dominate the financial sector in many countries during the first few years after independence, narrowing the possibilities for African managers to gain significant experience and handicapping bank officers even more. The same was true for staff in central banks and supervisory agencies.

African governments have recently placed more emphasis on developing regulatory capabilities and skills. Many of the early financial adjustment programs in West Africa focused on restructuring balance sheets, with regulatory issues often relegated to studies. The 1988–89 programs in Ghana and Kenya were the first to emphasize the development of the legal and regulatory framework. More attention has also been given to improving the financial infrastructure, typically through a

Table 4.6 Government Participation in the Capital of Commercial Banks *(number of banks)*

Country	1982 (213 banks)			1992 (245 banks)		
	Majority shareholder	Minority shareholder	No share	Majority shareholder	Minority shareholder	No share
Benin	3	0	0	0	0	5
Burkina Faso	4	0	1	4	1	0
Burundi	3	0	3	3	4	0
Cameroon	5	6	0	1	7	2
Central African Republic	1	2	0	1	0	2
Chad	1	2	1	1	2	0
Congo	4	0	0	3	0	0
Côte d'Ivoire	2	5	5	2	4	9
Gabon	1	4	1	2	4	5
The Gambia	1	1	0	1	0	2
Ghana	7	2	2	5	3	4
Guinea	6	0	1	1	2	3
Guinea-Bissau	—	—	—	—	—	—
Kenya	3	1	9	4	2	20
Madagascar	3	0	0	2	1	1
Malawi	3	1	1	1	3	1
Mali	3	1	2	2	2	2
Mauritania	4	1	0	1	0	3
Mozambique	1	1	0	0	0	3
Niger	4	0	5	2	1	4
Nigeria	24	4	9	22	6	24
Rwanda	1	1	0	1	2	0
Senegal	2	5	3	2	3	3
Sierra Leone	3	1	3	2	0	4
Tanzania	6	0	0	5	0	0
Togo	3	2	2	3	2	2
Uganda	2	5	2	2	4	3
Zambia	4	1	4	2	0	10
Zimbabwe	2	1	6	1	1	3
Total	106	47	60	76	54	115

— Not available.
Sources: Tenconi (1992); World Bank staff.

variety of technical assistance operations. The tasks range from simple training activities (teaching domestic bank officials how to shorten the time that a check takes to clear) to more complex operations (designing an adequate legal and regulatory framework). Ghana, Kenya, Madagascar, and Mauritania have made efforts to strengthen supervision and financial expertise. In general, though, not enough has been done to develop accounting and audit standards or to form a core of accounting professionals—tasks that go beyond the short time-frame of adjustment programs.

Changing regulatory standards is one thing; getting the information to apply them, given the scarcity of accountants, is another. Eighteen countries in the region have fewer than fifty fully qualified accountants (UNCTC 1991). In some countries, such as Rwanda, the banks must go outside the country to hire an external auditor, because they have no qualified chartered accountants. Requiring a bank (much less an enterprise) to be audited becomes time-consuming and expensive. Audit standards for banks and enterprises are often uneven and haphazardly enforced, and even if institutions conform to the letter of the regulations, their financial data may be of such questionable quality as to make the audit report meaningless.

Progress in creating new financial instruments, such as interbank and money markets, has been mixed, and it is clear that efforts to develop money and capital markets cannot succeed where competition is lacking or where governments still intervene extensively to set interest rates. The most advanced money markets, in Ghana and Zimbabwe, consist of an interbank market and discount houses. The discount houses trade in short-term instruments that are usually rediscountable by the central bank, such as central bank or treasury bills, crop bills, export and import bills, and bankers' acceptances. Short-term markets deepen and diversify financial markets, and they can develop if the fiscal and budgetary situations remain stable.

Improving Public Sector Management: A Long-Term Challenge

ACHIEVING BETTER MANAGEMENT IN THE PUBLIC SECTOR IS essentially a long-term development objective, and evaluating Africa's success in this regard is beyond the scope of this report. Upgrading the quality of the civil service, developing career streams, putting in place promotion and pay systems based on merit, strengthening budgetary and investment management, and building policy analysis and regulatory capacity—all these take considerable time and require considerable improvements in the institutional environment. They also require good governance. Adjustment programs have laid some of the foundations, but the efforts will have to continue long after the basic reforms are in place. The main short-term objectives of adjustment reforms have been to trim the civil service to a manageable size, increase real public sector wages to reasonable levels where necessary, get control of the payroll system, eliminate the worst "white elephants" from investment programs, create a rolling investment plan that includes all the investment projects being undertaken, and reform tax policy and administration. Progress even in these areas is difficult to quantify, partly because well-defined norms for measuring progress do not exist.

Civil Service Reform

Since independence, most African countries' policies toward the civil service (and public sector employment) have had three common features, each undermining institutional capacity. First, they expanded the size of the public sector faster than the economy grew. Second, they favored employment growth over income growth in the public sector, driving down the real wages of public sector employees. Third, they favored pay increases in the lower ranks, reducing pay differences between skilled and unskilled employees. The result: civil services are larger than countries need, more costly than they can afford, and less effective and productive than they should be. Reform programs have responded to these problems with short-term cost-containment measures and medium-term programs to build institutional capacity to increase productivity.

A narrow, short-term approach to civil service reform is likely to yield limited benefits where governance problems are serious (Dia 1993). In such settings, recruitment is based on subjective criteria, public employment is part of the social welfare system, pay levels are unrelated to productivity, and loyalty is to the political leader in power rather than to the state. Building a clear public consensus on the need for good governance may be a precondition for creating a more effective civil service. Encouraging professional and other interest groups, allowing freedom of association and expression, and reforming the judicial and legal systems will enable a more productive and responsive public sector and sharply curtail patronage and corruption.

The short-term record of civil service reform is mixed. Most adjusting countries tried to trim excessive public sector wage bills, shed "surplus" civil service staff, reverse salary erosion, and decompress the wage structure. There has been some progress in reducing public sector wages and salaries as shares of GDP and current expenditure (net of interest). Between 1985–86 and 1990–91, fifteen countries cut their wage bill as a share of GDP, while eleven increased it (figure 4.1). That eleven of fifteen countries with flexible exchange rates managed to cut their wage bill, while increases were recorded for seven of eleven fixed exchange rate countries, suggests that real depreciations and the relatively greater wage flexibility in the flexible exchange rate countries were important in reducing the wage bill.

Progress in controlling the wage bill has been mixed.

Many countries also took steps to reduce the number of surplus civil servants. They used a variety of measures: ensuring attrition through hiring freezes, enforcing mandatory retirement ages, abolishing job guarantees for high school and university graduates, introducing volun-

Figure 4.1 Public Sector Wage Bill

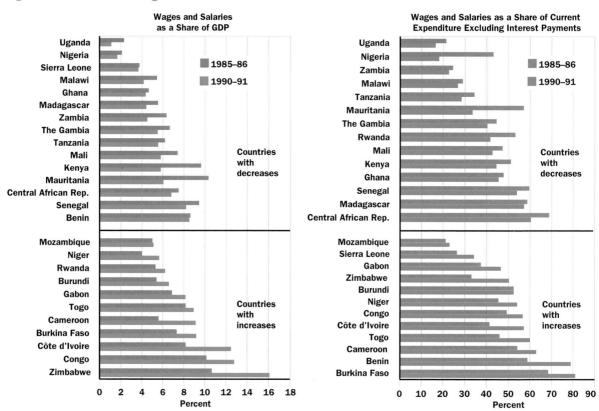

Note: Chad, Guinea, and Guinea-Bissau are excluded because of insufficient data.
Sources: IMF staff estimates; Nashashibi and Bazzoni (1994).

tary departure schemes, and making outright dismissals. Cameroon, Ghana, Guinea, Tanzania, and Uganda significantly reduced employment by exorcising payroll "ghosts"—paycheck recipients who did not actually work. The Central African Republic, Congo, Gabon, Ghana, The Gambia, Kenya, Mauritania, Mali, Nigeria, and Senegal used various forms of hiring freezes. Guinea and other countries achieved reductions by strictly enforcing the retirement-age provisions. And several countries adopted early retirement and voluntary departure schemes— the Central African Republic, Ghana, Guinea, Guinea-Bissau, Mali, and Senegal. Dismissals were less widely used, primarily in the Central African Republic, Guinea, Ghana, and Senegal. Despite these efforts, the gross reductions shown in table 4.7 considerably overstate net reductions, because of new hiring.

Only a handful of countries have cut the number of civil service employees by more than 5 percent since they began structural adjustment

Table 4.7 Reductions of Civil Service Personnel in Selected Countries, 1981–90

Country	Removal of "ghost" employees	Enforced/ early retirement	Voluntary departure	Retrenchment Regular staff	Retrenchment Temporary staff	Other mechanisms	Total[a]
Cameroon	5,840[b]	5,000	—	—	—	—	10,830
Central African Republic	2,950[b]	—	1,200	350–400	—	—	4,500–4,550
Congo	—	—	—	—	—	2,848[c]	2,848
The Gambia	—	—	—	919	2,871	—	3,790
Ghana	11,000[d]	4,235[e]	—	44,375[e]	—	—	48,610
Guinea	1,091[f]	10,236	1,744	—	—	25,793[g]	38,864
Guinea-Bissau	800[d]	945	1,960	921	—	—	3,826
Mali	—	—	600	—	—	—	600
Senegal	497	747[h]	1,283	—	—	—	2,527
Uganda	20,000[i]	—	—	—	—	—	20,000

a. Gross figures, not adjusted for new recruitment and attrition.
b. Includes elimination of double payments as well as "ghosts" (fictitious employees).
c. Attrition and hiring freeze.
d. Includes "ghosts" identified but not necessarily removed.
e. Includes staff in district assemblies and in the education sector.
f. Includes "ghosts" in the Conakry area only. A second census in 1989–90 identified many more "ghosts."
g. Parastatal liquidations and the transfer of joint-venture mining workers to company rolls accounted for 14,983 of these. The remaining 10,810 officials were assigned to a personnel bank and placed on administrative leave; it is unclear whether all have left the civil service.
h. An additional 2,133 officials applied for voluntary departure or early retirement.
i. Estimate based on savings from "ghost" removal divided by average civil service wages.
Source: World Bank (1991b).

(table 4.8).[8] Moreover, personnel cuts have usually had little fiscal impact, because the cuts disproportionately affected low-paid employees at the bottom of the civil service. Salary erosion has continued and has frequently been more important in reducing the wage bill than personnel reductions. Although a few countries, notably Guinea, reversed real wage erosion before the adjustment period, this has been the exception rather than the rule. Scattered evidence suggests that the erosion of real wages has been more prevalent in countries with higher inflation.

Few adjusting countries have effective control over the payroll system; in fact, all but six have significant problems (table 4.9). To manage the payroll system, governments need to maintain information on who is employed in the public sector and verify the information against the payroll. Personnel censuses can become quickly outdated unless systems are in place to maintain them and link them to the payroll. Again, governance problems undermine reforms in these areas.

The democratic transition in Africa has also led to reversals of wage containments and personnel reductions in some countries. In Congo the wage bill ballooned by about 60 percent in 1991 because of salary increases and a 15 percent increase in the number of public employees. In Ghana in 1992—a year of political transition—wage increases of about 80 percent compromised the fiscal stability maintained since 1986, casting doubt on the sustainability of the present level of public spending. Restoring fiscal balance has proven difficult.

Table 4.8 Change in the Number of Civil Service Personnel, 1985–92

Increase of 5 percent or more	No significant change	Decrease of 5 percent or more	Information not available
Burundi	Burkina Faso	Central African Rep.	Benin
Cameroon	Chad	The Gambia	Gabon
Congo	Guinea-Bissau	Ghana	Madagascar
Côte d'Ivoire	Togo	Guinea	Mozambique
Kenya	Zimbabwe	Mali	Nigeria
Malawi		Mauritania	Rwanda
Niger		Senegal	
Tanzania		Sierra Leone	
		Uganda	
		Zambia	

Source: World Bank staff.

Public sector salary spreads have widened substantially in several countries—a desirable development in that it may facilitate recruitment of talented individuals and provide public employees greater incentives to improve performance. But the data are too limited to establish whether this is a regionwide trend. In Ghana the ratio of the highest-paid echelon to the lowest-paid widened from about 5:2 in 1984 to 10:1 in 1991, and in Mozambique from 2:1 in 1985 to 9:1. Salary spreads appear also to have widened in Guinea and The Gambia, though they remained unchanged in the Central African Republic.

Several countries have also begun devising new administrative structures, redeploying personnel, redefining career streams, adopting formal hiring and promotion procedures, and instituting incentive-based compensation systems. These exercises, while useful, are very complex and may yield few long-term benefits unless underlying governance problems are also addressed.

Public Expenditure and Investment

Adjustment programs (and related technical assistance) have aimed at improving the budgeting processes in the public sector, the monitoring and reconciling of expenditures, and the allocation of public funds. But such efforts are complex, and it takes time to develop the necessary local capacity. A recent assessment of efforts among countries benefiting from the Special Program of Assistance for Africa (SPA) noted improvement in the government's capacity to plan and monitor public expenditure.[9] The strength of that capacity remains a concern, though, as does the sustainability and composition of government spending. Public spending is difficult to track because of numerous off-budget accounts (many established for donor-funded projects), the opacity of military budgets, and the financial operations of public enterprises and the banking systems. There is still a long way to go in improving the monitoring of implicit and explicit financial flows between public enterprises and government.

With respect to public investment, adjustment programs have tried to ensure that resources are used wisely and that low-priority projects are eliminated. One of the first steps necessary is to develop a rolling investment plan that takes account of all projects. As of late 1992, eighteen of the twenty-nine adjusting countries had not put in place an effective system for tracking all projects in the investment program, and Cameroon, the Central African Republic, Chad, Guinea-Bissau, Nigeria, and Tanzania

Table 4.9 Public Sector Management of the Payroll System, Late 1992

Country	Effectiveness
Benin	◑
Burkina Faso	○
Burundi	○
Cameroon	●
Central African Rep.	●
Chad	●
Congo	●
Côte d'Ivoire	◑
Gabon	●
The Gambia	◑
Ghana	◑
Guinea	●
Guinea-Bissau	●
Kenya	◑
Madagascar	◑
Malawi	◑
Mali	○
Mauritania	○
Mozambique	●
Niger	●
Nigeria	◑
Rwanda	○
Senegal	●
Sierra Leone	○
Tanzania	●
Togo	◑
Uganda	◑
Zambia	◑
Zimbabwe	◑

● Substantial problems.
◑ Some problems.
○ No significant problems.
Source: World Bank staff.

Table 4.10 Public Investment Program, Late 1992

Country	Recording of all projects
Benin	◗
Burkina Faso	◗
Burundi	◗
Cameroon	●
Central African Rep.	●
Chad	●
Congo	○
Côte d'Ivoire	◗
Gabon	○
The Gambia	○
Ghana	◗
Guinea	◗
Guinea-Bissau	●
Kenya	○
Madagascar	○
Malawi	○
Mali	○
Mauritania	◗
Mozambique	◗
Niger	◗
Nigeria	●
Rwanda	○
Senegal	◗
Sierra Leone	○
Tanzania	●
Togo	○
Uganda	◗
Zambia	◗
Zimbabwe	○

● Substantial problems.
◗ Some problems.
○ No significant problems.
Source: World Bank staff.

were assessed as having substantial problems (table 4.10). In some cases, the sheer number of projects financed by external donors makes effective control difficult. The public investment program in Burundi varies from 500 to 600 projects. In Tanzania the development budget lists about 2,000 projects, and even this list excludes many that are donor-funded.

Maintaining a rolling investment program that includes all investment projects, even those financed by donors, is only the first step in ensuring adequate quality of investment. Nigeria improved the monitoring of investments, but it is planning large investments with dubious rates of return. Because there are no established benchmarks that would enable us to compare the quality of public investment programs across countries, we were not able to systematically rank countries on the basis of their efforts to reform their public investment programs.

Creating a core program of the most worthwhile investment projects has been useful in improving the management of aid. Core programs push governments to set priorities for spending and to devise more effective mechanisms for channeling domestic counterpart resources to important foreign aid–financed projects. Such a program helped Ghana meet its most critical investment objectives (box 4.3). But in many countries, noncore projects have remained in the public investment program and competed (often successfully) for funds. So, designating a core program may not be as effective as properly sizing and ranking public investments in the first place.

Many countries have made progress in consolidating expenditures and revenues in the government budget, including better accounting of foreign aid and increased measurement of tax exemptions and quasi-fiscal expenditures. The composition of public expenditure is generally poor, however (see box 4.4 for a discussion of this as it relates to Kenya). Common problems include underspending in the sectors most vital for development, funding of investment projects without allocation of sufficient resources to meet future recurrent charges, poor maintenance of existing capital stock, overspending on wages, and high levels of military spending. Only two of the twenty-one countries covered by a 1991 survey for the SPA had a reasonable degree of efficiency in spending.

Tax Reform

Tax reform in Sub-Saharan Africa appears to have been driven by short-term revenue needs as much as other considerations, such as se-

Box 4.3 Public Finance Reform in Ghana

AT THE START OF ITS ADJUSTMENT PROGRAM IN 1983, Ghana faced a number of critical public expenditure problems. Economic decline and a shrinking revenue base had severely compressed government spending. Civil service wages and salaries had eroded, wage differentials were narrow, and employment rolls were padded. Nonwage operations and maintenance were neglected, while public investment declined to less than 1 percent of GDP. The result was a near-collapse of the country's economic infrastructure and severe cutbacks in social services.

In the course of adjustment, Ghana made substantial progress in addressing several of these problems. Increased revenue and foreign financing (including project and nonproject assistance) permitted total central government expenditure to rise from 11 percent of GDP in 1984 to 19 percent in 1986, where it stayed for the rest of the decade. Capital expenditure for infrastructure rose to about 8 percent of GDP by the end of the decade. The composition of expenditure was restructured to increase the share of nonwage operations and maintenance expenditures in health, education, and agriculture. The share of social services (including education and health) in total expenditure increased dramatically—from 34.5 percent in 1984 to about 50 percent in 1989. Real per capita education spending increased by 150 percent between 1984 and 1989, while real per capita health expenditure tripled. The share of primary education also grew, and there was greater cost recovery and a reduction of subsidies at higher levels. As a result, basic education enrollments are up and a range of health indicators have improved.

The government also shed about 50,000 surplus civil service staff, increased average pay levels, and widened the salary differential between the highest- and lowest-paid workers. Another priority was reshaping public investment. A task force prepared Ghana's first rolling public investment program in 1986 and established objective screening criteria for projects, scaling down to a core program of about 100 projects consistent with the country's implementation capacity. That program emphasized rehabilitation rather than new projects. In 1987 an inner "super-core" program was identified, with twenty-nine projects of special importance to be protected in budget implementation.

Source: World Bank (1992a).

curing a given level of revenue while minimizing efficiency losses, moving toward a more equitable distribution of income, and making the tax system simple and transparent both to ensure better voluntary compliance by taxpayers and to lower administrative costs. Despite the short-term focus on raising revenues, the ratios of tax revenue to GDP have been low in Sub-Saharan Africa, ranging from 6 to 20 percent at the start of the adjustment period in 1986 and ending with a median improvement of less than 1 percent by 1992, with considerable variation among countries (appendix table A.14). There were wide-ranging discretionary rate and base changes, while the expenditure-to-GDP ratio remained stubbornly higher, at 20–25 percent. These discretionary changes have taken several forms: eliminating exemptions for all nondiplomatic imports, imposing a minimum import levy, converting

Box 4.4 Changes in Public Spending in Kenya

KENYA MANAGED TO REDUCE ITS FISCAL DEFICIT in the 1980s and contain the total level of public spending. Like many other African countries, however, it was less successful in improving the composition of that spending.

Rapid growth in current expenditure, primarily for wages, was fueled by growth in central government employment (5.4 percent a year during 1981–87). Employment of teachers by the Teachers' Service Commission grew particularly rapidly, at 8 percent a year. Meanwhile, expenditures on nonwage operations and maintenance declined both in real terms and as a percentage of total expenditure for much of the 1980s, and recent increases have been insufficient to reverse the decline. Cuts in public investment were instrumental in reducing expenditures and the deficit until the early 1990s, when both shot back up. But the government has not established priorities for its public investment program.

Intrasectoral imbalances remain in both education and health. Budgetary costs per university student are more than seventy times those per primary student. At the university level, 30 percent of spending goes for boarding and allowances, and the government has taken some steps toward cost recovery. In primary education, teacher salaries account for 85 percent of spending, and milk distribution for another 13 percent. The number of teachers has been growing much faster than the number of students, leading to falling student-teacher ratios and rising costs. Nonwage expenditure has dropped sharply, to less than half the price of one textbook per student per year. More recently, some efforts have been made to improve the composition of public spending in the education sector.

The health sector also faces growing imbalances between personnel costs and other operating expenditures. Personnel expenditures increased an average of 6.4 percent a year in real terms over fiscal 1985–88, while nonwage operating expenditures fell by 4.4 percent, resulting in shortages of drugs and supplies.

Source: World Bank (1992a).

import and excise duties from specific rates to higher ad valorem rates, raising tax rates for petroleum products, and moving to a current-year basis for assessing corporate income. The most prominent trend has been for taxes of goods and services to replace taxes on international trade as the main source of tax revenue, while the share of taxes on income and profits has stagnated.

Efficiency considerations have been taken into account indirectly in several ways. High marginal rates of taxation on personal and corporate income have been significantly reduced. This, coupled with inflation-proofing of personal exemptions and tax brackets, has strengthened the incentive to work. In addition, taxing consumption rather than income has been stressed as a way to broaden the tax base while limiting adverse effects on the poor.[10] Tax reform has also promoted tax neutrality between the consumption of domestically produced goods and the consumption of imports by reducing the average level of effective protection for the former and reducing rate dispersion for the latter. Income redistribution objectives, however, have been pursued primarily through expenditure programs rather than tax programs, using implicit subsidies and explicit income transfers.

Some countries have also improved their tax administration procedures. Value-added taxes (VATs) or turnover tax thresholds reduce the number of taxpayers to a level compatible with administrative capability. A broad-based VAT and a single rate or a limited number of rates (as in Benin or Burkina Faso) also simplify administration. Simple business license fees and other systems of presumptive taxation aimed at small businesses are a step in the right direction. Benin and Senegal simplified their penalty systems for tax evasion, and Benin, Chad, and Niger enforced a temporary shutdown of taxpayers' premises to improve compliance. Some countries have also set up special units to monitor compliance of large taxpayers, in order to stabilize the major share of tax revenue. Improving compliance is difficult when tax administration is weak and perceived to be applied in a manner favoring the politically well connected.

Notes

The final section of this chapter, on tax reform, is based on a contribution by the Fiscal Affairs Department of the International Monetary Fund.

1. See World Bank (1991a) for a discussion of an initiative to build institutional capacity.

2. Burundi, Cameroon, Congo, Côte d'Ivoire, Ghana, Guinea, Kenya, Madagascar, Mozambique, Nigeria, Senegal, Tanzania, Togo, Uganda, and Zambia all had at least seventy-five public enterprises.

3. Those countries include Benin, Burkina Faso, Congo, Côte d'Ivoire, Ghana, Guinea, Malawi, Mozambique, Nigeria, Tanzania, Togo, and Zambia.

4. This was not the case in Cameroon, Congo, Gabon, or Kenya. Data are from the International Monetary Fund.

5. See McKinnon (1973), Fry (1988), King and Levine (1992), and World Bank (1989b), for example.

6. Giovanini and de Melo (1993) and Chamley and Honohan (1992) show that Africa's formal financial systems are indeed subjected to higher implicit taxation than other sectors. High reserve requirements on deposits and forced lending to the government at low real interest rates are forms of implicit taxation.

7. Guinea had one privately owned bank in the pre-reform period, which was the sole survivor of the massive banking liquidation of 1985.

8. A few countries, such as Rwanda, may not need large reductions in civil service personnel.

9. The SPA coordinates balance-of-payments assistance to low-income, debt-distressed African countries that are committed to adjustment programs.

10. Noncascading value-added taxes and final-stage retail sales taxes that exempt staples are examples of consumption taxes.

CHAPTER 5

The Payoffs to Reforms

I S ADJUSTMENT PAYING OFF IN SUB-SAHARAN AFRICA? THE answer is a qualified yes. Adjustment programs may not have raised all countries' GDP growth, exports, savings, and investment rates to those of adjusting countries in other regions. But the stronger reformers in Africa have turned around the decline in economic performance and are growing for the first time in many years. There also are signs that new firms are being created, that exports are growing, that private investment is picking up, and that savings performance is improving.

For the six countries with large improvement in macroeconomic policies:

- Median annual GDP per capita growth was almost 2 percentage points higher during 1981–86 than during 1987–91; it was 2.6 percentage points lower for countries with deterioration in macroeconomic policies.
- Median industrial growth was up 6.1 percentage points, compared with an improvement of 1.7 percentage points for countries with deteriorating policies.
- Median export growth increased 7.9 percentage points; it declined 0.7 percentage points for countries where policies worsened.
- Median gross domestic savings climbed 3.3 percentage points; the median fell 3.3 percentage points for countries with policy deterioration.
- Domestic investment also recovered, albeit slightly.

Furthermore, for the seven countries that substantially reduced taxation of their export crop producers, median agricultural growth rose 2 percentage points; it declined 1.6 percentage points for countries that raised taxes on producers. Overall, countries with better macroeconomic policies and limited government intervention in markets are enjoying GDP per capita growth, while those with a poor policy stance and more market intervention are facing further declines.

The strong acceleration in GDP per capita growth between 1981–86 and 1987–91 for African countries with improving macroeconomic policies compared favorably with that in other regions. Mozambique and Nigeria managed bigger shifts in growth than did Bolivia, the Philippines, or Thailand. Ghana, Sierra Leone, and Tanzania accelerated growth more than Mexico or Colombia and about as much as Costa Rica. After controlling for policy changes and initial conditions, the increase in GDP per capita growth among African adjusters appears to be no less robust than the increase among adjusting countries elsewhere.[1]

These outcomes, while encouraging, are not as positive as they might be. Current growth rates among the best African performers are still too low to reduce poverty much in the next two or three decades. So far, the rebounds have merely brought countries back to their historical trend of low growth, and it is not yet clear whether they are shifting onto a higher-growth path. Without further substantial increases in agricultural, investment, export, and GDP growth, Sub-Saharan Africa will continue to lag behind other developing regions.

How to Assess the Payoffs to Reforms

IS ADJUSTMENT WORKING? TO ANSWER THIS QUESTION, WE NEED to determine the most appropriate indicators of both adjustment effort and adjustment outcomes. In this report we use the indexes of policy change described in previous chapters to measure the extent of reform. It is worth highlighting that we are not using adjustment lending as a proxy for reform efforts, but rather assessing how much reform has actually occurred.[2]

We argue further that the most telling indicator of the success of adjustment efforts is the *change* in GDP per capita growth. The *rate* of growth that countries attain after implementing adjustment programs, though important in the long term, is not the best measure of how well adjustment is working in the short and medium terms. For decades, GDP per capita growth has been slower in Sub-Saharan Africa than elsewhere, and adjustment policy reforms are not likely to remove deep-rooted impediments to growth. That is the broader task of development, which encompasses much more than the implementation of an appropriate policy framework. It is not fair, then, to measure the short-term success of adjustment policies in Sub-Saharan Africa only by the yardstick of growth rates in other regions.

Furthermore, most adjustment programs in Sub-Saharan Africa are young, with many reforms implemented only recently, and it is too soon to realize big payoffs. But to the extent that the programs are addressing major macroeconomic imbalances and improving the overall policy environment, some positive outcomes—however modest—should be expected. In particular, programs that removed the import constraints of the early 1980s and restored external competitiveness while controlling inflation should have resulted in some improvement in growth.

In addition to growth, what other payoffs would be likely? Export performance is the leading indicator of whether adjustment policies are working, because adjustment programs seek to redress external imbalances. But there is no reason to anticipate an improvement in the trade balance or the current account early on. In fact, an initial deterioration in the trade balance is in some cases desirable: because most African economies were initially import-constrained, growth could not recover without an increase in imports.

The improved incentives for farmers (proxied by higher producer prices or lower rates of explicit taxation) should also lead to higher output of some agricultural commodities. But not much can be expected during the first years of adjustment, because aggregate supply responds slowly. Likewise, there should be modest increases in investment, primarily in countries with stable inflation, a clear direction in policy reforms, and a larger domestic savings effort. Industrial performance should improve too, as greater availability of inputs relieves production capacity constraints.

Better Macroeconomic Policies Boost Growth

FOURTEEN OF THE ADJUSTING COUNTRIES INCREASED THE average annual rate of growth between 1981–86 and 1987–91, while fourteen others decreased it (figure 5.1).[3] Mozambique, Nigeria, Uganda, and Ghana had the largest gains, exceeding 3 per-

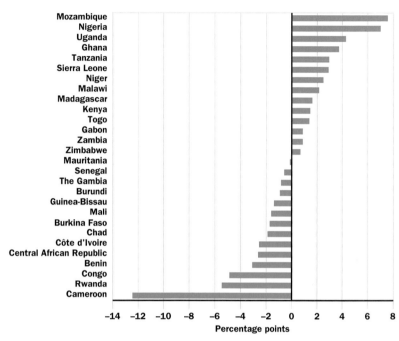

Figure 5.1 Change in Average Annual GDP per Capita Growth, 1981–86 to 1987–91

Half of the adjusting countries increased GDP per capita growth rates.

Note: Guinea is excluded because of insufficient data.
Source: Table 5.1.

centage points, while Cameroon, Rwanda, Congo, and Benin had declines of more than 3 percentage points. Eight countries went from negative to positive rates of growth, representing a strong turnaround.

What explains the differences in performance? One hypothesis is the difference in policies. Countries that moved toward macroeconomic stability and improved the relative prices for exports (especially agricultural exports) would be expected to enjoy the biggest payoffs. To the extent that a better policy environment remains in place, the improved growth should be sustainable—possibly heralding the start of a new period of accelerated growth. An alternative hypothesis is that external factors have driven the better performance—and the worse. Some observers emphasize the recent increase in external transfers and argue that it is a key to the improved performance. Others stress the recent deterioration in the terms of trade and argue that it is a key to poorer performance. Our conclusion: both policies and external factors were forces in the turnaround, with improved policies more strongly correlated with increases in growth.

External Factors Explain Some of the Change in Growth—But Not All

Much of the evidence in chapter 1 shows that the external environment has not been a major direct factor in Africa's long-term growth. But short-run growth can be affected by large and sudden changes in the external environment—that is, changes in net transfers or the terms of trade. For instance:

- More foreign exchange (from higher external transfers or better terms of trade) permits more imports, making it possible for firms to buy imported intermediate products and spare parts for their machinery and rapidly expand their production capacity.
- Larger aid flows finance productive investments that would otherwise not be made.
- Greater external income in Sub-Saharan Africa (from higher transfers or commodity booms) means higher domestic consumption, which in turn expands output (a Keynesian effect). The impact on growth persists only as long as external income keeps rising.

Looking first at changes in external transfers, the analysis here does not support the assertion that they are largely responsible for changes in growth. The median increase in external transfers between 1981–86 and 1987–91 was equivalent to 0.4 percentage points of GDP, compared with a median increase in GDP growth of 0.7 percentage points. But there was significant variation among countries, so it is useful to examine the relative importance of transfers on a country-specific basis. Using Easterly and others' (1993) finding that an annual increase in external income equal to 1 percentage point of GDP raises growth by 0.6 percentage points, we predicted the change in GDP growth that should have occurred between 1981–86 and 1987–91 due to the change in external transfers over the same period.[4] We then compared the predicted change with the actual change (figure 5.2). For none of the fourteen countries that accelerated GDP per capita growth do external transfers fully explain the improvement—not even in Mozambique, which benefited from the largest increase in external transfers as a share of GDP, nor in Tanzania, another country with substantial aid flows. In the former, higher transfers account for 52 percent of the increased growth; in the latter, 67 percent. In the other countries with increases in growth, external transfers explain a far smaller share. Four countries even improved their growth rates while transfers fell. Nigeria, despite declining external

Figure 5.2 Average Annual GDP per Capita Growth: Actual Change between 1981–86 and 1987–91 and Predicted Change Based on External Transfers

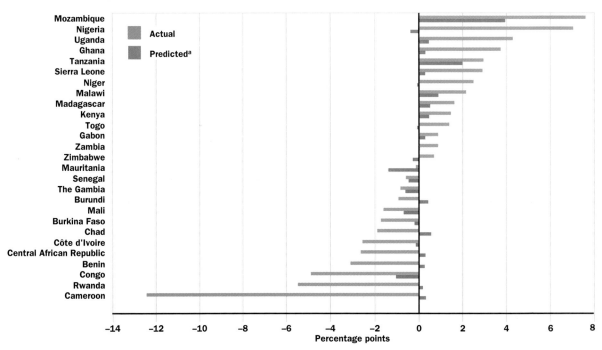

Note: Guinea is excluded because of insufficient data.
a. Predicted change in growth was calculated by applying a multiplier of 0.6 to the change in external transfers.
Source: World Bank data.

External transfers accounted for only part of the change in GDP per capita growth.

transfers, had a turnaround in GDP per capita growth of 7 percentage points!

Changes in external transfers also fail to fully explain the declining growth in the remaining thirteen countries. Growth slowed in six countries despite increases in external transfers. In six of the remaining seven, the decline in growth was larger than that predicted by the fall in transfers (Mauritania being the exception). The two countries in which the decline in external transfers had the largest negative impact were The Gambia and Senegal—with the predicted declines in growth about 75 percent of the actual ones.

Although changes in transfers do not explain the entire change in growth, there is a positive association between the two. Countries with increased transfers had a median rise in GDP per capita growth of about 1.2 percentage points—and those with declining transfers, a median decline of about 0.6 percentage points. External transfers helped because they provided much-needed foreign exchange, allowing countries to move out of the import-compression phase (Helleiner 1992). Recent estimates show that external transfers financed 40 percent of the 12 percent increase in real imports between 1981–86 and 1987–91 in the countries benefiting from the Special Program of Assistance for Africa (Demery and Husain 1993).

As for the terms of trade, another part of the external environment, almost all countries had declines, but many countries increased their GDP per capita growth rates nonetheless. The median loss of income from changes in the terms of trade averaged 0.2 percent of GDP a year and so was more than offset by the increase in external transfers. Thus terms-of-trade changes do not appear to have been an important factor explaining changes in growth during the adjustment period.

Even when the two sources of external income are added together, these external factors still explain only part of the increase in growth. Among countries with increases in external income, a median increase of 0.7 percent of GDP was associated with a median increase in GDP per capita growth of 1.5 percentage points (figure 5.3 and appendix table A.15). By contrast, in countries that had declines in external income, growth rates fell. But there was much variation: in ten of the twenty-seven countries, changes in external income and GDP growth moved in

Figure 5.3 Relation between the External Environment
and GDP per Capita Growth, 1981–86 to 1987–91

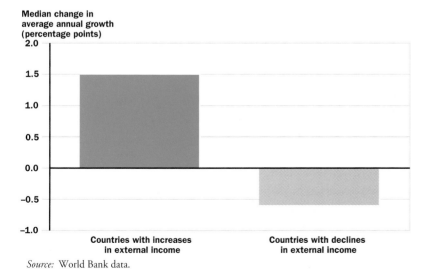

Median change in
average annual growth
(percentage points)

Increases in external income
contributed to higher growth.

Source: World Bank data.

Table 5.1 GDP per Capita Growth

Country	Average annual growth rate (percent)		Difference between the two periods (percentage points)
	1981–86	1987–91	
Large improvement in macroeconomic policies[a]			
Ghana	-2.4	1.3	3.7
Tanzania	-1.7	1.3	2.9
The Gambia	1.2	0.3	-0.8
Burkina Faso	2.2	0.4	-1.7
Nigeria	-4.6	2.4	7.0
Zimbabwe	0.3	1.0	0.7
Mean	**-0.8**	**1.1**	**2.0**
Median	**-0.7**	**1.1**	**1.8**
Small improvement[a]			
Madagascar	-3.7	-2.1	1.6
Malawi	-1.4	0.7	2.2
Burundi	2.1	1.2	-0.9
Kenya	-0.5	0.9	1.5
Mali	0.4	-1.2	-1.6
Mauritania	-0.9	-1.0	-0.1
Senegal	0.4	-0.2	-0.6
Niger	-4.9	-2.4	2.5
Uganda	-1.5	2.8	4.3
Mean	**-1.1**	**-0.1**	**1.0**
Median	**-0.9**	**-0.2**	**1.5**
Deterioration[a]			
Benin	1.1	-2.0	-3.1
Central African Republic	-0.1	-2.8	-2.6
Rwanda	0.4	-5.0	-5.5
Sierra Leone	-2.1	0.8	2.9
Deterioration[a] (continued)			
Togo	-2.8	-1.4	1.4
Zambia	-3.2	-2.3	0.9
Mozambique	-5.9	1.7	7.6
Congo	4.1	-0.7	-4.9
Côte d'Ivoire	-4.2	-6.8	-2.6
Cameroon	4.6	-7.9	-12.5
Gabon	-2.7	-1.9	0.9
Mean	**-1.0**	**-2.6**	**-1.6**
Median	**-2.1**	**-2.0**	**-2.6**
Unclassified			
Chad	4.5	2.6	-1.9
Guinea	—	—	—
Guinea-Bissau	2.9	1.5	-1.4
Medians			
All countries	-0.7	0.1	0.3
Low-income countries	-1.2	0.6	1.1
Middle-income countries	0.3	-1.3	-1.6
Countries with fixed exchange rates	0.4	-1.7	-1.8
Countries with flexible exchange rates	-1.5	0.9	1.5
Oil-exporting countries	0.7	-1.3	-2.0

— Not available.

a. Classifications are based on the overall scores reported in appendix table B.1.

Source: World Bank data.

opposite directions. Some countries (Benin, Burundi, the Central African Republic, Chad, and Rwanda) had declines in growth, despite increased external income.

Improving Policies Makes a Difference

Do changes in policies affect growth? Yes. Countries that improved their exchange rate policy and reduced inflation and budget deficits generally increased their GDP per capita growth rates (table 5.1). Our methodology was to divide countries into three groups, depending on whether they had large positive changes in macroeconomic policies, small positive changes, or negative changes, and to determine whether the groups differed in their economic performance. The six countries that improved policies the most had the largest median improvement in GDP per capita growth (1.8 percentage points), and all countries in the group returned to positive (though very low) growth rates. In contrast, among the countries where policies worsened, median growth declined 2.6 percentage points. This group includes the six countries with the sharpest downturns in growth. Finally, the countries that made small improvements in macroeconomic policies had a median increase of 1.5 percentage points. This was progress, but not enough to restore positive GDP per capita growth (this group had a median decline in growth of 0.2 percent a year during 1987–91).[5]

We also used econometric analysis to investigate the relationship between policies and growth, controlling for the initial rate of growth and external factors (box 5.1). The objective was to establish whether changes in policies affect growth even after taking into account the effects of changes in external income (discussed above) and a country's initial performance (because countries starting with negative rates of GDP growth are likely to show more improvement). The analysis supports the foregoing conclusion: changes in macroeconomic policies have a positive and statistically significant effect on growth (figure 5.4). However, the econometric analysis does not provide conclusive evidence on the impact of external factors on growth. While transfers are positively associated with growth, the recent improvement (or deterioration) in growth performance has been largely unrelated to changes in the terms of trade.

Improvements in macroeconomic policies are correlated not only with larger *changes* in the rate of GDP per capita growth but also with higher *levels* of growth. Countries that improved macroeconomic poli-

Box 5.1 Explaining the Increase in GDP per Capita Growth

THE FIVE REGRESSIONS IN THE TABLE BELOW IL-
lustrate the impact of changes in policies and external
income on growth. The regressions control for the rate
of growth before adjustment, because countries that
were doing particularly poorly (or well) are more likely
to experience an improvement (or decline). The five
regressions are robust for the importance of policies
and the initial growth rate, which are statistically significant and have the right sign. External transfers are
generally positive, though not statistically significant at
the 10 percent level. The coefficient ranges between
–0.06 and 0.58, with the average less than the coefficient used to predict growth rates in figure 5.2. The
terms-of-trade effect is not significant and generally
has the wrong sign (an improved terms of trade slows
growth). This result reflects the peculiarities of the
short time period under study and should not be taken
to contradict the well-established positive relation in
the long run between growth and the terms of trade.

The main difference across regressions is the
choice of policy indicators. Regression I shows the results for the change in GDP per capita growth using
the index of change in overall macroeconomic policy
described in appendix B. Regressions II through V examine the link between the change in the growth rate
and the changes in the individual policy indicators
that are components of the overall change index. The
policy variables have the right sign, and with the exception of inflation they are statistically significant at
the 5 percent level. Inflation is statistically significant
(at the 10 percent level) in regression II, but not in regression IV, where it is the only policy variable.

Box Table 5.1 Regressions for Analyzing the Change in Growth
(dependent variable: change in GDP per capita growth, 1981–86 to 1987–91)

		Change in							
Regression	Constant	Overall macro-economic policies	Exchange rate policy	Inflation	Overall fiscal deficit	Net external transfers	Income from changes in the terms of trade	GDP per capita growth, 1981–86	Adjusted R^2
I	−1.84	2.11					0.45	−0.55	−1.04	0.75
	(−3.5)	(4.4)					(1.6)	(−1.3)	(−6.3)	
II	−1.85		0.59	−0.43	−1.04	0.20	−1.08	−0.98	0.85
	(−4.4)		(2.6)	(−1.8)	(−4.5)	(0.8)	(−2.9)	(−7.2)	
III	−1.13	1.09				−0.06	−0.05	−0.84	0.70
	(−2.2)	(3.8)				(−0.2)	(−0.1)	(−5.1)	
IV	−0.62			−0.47		0.22	0.04	−0.92	0.53
	(−1.0)			(−1.1)		(0.6)	(0.1)	(−4.4)	
V	−2.00				−1.28	0.58	−1.06	−1.16	0.79
	(−4.0)				(−5.0)	(2.2)	(−2.5)	(−7.5)	

Note: Numbers in parentheses are *t*-statistics.

Figure 5.4 **Changes in Macroeconomic Policies and GDP per Capita Growth, 1981–86 to 1987–91**

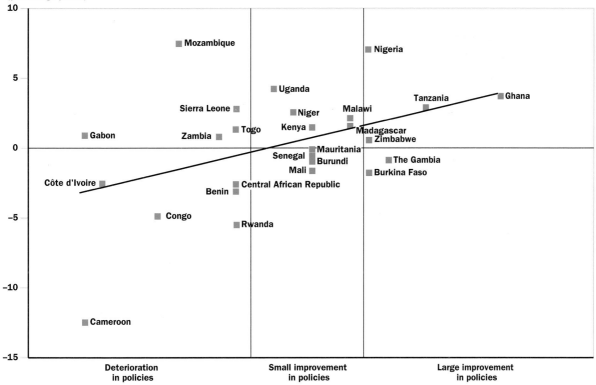

Note: Chad, Guinea, and Guinea-Bissau are excluded because of insufficient data.
Sources: Table 5.1 and appendix table B.1.

Changes in macroeconomic policies are positively correlated with increases in GDP per capita growth.

cies the most had positive rates of GDP per capita growth during 1987–91, while those whose policies deteriorated had negative rates. But even for the top improvers, the growth rates remained low (at a median of 1.1 percent a year). Adjustment policies, though instrumental in generating the conditions for higher growth, are thus only part of the solution. Shifting economies to a new growth path requires a good overall policy environment and better use of more traditional development instruments, such as investments in education and infrastructure.

To the extent that macroeconomic policies matter—and they do— getting the exchange rate right is one of the top priorities for short-term growth. Countries that significantly reduced the parallel market premium (by devaluing) and adopted realistic macroeconomic policies enjoyed the biggest payoffs. Dividing countries into three groups based on the real depreciation during adjustment shows that countries that managed large real depreciations (40 percent or more) enjoyed the largest turnaround, with a median increase in GDP per capita growth of 2.3 percentage points (appendix table A.16). Of this group, Burundi was the only country whose GDP growth declined. In contrast, countries that experienced real appreciations suffered a median decline of 1.7 percentage points. There is a difference of 4 percentage points in the median changes for the top and bottom groups. The gap between the fixed and flexible exchange rate countries is also sizable (3.4 percentage points), because of the different adjustment strategies followed (box 5.2).

African countries had a clear need for real depreciations in the early 1980s because of deteriorating terms of trade and unsound exchange rate policies. These initial conditions largely explain the effectiveness of devaluations in increasing growth. For countries that already have realistic real exchange rates, there is little scope to further boost growth by depreciating, though gains would be expected from maintaining external competitiveness. But for countries with unrealistic exchange rates, the expected payoffs to real depreciations are large.

Having Good Policies Also Makes a Difference

We have argued that the *change* in GDP growth rates is the most appropriate indicator of whether policy reforms are working in the short and medium terms. Over the long term, however, it is the *rate of growth* itself that ultimately matters. And over the medium to long term, the policy stance is more important than the change in policies in explaining the rate of growth. This is because changes in policies are not necessarily correlated with a country's policy stance. Tanzania showed large improvements in macroeconomic policies, and yet it still had a very poor policy stance in 1990–91 because its policies were so poor to begin with. By the same token, a country starting with reasonable policies might maintain an adequate stance even if its policies deteriorate. In Togo, macroeconomic policies worsened in the second half of the 1980s (as the real exchange rate appreciated and the budget deficit increased), and yet the country's policy stance remained fair thanks to a sound macroeconomic framework in the early 1980s.

What do we find when we examine the link between policy stance and the rate of growth? Median GDP per capita growth in countries with adequate or fair macroeconomic policies was 0.4 percent a year—low but at least positive, and better than the decline of 1.2 percent a year during 1981–86 (appendix table A.17). Meanwhile, countries with poor or very poor macroeconomic policies had staggering declines in GDP per capita, with the median at –2.1 percent a year during 1987–91. The median growth rates were also quite different for countries with limited, medium, and heavy government intervention in markets: 1.9 percent, –1.1 percent, and –1.4 percent, respectively. More than 4 percentage points separated the three countries with the best macroeconomic policies and the least intervention from the two countries with the worst macroeconomic policies and heavy intervention—a powerful incentive for moving toward good policy.

Agriculture Is Growing Faster

THE MOST IMPORTANT WAYS THAT ADJUSTMENT AFFECTS agriculture are by reducing taxation through macroeconomic policy changes and by reforming the arrangements for marketing. Chapter 3 showed that reforms shifted the terms of trade in favor of agriculture in many countries. The taxation (both explicit and implicit) of export crop producers fell in about two-thirds of the countries, and in ten countries real prices for export crop producers were higher at the end of the decade than at the beginning. Few reliable data series are available on producer prices for food crops, but several countries eliminated food crop marketing boards or substantially cut back on their activities, virtually eliminating the parallel market.

These reforms, proxied by the change in real producer prices for export crops and the change in overall taxation of export crop producers, appear to have buoyed agricultural growth.[6] Countries that improved the real prices for agricultural exporters increased agricultural growth, while countries that let prices decline saw agricultural growth fall, for a difference in medians of more than 2 percentage points (top of figure 5.5 and appendix table A.18). Even more striking is a comparison of the countries that substantially reduced the level of taxation and those that increased it: the difference in median growth rates was 3.6 percentage points (bottom of figure 5.5 and appendix table A.19).[7] But no clear pattern emerged distinguishing countries in which macroeconomic

Box 5.2 The Payoffs to Fixed and Flexible Exchange Rate Regimes

WHEN REAL DEPRECIATION IS NEEDED, A FLEXIBLE exchange rate generally reduces the output costs of depreciating because it allows a quick initial real depreciation to raise competitiveness. But it increases the risk of a *permanent* increase in inflation. A fixed exchange rate reduces that risk, generally at the expense of output, because recession is needed to bring down domestic prices to achieve the required real depreciation. The stronger the resistance of workers to wage cuts and the more opposed producers of nontradables are to price cuts, the longer it will take to effect the real depreciation—and the more costly (in forgone output) the fixed exchange rate strategy becomes. In both, a well-designed adjustment package needs to include tight domestic credit and fiscal policies to reduce domestic absorption.

The median real depreciation between 1981–86 and 1987–91 in the flexible exchange rate economies was 50 percent, compared with an 8 percent real appreciation in the fixed exchange rate economies (appendix table A.16). The devaluations in the flexible exchange rate countries had an unavoidable short-term impact on inflation, but by 1990–91, once the initial effects had worked themselves out, inflation fell back to the levels of the first half of the 1980s. The annual inflation rate declined in nine of sixteen countries with flexible exchange rates, and overall, the median remained virtually unchanged—19 percent during 1981–86 and just under 21 percent during 1990–91 (appendix table A.3). Meanwhile, the fixed exchange rate countries continued to have low inflation—a median of 6.3 percent during 1981–86 and 0.5 percent during 1990–91.

Overall, however, the macroeconomic performance of the fixed exchange rate countries deteriorated significantly in the second half of the 1980s and was clearly worse than in other African adjusting countries (box figure 5.1). In the countries with fixed exchange rates, median real GDP per capita growth fell on average by 1.7 percent a year during 1987–91, and export growth stagnated. The flexible exchange rate countries did better. Median GDP per capita growth climbed from –1.5 percent a year during 1981–86 to 0.9 percent a year during 1987–91, with real export growth showing even more improvement.

The disparity in outcomes for the two groups of countries extended to other economic indicators. Gross domestic investment as a share of GDP fell about 3 percentage points in the fixed exchange rate countries, but increased slightly in the flexible exchange rate countries. And gross domestic savings in the fixed exchange rate countries, while increasing from low levels, still fell short of the median level of savings in the flexible exchange rate countries. Poverty worsened in the fixed exchange rate countries because of the loss of income-earning opportunities and the inability of fiscally constrained governments to provide basic social services. And because the reforms did not lower nominal wages or the prices of nontradables relative to the prices of tradables, the attempted internal adjustment failed to restore competitiveness and growth.

Relying solely on internal adjustment measures is best for correcting small losses of competitiveness, particularly those from excess internal demand. Under an internal adjustment, competitiveness can be regained only at the rate by which international inflation exceeds domestic inflation. The fixed exchange rate countries have been able only to freeze—not reduce—domestic wages and prices. Meanwhile, because international inflation decelerated in the 1980s to 2 to 4 percent annually, the countries with fixed exchange rates can at best improve their competitiveness by 2 to 4 percent a year. At that rate, it will take them a decade or more to become competitive—longer if their competitors further depreciate their exchange rates. Without big changes in policies to restore competitiveness, the outlook for these countries is grim: low investment, financial crises, worsening poverty, falling exports, and continuing declines in per capita income.

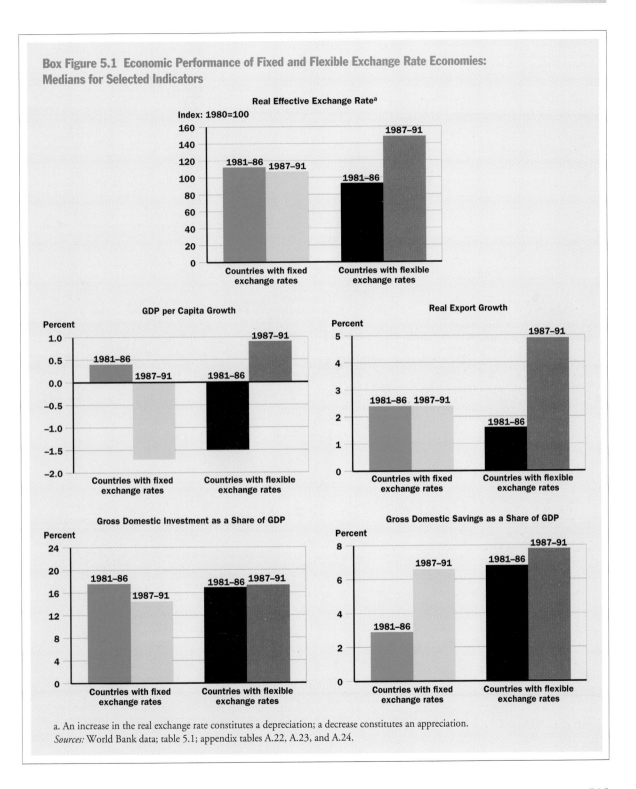

Box Figure 5.1 Economic Performance of Fixed and Flexible Exchange Rate Economies: Medians for Selected Indicators

Real Effective Exchange Rate[a]

Index: 1980=100

a. An increase in the real exchange rate constitutes a depreciation; a decrease constitutes an appreciation.
Sources: World Bank data; table 5.1; appendix tables A.22, A.23, and A.24.

Figure 5.5 Relation between Agricultural Growth and Two Measures of Agricultural Policy, 1981–86 to 1987–91

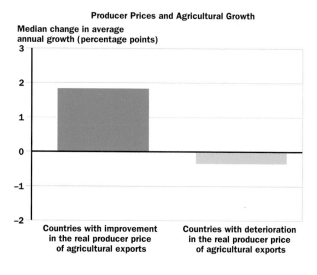

Producer Prices and Agricultural Growth

Median change in average
annual growth (percentage points)

Countries with improvement
in the real producer price
of agricultural exports

Countries with deterioration
in the real producer price
of agricultural exports

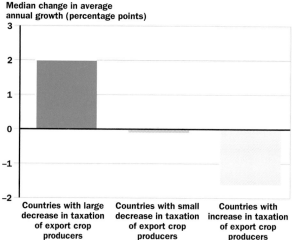

Taxation and Agricultural Growth

Median change in average
annual growth (percentage points)

Countries with large
decrease in taxation
of export crop
producers

Countries with small
decrease in taxation
of export crop
producers

Countries with
increase in taxation
of export crop
producers

Better prices for farmers and less taxation meant faster agricultural growth.

Sources: Appendix tables A.18 and A.19.

policies improved from those in which they deteriorated (appendix table A.20). This is not too surprising, given that macroeconomic policy changes do not always translate into higher producer prices because of lags in marketing board reforms and other government interventions.

Policy changes may be moving some countries back to their long-run agricultural growth trends, but the conditions are not yet in place everywhere for accelerated agricultural growth rates. Per capita agricultural growth rates are still negative for most countries. Many countries, such as Tanzania and Burundi, continue to operate below their agricultural potential because of macroeconomic and agricultural pricing distortions and inefficient marketing arrangements. Moreover, both policy and institutional factors have strong effects on supply response, as the difference in the agricultural performance of Ghana and Nigeria shows (box 5.3). The aggregate supply response takes time to materialize, and extrapolations of short-term supply responses may underestimate the long-term response to policy reforms (box 5.4).

Box 5.3 Why Agriculture Is Growing Faster in Nigeria Than in Ghana

ALTHOUGH GHANA IS REGARDED AS HAVING made the most progress of any adjusting country in Sub-Saharan Africa, its performance in the agricultural sector has lagged behind that of others. Nigeria, for example, has had substantially stronger growth in agriculture. Whereas Ghana's agricultural sector grew about 2 percent a year during 1987–91, Nigeria's grew about 4 percent a year, and the net real return to farming increased fourfold.

Several factors account for this difference:

- First, Nigeria eliminated its export crop marketing boards, which has allowed Nigerian producers to obtain a larger share of export prices. In Ghana a number of marketing boards, including the Cocoa Board and the Cotton Mills, continue to exert a major influence on producer prices.
- Second, Nigeria's investment in research and extension services has provided farmers with the technical know-how to improve small-scale irrigation and soil fertility.
- Third, rural infrastructure in Nigeria is more extensive than in Ghana, which can be characterized as largely a "footpath economy." The cost of poor rural infrastructure is significantly reduced labor productivity and higher production costs, which translate into reduced profits and fewer production incentives.

- Fourth, Ghana's main crop, cocoa, has suffered an extended period of depressed world prices. Cocoa does not account for as large a share of Nigeria's agricultural exports, and the terms-of-trade effects on its other export crops have been less severe.
- Fifth, while Ghana implemented overall adjustment policies earlier, reforms within agriculture did not get under way until the late 1980s. Nigeria proceeded quickly on agricultural reform in 1986.

The lesson from this comparison is the importance of removing bottlenecks in the agricultural sector. Structural differences seem to outweigh different exchange rate policies in explaining outcomes. On the policy side, Ghana appears to have an advantage in allowing the exchange rate to adjust quickly. Nigeria has relied upon periodic devaluations, a practice that leads to occasional misalignments. Structural conditions in Nigeria, however, are more favorable to agricultural growth. In addition, experience in Nigeria suggests that small-scale irrigation schemes in which farmers participate in design and implementation are more effective and less costly than large public irrigation systems. Furthermore, farmers are more likely to adopt new technologies if they see the linkage to higher financial returns.

Box 5.4 Aggregate Supply Tends to Respond Slowly in the Short Term

JAEGER'S (1992) ANALYSIS OF THE RESPONSE OF export crops and food crops to policy changes in Africa provides further evidence that aggregate supply responds to favorable policy changes. Specifically, Jaeger examines the response of export crops to changes in real producer prices, the real effective exchange rate, and variables representing weather and disasters (war, civil strife, famine) for twenty-one Sub-Saharan countries having data for 1970–87 (countries that overlap with our sample of adjusting countries). The estimated price elasticities of export supply range from 0.1 to 0.3, and the elasticities with respect to the real effective exchange rate (where a fall indicates an appreciation) range from –0.01 to –0.25. Countries exporting annual crops had higher elasticities than countries exporting tree crops. The results support the conclusion that the aggregate response in the short run is positive but not large.

Jaeger also finds that total agricultural production, total food production, and staple food production respond to increases in export crop prices and depreciations of the real effective exchange rate. The results suggest no tradeoff between food and export crop production—results consistent with other empirical findings of a positive correlation between the growth in export crops and that in food crops (see von Braun and Kennedy 1987).

Jaeger offers several explanations for this. First, food crops can benefit from applications of fertilizer to export crops when they are grown together or in succession. Second, higher income from export crop production can lead to higher investment in food crops. In addition, farmers may not have to supplement their incomes with off-farm employment outside the growing season, so they may be able to devote more labor to food crops. Third, a better policy environment, proxied by higher export prices and more competitive exchange rates, helps both export and food crops by promoting growth and thus increasing aggregate demand. The dismantling of food crop marketing boards stimulates food crop production.

And real effective exchange rate depreciations may increase the (official) price of imported staple foods—and thus the domestic price of foodstuffs that can substitute for imports. The effect on domestic prices may be minor, however, since prices in the parallel markets in large part reflect the foreign exchange premium before the liberalization of import markets.

Jaeger's analysis squares with other research findings that document the responsiveness of African farmers to changes in the prices of individual crops (see Bond 1983). The price elasticities of supply for individual crops are high in the short run—and even higher in the long run. But as Binswanger (1989) points out, the aggregate supply response is more contentious. In the short run, the supply of the main factors of agricultural production tends to be fixed, so that a relative price shift in favor of one crop shifts factors of production into that crop at the expense of another. Consequently, aggregate agricultural supply elasticities tend to be small even if individual elasticities are large. But over the long run—and long can be ten to twenty years—the supply response can be large, with less rural outmigration and greater investment in agriculture, roads, markets, education, and health.

The short-run price elasticities of aggregate supply for various countries reported in Binswanger (1989) ranged from 0.05 to 0.25. Those for Sub-Saharan Africa were no lower than for other areas, suggesting that the lower levels of infrastructure and other factors do not pose significantly greater constraints to a supply response in Sub-Saharan Africa. Very few methodologically sound studies have looked at the long-run supply response—with none for Africa—but one for Argentina estimated a supply elasticity of 0.4 after five years and 1.8 after twenty years. A study of Chilean agriculture cited by Valdes (1989) found an aggregate supply elasticity of 0.3 after three years, 0.6 after four and five years, and more than 1.0 after ten years. This evidence suggests that, if policies improve, we should expect substantial increases in aggregate supply not in the short run but in the medium and long run.

Industry Is Expanding

CRITICS OF STRUCTURAL ADJUSTMENT PROGRAMS IN AFRICA point to an anti-industrial bias in the policy package (see Lall 1992; Stein 1992). They fault policies that suddenly reduce trade protection, devalue the currency, cut public spending, remove government subsidies and price controls, increase real interest rates, and promote privatization. Such policies, they argue, not only cause industrial production to stagnate or decline in the short run, but also erode an important part of the industrial base for future growth.

Put simply, the critics claim that structural adjustment programs are causing the deindustrialization of Africa. One piece of evidence cited is that about half the countries in Sub-Saharan Africa had declines in industrial output in the first part of the 1980s, while the rest of the region had output growth of less than 2 percent (Stewart, Lall, and Wangwe 1992). But many of the countries with negative growth had not implemented adjustment programs, or had done so only recently, so their poor performance cannot be blamed on adjustment.

Assessing whether deindustrialization has occurred is not easy, but there is no systematic evidence of it in our sample of adjusting countries (box 5.5). Countries that made large improvements in their macroeconomic policies had strong increases in the growth of industry and manufacturing—with median increases close to 6 percentage points between 1981–86 and 1987–91 (figure 5.6 and appendix table A.21). The response was weaker in countries with small improvements in macroeconomic policies and weakest for countries with deterioration in policies. In all, only eight adjusting countries had contractions in their industrial sectors, and five of those were from the group with worsening policies.

Surveys of manufacturing firms in Ghana, Kenya, and Tanzania further support the contention that strong reform efforts do not cause deindustrialization.[8] The picture in Ghana, the country with the most extensive adjustment, is not one of stagnation and deindustrialization; instead, it shows much activity, particularly among smaller enterprises not included in official statistics. Aggregate employment and output have been increasing about 2 percent a year for a sample of manufacturing firms in four sectors representing about 80 percent of manufacturing employment—food processing, metalworking, woodworking, and textile and garment manufacturing. Both old firms (those operating before adjustment) and new firms (those started after adjustment) have

Box 5.5 How to Know Whether Deindustrialization Is Occurring

PROPONENTS AND DETRACTORS OF STRUCTURAL adjustment agree that Africa's industrial growth was generally inefficient before adjustment (Stewart, Lall, and Wangwe 1992). In many cases, heavy-handed government policies to promote import-substituting industrialization—at the expense of agriculture and other sectors—expanded the manufacturing sector beyond its efficient size and distorted its structure. Such policies can lead to rapid growth of output and employment in the short run, but that growth generally is not sustainable and soon peters out, leaving in its wake internal and external imbalances—and often economic crisis. The economy, distorted and pushed beyond its efficient limits, requires downsizing and restructuring. In such cases, any deindustrialization is a move toward more efficient outcomes, not toward a structural maladjustment of the economy. But it is also possible that downsizing and restructuring could be the unintended consequences of a policy package that inhibits manufacturing growth.

To make the case that structural adjustment programs cause deindustrialization in Africa, one would have to show that (a) there are significant declines in industrial output, output shares of GDP, and employment because of policy reforms, (b) the declines in output and employment are more than temporary outcomes of efficient adjustment, (c) the changes in the industrial sector are not shifting the economy toward greater efficiency, and (d) the policy reforms are impeding long-run industrial growth and transformation by inhibiting the pace and pattern of investment and thus the shift to a higher growth trajectory.

What indicators might be used to examine these issues?

- Trends in industry's contribution to the domestic economy, including changes in the growth of real manufacturing value added over a period long enough for the economy to move through the difficult transition phase immediately after policy reforms. Another indicator, though more flawed, is the relative share of manufacturing output (in constant prices) in GDP over the same period.
- Employment. Changes in employment indicators need to be interpreted carefully, because adjustment programs can lead to a rationalization of the manufacturing sector and thus possibly to a short-term reduction in jobs. As adjustment proceeds, however, employment should increase as new activities come on stream and overall production capacity rises.
- Indicators of trends in production capacity: the number of manufacturing company bankruptcies, the number and size of establishments, and the average capacity in plants.
- Shifts in resources from activities with high domestic resource costs to those with low costs, providing evidence of efficiency improvements.
- Trends in productivity growth and changes in the growth rate of manufactured exports.

Time series for most of these indicators are not available, making it impossible to resolve the deindustrialization debate conclusively. But the data we have assembled from national accounts and from surveys of manufacturing firms do not support the hypothesis that structural adjustment programs have led to deindustrialization in Africa.

been growing, but new firms outpace older enterprises in every size class. Some old, larger firms are downsizing to become more efficient in response to adjustment policy changes, and some have shut down. Of forty-three medium-sized and large old firms, 63 percent had fewer employees in 1991 than in 1983 (at the start of adjustment). For all new firms in these size classes, however, the number of employees rose be-

Figure 5.6 Changes in the Growth of Industry and Manufacturing, 1981–86 to 1987–91

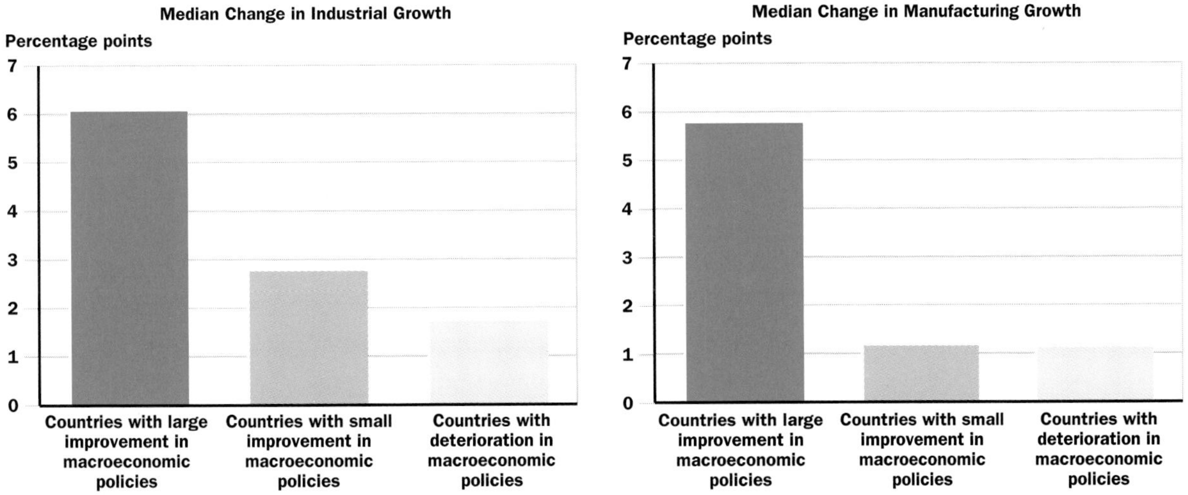

Median Change in Industrial Growth

Median Change in Manufacturing Growth

Source: Appendix table A.21.

tween startup and 1991. Almost two-thirds of the increase in manufacturing employment since the start of adjustment was attributable to new entrants. A significant proportion of new entry has been concentrated in small enterprises in the woodworking and metalworking sectors, where domestic resource costs are relatively low.

Adjustment programs radically change relative prices and the incentive environment that firms operate in—and thus the characteristics and behavior of firms that survive and prosper. For example, surviving entrepreneurs would be expected to focus more on raising production skills and cutting costs than on seeking rents. The new firms in Ghana (those started after 1963) are run by entrepreneurs with better-educated employees.[9] Among small firms, three-fourths (77 percent) of the owners of new firms have gone through apprenticeship programs, compared with 53 percent of the owners of older firms. New firms also have a higher propensity to invest, and this has increased since 1987. And of the medium-sized and large firms, more new firms export than old.

Contrary to the conventional view that policy conditions in Africa inhibit enterprise growth, there has been substantial movement of enterprises from one size class to the next during the adjustment period. For example, 67 percent of the new medium-sized firms in Ghana began as small firms, compared with 50 percent of the old medium-sized firms. This greater upward mobility, combined with differences in en-

Macroeconomic policy reform spurred industrial and manufacturing growth.

terprise attributes, suggests that new firms may be better able to take advantage of new economic opportunities.

The big question is whether the activity of small firms is a structural break with the past or simply a sign of distress. Are many of the smaller new entrants simply household efforts to survive at the margin, or are they dynamic new enterprises that can significantly increase employment in the future? In every size class, the new entrepreneurs have more human capital than old firms—and new firms, on average, have higher export intensities, higher propensities to invest, similar or higher levels of total factor productivity, and faster movement through the size classes. All this supports the view that adjustment programs are leading to more efficient outcomes in the industrial sector.

What is not yet clear is whether the conditions are in place to shift the adjusters to a much higher growth trajectory. Given Africa's lack of industrial experience, an increase in technological capability would seem to be a prerequisite for further, fast-paced industrial growth. As Pack (1993, p. 1) argues, "prices are one-half of a scissor, the other being technical skill." In Africa one might add upgraded infrastructure and business support services to that other blade of the scissor.

Exports Are Growing

AFRICA'S EXPORT PERFORMANCE BEFORE ADJUSTMENT WAS poor. Between 1965 and 1986, real exports from Sub-Saharan Africa merely doubled, while those of non-African adjusting countries quintupled. Between 1987 and 1991, the median rate of export growth for the African adjusting countries was 3.6 percent a year, compared with 9.2 percent in other developing countries. Although this is an improvement from 1.3 percent a year between 1970 and 1986, export growth needs to accelerate.

Exports are expected to expand early in successful adjustment programs, because successful programs increase external competitiveness and rely on export growth to offset the output costs of stabilization efforts. Although export growth remained positive in most adjusting countries—the exceptions being Benin, Cameroon, the Central African Republic, Mauritania, Sierra Leone, and Zambia—the performance was uneven, and for ten countries the rate of export growth slowed. Coun-

Figure 5.7 Median Change in Real Export Growth, 1981–86 to 1987–91

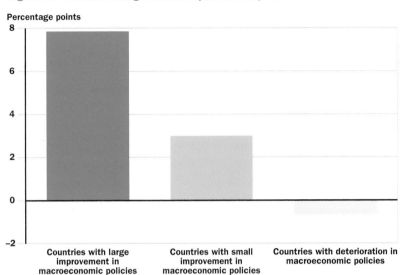

Percentage points

Source: Appendix table A.22.

Macroeconomic policy reform paid off in faster real export growth.

tries with the largest improvements in macroeconomic policies enjoyed the highest median growth in exports and had by far the largest surge in export growth, with a median of almost 8 percentage points (figure 5.7 and appendix table A.22). In contrast, exports lost ground in countries with deteriorating macroeconomic policies, where the median growth rate fell 0.7 percentage points.

Despite the higher exports, few African countries have managed to diversify their export base much. Almost all African countries continue to depend heavily on primary commodities for their export earnings, with no more than three primary commodities constituting over 70 percent of the value of exports. There are, however, signs of export diversification in countries such as Burundi and Kenya (Husain and Faruqee forthcoming).

No Quick Response in Investment or Savings

ALTHOUGH INVESTMENT IN MANY COUNTRIES HAS NOT YET reached levels consistent with sustainable long-term growth, there are indications of improvement in some countries. The share of private investment is also increasing, albeit from a very small base. Savings have traditionally been low throughout the region, and adjustment has had little impact on them so far.

Investment

Investment generally responds slowly to adjustment programs—in Africa and elsewhere (World Bank 1992a; Serven and Solimano 1992; Mosley, Harrigan, and Toye 1991). This slow response is understandable. Governments cut capital spending as part of their fiscal stabilization, while the private sector adopts a wait-and-see attitude during the early phases of adjustment, mindful of the irreversibility of investment decisions and the reversibility of key policy changes (indeed, policies have frequently been reversed in the past). The problem is particularly serious where there is no consensus about the importance of private sector–led growth.

Median gross domestic investment in African adjusting countries declined from more than 21 percent of GDP in the second half of the 1970s to 17 percent in the early 1980s and 16 percent in the second half of the decade. By comparison, investment in other adjusting countries remained stable at about 23 percent of GDP during the 1980s, after declining from 26 percent of GDP in the late 1970s. Africa needs to increase investment to about 25 percent of GDP to sustain GDP growth of about 6 percent a year.

Investment fell in thirteen of twenty-eight African adjusting countries in the second half of the 1980s, with performance related to changes in macroeconomic policies (appendix table A.23). It is important here to distinguish the oil exporters from the other countries, because the oil exporters entered the adjustment period with much higher (and many times unsustainable) investment-to-GDP ratios (about 40 percent in Congo and Gabon). So, unlike most other adjusters in the region, the large cuts in investment that these countries made were expected and desirable. The ratio of investment to GDP declined significantly in the oil-exporting economies (a median fall of 7.7 percentage points). Despite the large reductions, the investment-to-GDP ratios in these countries were still among the highest in the region.

Investment increased in the non–oil exporters that improved their macroeconomic policies and declined markedly in those where policies worsened (figure 5.8). The median change in investment as a share of GDP was 1.1 percentage points for countries with large policy improve-

Figure 5.8 Median Change in Gross Domestic Investment as a Share of GDP, 1981–86 to 1987–91

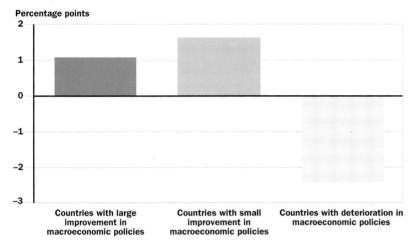

Percentage points

Countries with large improvement in macroeconomic policies

Countries with small improvement in macroeconomic policies

Countries with deterioration in macroeconomic policies

Macroeconomic policy reform yielded higher investment rates.

Note: Oil-exporting countries are excluded from the country groups.
Source: Appendix table A.23.

ments, 1.6 percentage points for those with small improvements, and –2.4 percentage points for those with deteriorations.

A fall (of 1 percentage point) in median public investment as a share of GDP partly explains the decline in total investment from the first half of the 1980s to the second half. Macroeconomic stabilization required a cut in overall public spending, and most countries preferred to protect current noninterest spending at the expense of capital spending. Public investment fell in sixteen of twenty-six adjusting countries, and the cuts were particularly steep in the oil-exporting countries (a median of –7.3 percentage points).

The data on private investment are more scarce (available for only thirteen countries), but they provide a more favorable outlook. Nine countries increased investment, and in seven of them the increase coincided with an improvement in macroeconomic policies. In only three countries did private investment and policies move in opposite directions. The investment response thus is moving in the right direction.

Foreign direct investment increased slightly during adjustment, especially in countries that improved macroeconomic policies. It rose in nine of the thirteen countries where policies improved and data were available—and declined in six of the eleven countries where policies deteriorated. The region's resistance to foreign capital and the lack of investment opportunities do little to attract foreign direct investment. Foreign investment flows (as a share of GDP) are half those in other regions, and they traditionally have not played a major role in the African adjusting countries, except in some of the oil and mineral exporters. Six of the seven countries where foreign direct investment exceeds 1 percent of GDP rely primarily on oil or minerals for their export revenues. (The Gambia, where investment in tourism is important, is the seventh.)

The relatively low investment rate in many African countries is not a major obstacle to restoring growth in the short term, especially if increases in the efficiency of investment compensate for the low levels. After all, despite much higher investment rates in the 1970s, the region did not grow any faster during that decade, because of the poor quality of many of the investments. Over the medium term, increases in high-quality investments will be necessary for steady growth. Experience shows that private investment will pick up if the initial growth spurt is sustained and if clear signals are given to firms about the present and future incentive systems.

Savings

The average savings rate for adjusting Sub-Saharan countries was about 8 percent of GDP in the late 1980s, compared with 22 percent for other adjusting countries, 20 percent for India, and more than 33 percent for the fast-growing East Asian economies. Apart from the oil exporters, only two Sub-Saharan economies—Kenya and Zimbabwe—had savings rates near 20 percent during 1987–91. It would be a mistake, though, to draw a simple line of causation from low domestic savings to low investment and slow growth. The evidence suggests that high savings largely followed growth in the East Asian economies. They managed to get into a virtuous circle in which high growth led to high domestic savings that financed the investment needed to sustain high growth. The key to starting this circle is not forcing up the savings rate (something the former Soviet Union did, with poor results), but establishing an environment that favors rapid accumulation, efficient resource use, and rapid productivity growth.

Domestic savings increased in the late 1980s in the countries that improved their macroeconomic policies (figure 5.9 and appendix table A.24), and fell in the countries where policies deteriorated. There were exceptions. Tanzania had a sizable reduction in its savings rate (primarily because of a large increase in external transfers equal to 19 percent of

Figure 5.9 Median Change in Gross Domestic Savings as a Share of GDP, 1981–86 to 1987–91

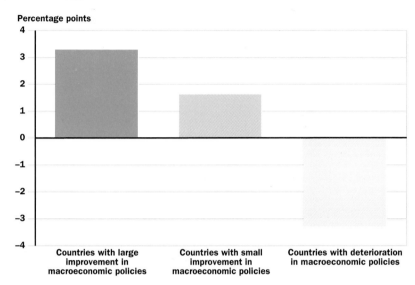

Percentage points

Macroeconomic policy reform boosted domestic savings rates.

Source: Appendix table A.24.

GDP), as did Malawi (which had an increase in net transfers of 9 percent of GDP).[10] Public savings declined in Kenya and Niger, explaining some of the fall in domestic savings, and only barely increased in Burundi. Among countries whose macroeconomic policies deteriorated, only Benin and the Central African Republic increased their savings rates.

Public savings (current revenue excluding grants minus current expenditure), like total savings, were low during 1981–86, and they stayed low during 1987–91. For the adjusting countries as a whole, the median performance was a dissavings of about 1 percent of GDP in both periods. But again there were strong differences in performance associated with changes in macroeconomic policies. Public savings generally increased in countries with improved macroeconomic policies and declined in countries with deteriorating policies. In a few countries—Ghana, Mali, Mauritania, Senegal, and Uganda—the improvement between the two periods was in excess of 3 percentage points. Changes in public savings were positively correlated, in turn, with changes in total revenue.

A big concern is that the large net external transfers (foreign savings) may be crowding out domestic savings. Across countries in the late 1980s, changes in net transfers did not completely offset changes in domestic savings (though they are significantly and negatively correlated). A 1 percentage point increase in net aggregate transfers was associated with an increase in investments of roughly 0.6 percentage points. So, net transfers financed both increased investment and consumption. That is neither surprising nor bad, because maintaining adequate consumption levels in poor economies, while pursuing policy reforms and higher investment, is important for poverty alleviation.

Notes

1. The comparison is based on data from the World Bank's third report on adjustment lending (World Bank 1992a). That report examined performance between 1981–85 and 1986–90, classifying countries by how intensively they used adjustment lending and comparing middle-income adjusting countries with the adjusting countries in Sub-Saharan Africa. (Data for low-income countries were not broken out separately. And although most Sub-Saharan adjusters were low-income countries, a few were classified as middle-income and thus were counted in both groups.) Growth improved 2.7 percentage points in the middle-income countries receiving intensive adjustment lending, and 2.4 percentage points in Sub-Saharan Africa. This difference is small, especially considering the differences in policy reforms and in institutional capacity and other endowments. For example, the African recipients of intensive adjustment lending depreciated their real effective exchange rates by about the same amount as middle-income recipients of intensive lending, despite having an average parallel market premium roughly five times higher. As for GDP growth among recipients of nonintensive adjustment lending, African countries did much better than their middle-income counterparts: growth declined only 0.1 percentage points in the former group, compared with 2.0 percentage points in the latter.

2. For an assessment of the impact of adjustment lending, see World Bank (1992a) and Elbadawi (1992).

3. There are strong indications that Guinea, the twenty-ninth country, went from negative to positive growth after a new government came to power in 1984 and adopted an adjustment program in 1985, but there is no consistent set of GDP data to confirm this.

4. Easterly and others (1993) calculate the impact that changes in the income terms of trade have on growth. Because we are not aware of other studies that estimate a quantitative relationship between external transfers and growth (holding policies constant), we used the average of the coefficients of 0.4 to 0.8 derived by Easterly and others and based on a large sample of countries. According to our estimates based on African countries (box table 5.1), the multiplier is smaller—about 0.3 on average.

5. Appendix B examines the robustness of the results by looking at the outcomes using alternative policy indicators and alternative time periods to calculate the index of change in macroeconomic policies.

6. Agricultural growth is defined here as value added in forestry, fishing, and hunting as well as agriculture. The ideal indicator of the effect of agricultural reforms would also control for weather and other exogenous factors.

7. The Food and Agriculture Organization (FAO) agricultural production indexes provide a more direct indication of changes in agricultural production, but because the data cover only agricultural crops, they are not as comprehensive as those for value added. Nonetheless, both data sets show a similar pattern: countries in which export producer prices increased had larger production gains than countries in which prices deteriorated. And countries that decreased taxation of export crop producers

had larger production gains than countries that increased taxation.

There are substantial discrepancies between the value-added data and the FAO production data for some countries, sometimes attributable to the wider coverage of the GDP data, sometimes not. For Tanzania, for example, the FAO data are at variance with other data on the agricultural sector. Other sources indicate that growth in marketed food output has been impressive, doubling between 1983 (when reforms began) and 1988. The increased availability of food essentially restored Tanzania's ability to feed itself and almost eliminated the need for food imports. Export crop sales have been restored to levels recorded in the early 1980s, and cotton exports have set records.

8. The surveys, conducted in 1992 and 1993, cover randomly chosen formal and informal manufacturing enterprises of all sizes, including unregistered enterprises excluded from official figures. The surveys provide detailed information on the entrance of new firms, on the growth of enterprises before and during structural adjustment, and on the age and size of growing firms. The surveys also yield information on the characteristics of old firms (those in business before adjustment) and new firms (those started after adjustment), shedding light on whether adjustment programs are leading to more efficient outcomes. The Ghana survey was conducted by the Centre for African Economic Studies at Oxford University, and the Kenya survey by the Department of Economics at Gothenburg University in Sweden. For details on the Tanzania survey, see Dutz and Frischtak (1993). All three surveys were sponsored by the World Bank's Africa Technical Department, Private Sector Development and Economics Division, as part of its Regional Program on Enterprise Development.

9. This, of course, partly reflects the fact that the number of educated people has increased in Ghana. Nevertheless, firm-specific assets have also increased because business opportunities for educated people have expanded.

10. Tanzania's low domestic savings rate may also be due partly to errors in classifying unofficial export revenues.

CHAPTER 6

Poverty and the Environment

R EDUCING POVERTY—THE MOST IMPORTANT GOAL of development—is particularly difficult in Sub-Saharan Africa because of slow economic growth, rapid population growth, and a fragile resource base. The share of people living in poverty is larger in Africa and the poor are poorer than in any other region. And Africa is the only part of the world where the number of poor is increasing. Tackling poverty requires an increase in GDP per capita growth, securing the right kind of growth, and investing in social services that will enhance the capabilities of the poor. A recent report by the World Bank (1993c) estimated that it would take annual growth of 4.7 percent in aggregate consumption to reduce the number of poor people in Sub-Saharan Africa—far more than the 0.8 percent achieved in the 1980s and well above the 3.3 percent projected for 1993–2000. Rapid population growth means that African economies must grow faster than other regions to reduce poverty. It also makes equitable growth more difficult, because it places more stress on the natural resource base and on the already-limited financial and institutional capacity of governments to provide basic social services.

Efforts to reduce poverty can have large payoffs for the environment as well, because poverty and the environment are often linked. As *World Development Report 1992* (World Bank 1992d) points out, the poor are both the victims and the agents of damage to the environment. Because the poor—especially poor women—tend to have access only to the more environmentally fragile resources, they often suffer high productivity declines because of soil degradation or the loss of tree cover. And because they are poor, they may have little recourse but to extract what they can from the resources available to them. The high fertility rates of poor households further strain the natural resource base.

Equitable economic growth, coupled with basic education and health services, can raise the incomes of the poor, hasten the transition to lower fertility rates, and enable the poor to make investments in protecting the environment that are in their long-term interest. Although broad-based growth is absolutely essential, it will need to be complemented by government action in specific areas to spur poverty reduction and protect the environment. Educating girls may have the highest payoff for poverty reduction, because it raises the economic productivity of women and leads to healthier, better-nourished, and better-educated children. Higher levels of education also lead to lower fertility levels, reducing population growth and pressure on the environment. Policies to protect the environment will often be specific to the diverse ecological conditions prevailing. Appropriate incentives to preserve rather than mine the soil, economic energy pricing, and sensible tax policy for forestry are examples of policies that benefit the environment and are consistent with poverty-reducing growth.

Adjustment, Growth, and Poverty

MOST AFRICAN SOCIETIES ARE PREDOMINANTLY RURAL (with upwards of 90 percent of the poor in rural areas) and relatively weak in providing basic social services. A development strategy that makes substantial inroads into the poverty problem must restore high growth, but it must also achieve broad-based growth with the participation of the poor. Growth in labor demand is key to this, with the expansion of agriculture (the most labor-intensive sector and the one that employs most of the poor) important given the current level of development of most Sub-Saharan African countries. Growth in rural, off-farm income and urban labor demand (especially in the informal sector) can be valuable, but it will be difficult or impossible to reduce poverty much without rapid agricultural growth. Expanding basic social services (especially educating girls) is the most important complementary area—both as an input for high growth and as a means of ensuring broad participation in the growth process.

Supporting agriculture, expanding labor-intensive industries, and investing heavily in basic social services were exactly the policies pursued by the fast-growing East Asian economies: the "four tigers" (Hong Kong, the Republic of Korea, Singapore, and Taiwan, China), as well as Indonesia, Malaysia, Thailand, and more recently China. They have had not only the fastest sustained growth of any group of countries in history, but also highly equitable growth, thus enjoying the most rapid reduction of poverty ever.

Getting the right kind of growth and investing in people are central, and it is likely that narrowly targeted interventions to reach specific groups of the poor will play only a small role in the poverty-reduction strategies of most African countries. With close to half the population below the poverty line, spread across vast rural areas, and eating the same staple foods as better-off households, targeting the poor through food subsidies or food-for-work programs is an institutionally demanding way of transferring income to a vast number of people. It is also likely to result in large income leakages. The returns to expenditures on basic social services are higher, and they benefit the poor disproportionately. Income transfers may have a role, but a much smaller one than, say, in the countries of the former Soviet Union.

Structural adjustment has often been accused of hurting the poor. To address this issue, it is useful to focus on two questions: Would the poor have benefited from less adjustment? And, to the extent that adjustment benefited the poor, could policy reforms have been designed differently to have benefited them more? Adjustment has contributed to faster GDP per capita growth in half the countries examined in this report, and there is every reason to think that it has helped the poor, based on the strong linkage between growth and poverty reduction elsewhere in the world (World Bank 1990). But in many adjusting African countries, policy implementation has been very partial, and growth has not shown much, if any, recovery. Often the poor would have benefited from *more* adjustment, not less—from more fundamental reform of agricultural marketing, more complete exchange rate unification and real depreciation, and more radical reform and redistribution of public spending. It is also true—as the United Nations Children's Fund (UNICEF) and others have pointed out—that many adjustment programs launched early in the 1980s did not pay enough attention to ensuring adequate provision of services to the poor. Since the late 1980s, more effort has gone into improving the composition of public expenditure and the delivery of social services. Policy reforms undertaken in the course of adjustment programs can lay the broad foundations for better social policies, but long-term development efforts to improve the delivery of social services must also be pursued to complement adjustment policy reforms.

Getting better information on the conditions and attributes of the poor and tracking changes in welfare during the adjustment process must be high on the agenda. It is a sorry state of affairs when we know least about poverty in the region where poverty is most a problem. There has been progress in systematically assessing living standards, notably under the Social Dimensions of Adjustment Program and the Living Standards Measurement Program. But much more needs to be done in the 1990s, with governments and the international community working together.

Economic Declines in the Early 1980s Hurt the Poor

In assessing the effect of adjustment on the poor, it is important to understand the economic conditions that led to adjustment in Africa—and *their* effects on poor households. The economic crisis of the early 1980s caused large declines in per capita income that especially hurt those below the poverty line. The fortunes of the poor are determined by the initial distribution of income, the level of economic growth, the way growth affects the poor, and the pattern of public spending. Most African countries were faring badly on all counts in the early 1980s. Growth was stalled or negative. It was strongly biased against agriculture, where most of the poor earn their living. And public spending and the provision of rationed goods were skewed to those better off.

As macroeconomic balances deteriorated further in the early to mid-1980s—often coupled with declining terms of trade—recessions became unavoidable, and governments initially responded in ways that made matters worse for the poor. In countries with flexible exchange rates, the strategy was to tighten foreign exchange rationing and defend the official exchange rate. From Ghana to Tanzania, this heightened the dualism in markets, with the influential getting greater and greater rents from scarce foreign exchange (or products) in official markets, and the bulk of the populace facing either high parallel market prices or rationing. The poor were hit by the general decline in economic activity and the worsening terms of trade for their products. The rural poor suffered a continuation and probably some worsening of the long-term biases against them in development strategy. But it was most likely the urban middle class who faced the largest welfare declines, as a result of the collapse of urban labor markets in many countries in the early 1980s.[1] The urban poor, a much smaller group, may have suffered as well. And women were probably especially hurt by falling incomes and rising prices and by a cutback in social services.

In countries with exchange rate convertibility there was generally no rise in rationing of either foreign exchange or other products. However, the failure to tackle fiscal problems and the decline of competitiveness led to worsening poverty, especially in rural areas. Household data from the Côte d'Ivoire Living Standards Survey show that the recession quickly trickled down to households (Grootaert 1993). If mean household expenditure had remained constant in Côte d'Ivoire during 1985–88, poverty would have fallen by 20 percent. But because GDP declined under an abandoned adjustment effort, the number of people living in extreme poverty increased by 57 percent. The decline in income (as opposed to a redistribution of income from the poor to the wealthy) was the biggest influence on poverty during the second half of the 1980s (box 6.1). Côte d'Ivoire's experience underscores the fact that poverty can increase in even a short period of economic decline and destabilization if countries are adjusting insufficiently. However, the lack of similar data for other countries precludes investigating whether stronger adjustment programs can reduce the incidence and depth of poverty.

Adjustment-Led Growth Has Probably Helped the Poor

In about half of the adjusting countries in our study, GDP per capita growth declined as governments did not take adequate measures to get back on the growth track (chapter 5). But the other countries implemented more successful adjustment reforms and saw GDP per capita growth increase. This faster growth in all likelihood reduced the deterioration in the conditions of the poor. Incomes have been rising (or not declining as fast), so the depth of poverty is likely to have been less severe, and the absolute number of people falling below the poverty line may have been reduced somewhat. Moreover, the gains from growth may well have benefited the poor, and especially the rural poor, disproportionately. Key reforms likely to have helped the rural poor include the reductions in disincentives to the production of tradable goods, as well as other agricultural reforms such as liberalizing marketing.

Box 6.1 The Costs of Recession and an Inadequate Adjustment in Côte d'Ivoire

DURING 1984–86, CÔTE D'IVOIRE BENEFITED from higher coffee and cocoa prices, which increased household spending. Poverty fell in most areas, with the greatest reductions among the poorest groups (Grootaert 1993; Demery forthcoming). But when the terms of trade plunged after 1986, the government abandoned its adjustment program, relying only on spending cuts to control macroeconomic imbalances. GDP declined in 1987, and poverty rose rapidly. The percentage of poor people rose from 30 percent in 1985 to 46 percent in 1988, and for urban areas from 19 percent to 25 percent. The deterioration of the urban economy hurt lower-paid public sector workers the most. But other urban groups were affected, too, indicating that public sector retrenchment was not the only cause of increasing urban poverty. Export crop farmers—the group that would have been expected to benefit the most if adjustment efforts had maintained external competi-

tiveness—suffered more than food crop farmers. Real producer export prices fell more than 50 percent between the beginning of the decade and the end.

The access to basic services was protected, but social indicators declined systematically for the poorest households, which cut back their educational spending. There was a significant decline in school enrollment for girls, and the age-grade mismatches in primary school increased among the poor. Preventive health care (mainly vaccinations) nevertheless reached more of the poor.

The main lesson: inadequate adjustment can seriously erode the living standards of the poor. Poverty in Côte d'Ivoire increased because of the recession, as the government cut spending to adjust to a terms-of-trade shock. The increase in poverty resulted not from the redistribution of income from the poor to the rich, but from the economic decline that affected all income groups.

Dorosh and Sahn (1993) summarize what is known about the poor in Sub-Saharan Africa and their sources of income.

- Most of the poor—80 percent in Ghana, 92 percent in Madagascar, 96 percent in Côte d'Ivoire, and 99 percent in Malawi—live in rural areas.

- The poor rely heavily on agricultural income, which constitutes more than 50 percent of all income in most countries studied (appendix table A.25). Crops grown for sale (as opposed to home consumption) vary in importance; they account for 45 percent of total income in the forest of Côte d'Ivoire and 35 percent in The Gambia, but less than 15 percent in Kenya, Malawi, Rwanda, and parts of Ghana and Madagascar.

- The majority of poor farmers' income comes from nontraded food products, either consumed by the household or sold locally (appendix table A.26). Nonetheless, export crops (such as cocoa, tobacco, cotton, coffee, cola nuts, rubber, and sugar) still account for a significant share of agricultural income in many regions.[2] In the forest of Côte d'Ivoire, sales of export crops are three times larger than those of tradable and nontradable foods. In southern Malawi, export crops account for 23 percent of agricultural income—more than 80 percent of the value of agricultural sales. In Ghana, where cocoa accounts for about 5 percent of total household income, the poor derive about 65 percent of their income from agriculture, with 36 percent from crops and 21 percent of that from cocoa (World Bank 1993b).

■ Off-farm income is also significant, accounting for at least 20 percent of total income in all but two of the areas studied and for more than a third of total income in many areas.

From these facts three conclusions emerge. First, although the high share of income from home consumption of agricultural production somewhat buffers the poor from market forces, they still rely on selling their produce for a significant part of their income. So, changes in market prices matter. Second, improvements in the price of tradable crops (as a result of real exchange rate depreciations and marketing reforms) are likely to have a positive, direct impact on the income of the rural poor in the short run, though the effect may not be large in cases where the share of tradable goods they produce is low. Third, because a big part of their income is from off-farm activities, the poor would also benefit from improvements in price (or other) incentives that induce the better-off rural households to employ more poor workers or purchase more locally produced goods and services.[3]

At the same time, real depreciations and agricultural reforms—though they may have played a large part in raising official prices of some consumer goods—probably had little impact on the consumption of the poor.

■ Most of the spending of the rural poor is on nontraded food products such as millet and cassava (appendix table A.27). Domestic production of nontradable foodstuffs has increased in recent years, holding down real price increases. So the poor—particularly net purchasers—have probably not been hurt on this score. And in many countries, the share of own-production in the consumption of nontradables is high, ranging from 32 percent in The Gambia to 88 percent in the west and south of Madagascar. This high share also insulates the poor to some extent from increases in the

prices of food imports resulting from real exchange rate depreciations and marketing reforms.

- Most of the poor had little access to cheap food imports before adjustment reforms. Instead, it was mostly—though not entirely—
the urban elites who had access to rationed (tradable) foodstuffs at
below-market prices. In countries with overvalued exchange rates,
monopoly import agencies often received import quotas for
traded food staples (to limit demand for cheap foreign exchange),
and they made the imported food available to the urban elites.
Most of the poor were forced to purchase imported food staples
on either the open or the parallel market.

- More liberalized marketing of domestically produced or imported staple foodstuffs has not pushed up real prices on the open
market, even when there have been large real depreciations. Limited supply kept parallel market prices high in the pre-adjustment
period. Indeed, real prices have fallen in some countries, such as
Tanzania, which had the severest rationing. Real consumer prices
for maize, rice, and beans all fell sharply between 1985 and 1987,
when food crop marketing was first being liberalized. Even in
1992, real prices for these staples remained well below those of
the early 1980s (Mayfield 1992; van den Brink 1993). Guinea's
and Madagascar's major reforms of the rice sector also have not
led to large real price increases relative to the open market prices
before liberalization.

There are, of course, instances in which agricultural reform has in-
flicted hardship on the poor. Poor urban consumers in Madagascar, having apparently benefited to some extent from controlled rice prices before the devaluation, were hurt by the removal of subsidies (although
they benefited from other reforms). And some poor groups have not
been helped as much as others. There is reason to think that the benefits
of growth may not be evenly distributed within households, because
labor and income are allocated according to the status, bargaining
power, and options of individual household members, which in turn are
related to control over assets and income. Women are at a disadvantage
to the extent that they have less wealth, lower income, and less access to
profitable income-generating activities and resources. As the major producers of nontradable food crops produced for home consumption,
women may not have benefited from increases in prices of crops grown

primarily for export, especially where they lack the resources to under-take export crop cultivation.

So, if the rural poor cultivate export crops and traded or tradable food crops, and if they are net sellers of tradable foods, exchange rate and marketing reforms raise their incomes to the extent that higher bor-der prices are passed back to producers. But if the poor do not get a large share of their agricultural income from tradable crops, the direct bene-fits may not be so large.

In summary, the increase in growth from the stronger adjustment programs has probably helped many of the rural poor. Economic mod-eling exercises to test the impact of alternative policy scenarios for Côte d'Ivoire (Lambert, Schneider, and Suwa 1991) and Cameroon, Mada-gascar, Malawi, and Niger (Dorosh and Sahn 1993) confirm that real exchange rate depreciations can reduce both poverty and income in-equality. Indeed, the poor might have benefited more if distortions had been reduced even further. Explicit and implicit agricultural taxation re-main high in many countries. Pursuing agricultural marketing reforms and other initiatives to lower marketing and transportation costs can both increase producer incentives and hold down real food prices—to the benefit of the poor.

Promoting Efficient Public Expenditures That Benefit the Poor

In general, adjustment programs in Africa have not cut public spend-ing in the aggregate, particularly current expenditure. The economic crisis before adjustment did: the declines in government revenue neces-sitated spending cuts, in some cases large cuts, especially where invest-ment had ballooned out of control as governments borrowed in the ex-pectation that terms-of-trade windfalls would persist. Although fiscal deficits are generally lower now than at the beginning of the 1980s for about half the adjusting countries—particularly those that had large real exchange rate depreciations—current spending and capital spending in these countries are higher as shares of GDP. In general, the high net ex-ternal transfers to Africa have also enabled governments to finance the costs associated with reforms and protect expenditures while reestablish-ing internal and external balances. But there is little evidence that the composition of spending has improved substantially in favor of the poor in any of the adjusting countries, though a few countries have started to make strong efforts in that direction.

Reducing public sector employment. Reducing civil service payrolls is a painful but unavoidable part of a shift toward spending more for basic services. Governments feared that the reduction in public employment would lead to major civil unrest and increase the number of poor people. For the most part, these fears have not been realized to any great degree, for four reasons. First, personnel reductions, while substantial in a few countries, have been circumscribed in many others. Second, governments have taken some measures to compensate retrenched workers. Third, retrenched workers have found other income-generating opportunities, often in the rural sector as the terms of trade for agriculture improved. Fourth, the real wages of public sector employees in many countries, particularly those in the lower echelons, had fallen to very low levels before the adoption of adjustment programs, so that many of them had already developed alternative income-generating activities outside the public sector. Nonetheless, the loss of public sector employment—a disguised form of welfare for many—led to increased hardship and income insecurity.

Surveys show that some retrenched public sector employees have not found income opportunities equal to their previous jobs (Alderman, Canagarajah, and Younger 1993; Mills and others, forthcoming). In Ghana the income of retrenched workers is roughly comparable to that of the general population, but a disproportionately large number of retrenched workers' households are in the top and bottom income deciles. Those who turned to agriculture fall into the bottom deciles, in part because they view it as stopgap work while they wait for more remunerative opportunities. In Guinea the retrenched employees who found other employment are earning at least as much as before leaving the public sector. But about a quarter of the workers retrenched between 1985 and 1988—generally those with the fewest human capital and financial assets—remain unemployed.

Retraining programs for retrenched workers have been costly—and generally ineffective. Severance payments may be more useful: survey data from Ghana and Guinea show that the marginal propensity to invest out of severance payments is relatively high. This suggests that severance payments stimulate small-scale investment and should not be viewed simply as income transfers. However, many social security funds have been used to cover (directly or indirectly) the losses of public enterprises or have been invested in projects with low returns, so public funds are no longer available to finance severance pay.

Reducing fertilizer subsidies. Lowering fertilizer subsidies has probably had little effect on the poor, given the spotty evidence that poor farmers were not major consumers of subsidized fertilizer in countries that rationed its supply. To the extent that subsidized fertilizer did reach the poor, they presumably used more fertilizer than in the absence of subsidies and increased their agricultural income. However, many people question whether such subsidies are the best use of scarce public (and donor) resources. The poor might, for example, gain far more from infrastructure investments that lower the costs of marketing and benefit both producers and consumers.[4]

Reorienting social expenditures. Overall cuts in spending have not been a central feature of adjustment programs in Sub-Saharan Africa, but it is still likely that there were spending cuts in social services that had previously benefited the poor to some degree. Poverty reduction was not an explicit central objective of early adjustment programs, and, until recently, little attention was given to the level and composition of social expenditures—a shortcoming that is being corrected.

Table 6.1 presents data on health and education spending for fourteen of the adjusting countries in our study sample. For these countries, median real health spending increased by about 5 percent between 1980–83 and 1987–89, whereas education spending decreased by roughly the same amount. Only four countries—Cameroon, Ghana, Kenya, and Zimbabwe—substantially increased their outlays for education, and in one or two cases, the increase may have gone for university rather than primary education. Real spending per capita, by contrast, increased only slightly in health and declined even more in education, as governments could not keep up with rapid population growth.

As shares of GDP, median health spending increased slightly between the first and second halves of the decade, while median education spending declined (table 6.2). Countries that improved macroeconomic policies allocated a marginally higher share of expenditure to health and education, but the difference among groups is not large. Public expenditure on education in six of the high-performing East Asian economies (Hong Kong, Indonesia, the Republic of Korea, Malaysia, Singapore, and Thailand) was about 3.7 percent of GDP in 1989—similar to that for Africa. But because their per capita gross national product was 4.5 times greater, and because their school-age population was shrinking (while Africa's was growing), the actual spending per student was much higher.[5]

Table 6.1 Changes in Real Health and Education Expenditures in Selected Countries, 1980–83 to 1987–89 *(percent)*

Country	Health	Education
Burkina Faso	11.7	13.4
Cameroon	18.5	60.4
The Gambia	—	–64.0
Ghana	—	136.4
Kenya	1.5	33.8
Madagascar	6.2	–12.8
Malawi	3.4	–15.8
Niger	36.7	–2.1
Nigeria	–50.5	–70.3
Sierra Leone	—	–82.8
Togo	—	–4.7
Uganda	–24.1	–4.5
Zambia	–3.4	–18.3
Zimbabwe	37.6	30.9
Mean	**3.8**	**0.0**
Median	**4.8**	**–4.6**

— Not available.
Source: Sahn (1992).

Table 6.2 Social Spending in Selected Countries

Country	Health expenditures as a percentage of GDP		Education expenditures as a percentage of GDP	
	1981–86	1987–90	1981–86	1987–90
Large improvement in macroeconomic policies[a]				
Ghana	0.8	1.3	2.2	3.4
Tanzania	1.3	0.6	—	—
The Gambia	2.3	1.5	4.6	3.3
Burkina Faso	0.7	0.6	1.9	1.6
Zimbabwe	2.3	2.9	7.5	8.7
Mean	**1.5**	**1.4**	**3.2**	**3.4**
Median	**1.3**	**1.3**	**3.4**	**3.3**
Small improvement[a]				
Madagascar	1.0	1.2	3.6	3.0
Malawi	2.0	2.0	3.7	3.0
Kenya	1.8	1.6	5.3	5.8
Mali	0.8	0.7	3.0	2.7
Niger	0.8	1.3	2.5	3.1
Uganda	0.4	0.4	1.3	1.3
Mean	**1.1**	**1.2**	**3.3**	**3.1**
Median	**0.9**	**1.2**	**3.3**	**3.0**
Deterioration[a]				
Sierra Leone	1.1	0.4	2.4	1.0
Togo	1.7	1.3	5.6	4.4
Zambia	2.3	1.7	4.5	2.2
Cameroon	0.9	0.8	2.5	3.1
Mean	**1.5**	**1.1**	**3.7**	**2.7**
Median	**1.4**	**1.1**	**3.5**	**2.7**
All countries				
Mean	**1.3**	**1.2**	**3.6**	**3.3**
Median	**1.1**	**1.3**	**3.3**	**3.0**

—Not available.

a. Classifications are based on the overall scores reported in appendix table B.1.
Source: Nashashibi and Bazzoni (1994).

There is no evidence of a systematic trend to shift health and education spending away from the secondary and tertiary levels and toward the primary level (Sahn 1993). This in part reflects country and donor priorities, since donor financing accounts for a very large proportion of investment spending in these sectors. Countries varied greatly in the share of education expenditures allocated to primary education: from a low of 33 percent in Uganda to a high of 86 percent in Ghana (appendix table A.28). For most countries, the share was between 40 and 55 percent, with a median of 52 percent—roughly in line with the median in Asia in 1985 (Tan and Mingat 1993).

Spending on higher education in African adjusting countries amounts to about 20 percent of total education expenditure (figure 6.1 and appendix table A.28). This is high relative to the high-performing Asian economies: in 1985, only 10 percent of the Republic of Korea's budget went to higher education, in Malaysia 15 percent, in Thailand 12 percent, and in Indonesia 9 percent. As Birdsall and Sabot (1993) note, Asian governments focused on public provision of primary and secondary education, stimulating a demand for higher education that they let the private sector satisfy. This is socially efficient, because the returns are higher to investment in basic education. It is also equitable, because government subsidies for higher education have gone disproportionately to families with relatively comfortable incomes, who could afford to pay a greater share of university fees.

There is also a misallocation between salary and other recurrent expenditures in the education budgets of African countries. Salaries consume about 90 percent of the recurrent budget for primary education, leaving little for textbooks, training, and other materials. Meanwhile, subsidies (such as scholarships) account for a large share of the expenditure on tertiary (and sometimes secondary) education. Many public spending programs are trying to tackle this misallocation of resources, but with great difficulty because they fear student protests.

The story is pretty much the same for health. Many countries have a strong bias toward secondary and tertiary care (in district and capital hospitals), and there is little discernible movement toward primary health care or basic health services. In addition, personnel expenditures tend to squeeze other critical expenditures. Averaged across countries, personnel costs absorb about 70 percent of the recurrent budget for health. A few countries, however, are making progress in shifting spending toward basic health facilities (which provide the most cost-effective health interventions) and toward nonsalary recurrent items. Throughout the 1980s, Zimbabwe, for example, pumped new investment into the completion of its basic health infrastructure, doubling the number of rural health centers from about 500 to over 1,000 during 1980–90.

The continuing misallocations of Africa's social spending clearly work against the poor, but trends in aggregate public spending do not tell the full story. First, the private sector provides many social services. Second, it could be misleading to make inferences about the delivery of

Figure 6.1 Allocation of the Education Budget in Selected African Countries

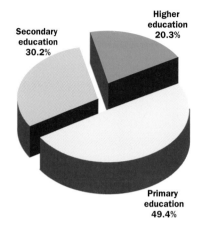

Note: Percentages are the means of both recurrent and development expenditures for the Central African Republic, Côte d'Ivoire, Kenya, and Zimbabwe in 1990; The Gambia and Uganda in 1989; Benin and Malawi in 1988; and Tanzania in 1986.

Source: Appendix table A.28.

Universities swallow one-fifth of the education budget in Africa—too large a share.

basic services from aggregate public spending. For example, in Côte d'Ivoire the poor were forced to cut their spending on education and health care in response to declining incomes, even though public spending for health was protected. Women and girls suffered particularly. Third, there could be regional differences in access within countries—differences that do not show up in national data. For example, the poor in remote regions may have little access to public services. Fourth, the poor also benefit from public spending on agriculture and infrastructure, so simply looking at social spending does not tell the whole story. One problem is the lack of disaggregated data on budgetary expenditures, which are needed for a detailed analysis of how much the poor benefit from public spending.

The Environment

THE NEXT FEW YEARS WILL SEE RAPID LEARNING ABOUT THE direction and magnitude of interactions between economic and environmental changes. For now, however, there is a very limited research base from which to draw conclusions. Much of the research that does exist was sparked by the concerns of environmentalists, who charge that adjustment reforms—particularly the shifting of production incentives and the rationalization of public expenditure—have brought harm to the environment. The following summary of the evidence is intended to add to the debate on how policy changes affect the environment.

Changing Incentive Structures and Environmental Degradation

The World Commission on Environment and Development published one of the earliest studies of the link between adjustment and the environment. Known as the Brundtland report, it observed that debt that cannot be amortized forces African countries dependent on raw materials to deplete their fragile soils, with the result that good land is turned into desert (WCED 1987). Many environmentalists picked up this point and made it the centerpiece of their criticism of structural adjustment programs. As a leading environmental organization noted, "a heavy external debt burden clearly contributes to the economic and exploitative pressures placed upon a country's natural resource base" (Conservation International 1989, p. 12). Similarly, a Friends of the Earth paper asserted that because of debt, "developing countries are forced to accelerate the exploitation of their natural resources" (Torfs 1991, p. 37).

The main argument in this criticism is that many countries reacted to the external shocks in the crisis years of the early to mid-1980s by exploiting land and forest resources in unsustainable ways. In other words, policy reforms intended to reduce distortions against the production of tradable goods expanded the production of exports—timber and other agricultural exports—and may have damaged the environment. For example, adjustment programs that called for devaluations motivated loggers to increase timber production for export and promoted the conversion of forest land to agriculture. Statements to this effect appear in studies by the Sierra Club (Glickman and Teter 1991) and the World Wildlife Fund (Reed 1992).

The evidence on all this is limited and contradictory. Pimentel and others (1991) suggest that the devaluations under adjustment reforms in the early 1980s promoted deforestation in Ghana—a conclusion inferred from substantial growth in timber revenues. One problem with this assessment is that data on timber cutting and exports are notorious for their imprecision. An increase in revenue could reflect an increase in volume cut, but it might just as easily reflect higher prices or better reporting of logging activity.[6] The World Wildlife Fund study, in attempting a similar assessment of the adjustment effort in Côte d'Ivoire, concluded that because of the complexity of intervening factors, the "net impact of adjustment on the environment remains ambiguous" (Reed 1992, p. 71).

The debt and deforestation issue is a subset of the more general issue of how policy reforms affect individual or firm incentives governing resource use. Economic reforms that change the relative prices of macroeconomic or sectoral variables—such as exchange rate reform, export tax reform, market-determined pricing of agricultural exports, marketing board liberalization, and privatization—can also change the incentives governing resource use and conservation.

Export crop expansion: varied effects on the environment. Cromwell and Winpenny (1991) analyzed the environmental impact of Malawi's structural adjustment reforms by looking at the spatial extent of production, the intensity of production, the crop mix, and the production techniques of estates and smallholders. They argued that poverty continued to grow in the early 1980s as a result of population pressure, declining real incomes, and the continuing strong dualism between the estates and smallholders. Smallholders, particularly those least secure for food, responded by intensifying their production of food staples on marginal flatlands, as well as extending their cultivation to marginal slopes. In addition, shifts in the relative prices for crops contributed to shifts in the crop mix, with environmental implications. When the returns to maize declined relative to export crop returns during the early to mid-1980s, smallholders increased their output of groundnuts, beans, and cotton. Because the production of groundnuts and beans is probably more beneficial to soil fertility than maize farming, the environmental effects may have been positive—until maize prices later improved and producers shifted back to maize.

For the estates, incentives and other policies (land tenure, credit) favored tobacco cultivation, which depletes soil fertility and requires a great deal of wood for curing tobacco and building barns. Recent policy shifts have tried to reduce the dualism of the economy by encouraging smallholders to grow tobacco. The environmental impact of these policies is not likely to be in just one direction. Cultivating more tobacco may mean more soil damage and more loss of trees, but an increase in smallholder incomes from the more profitable tobacco crop may reduce the pressure to cultivate marginal areas.

Malawi's experience shows that the choice of crops promoted (or discouraged) has major environmental implications. The same goes for the indirect incentives to produce various crops in West Africa, where different rates of implicit taxation of crops significantly affect land use. Many Sub-Saharan countries have favored export crops over domestic food crops, but "although many environmentalists argue that overemphasis on export crop production exacerbates soil degradation and ecological disturbance, their view is not valid as a general proposition" (Repetto 1989, pp. 71–72). One reason the proposition cannot be generalized is that export crops tend to be less prone to erosion than food crops. Export crops are usually tree crops or perennials that provide land cover and stable root structures, such as coffee, cocoa, rubber, palm oil, and bananas. Where tree and bush crops are grown with grasses as ground cover in West Africa, soil erosion may be a third of that from such crops as cassava and maize. So trade reforms can not only benefit export growth, they can reduce the environmental damage from soil erosion.

Institutional factors and resource management. The environmental problems of property rights and related institutional deficiencies fall into two categories. First, uncertain tenure reduces the incentives for resource conservation. Second, inequitable access to land resources can increase the population pressure on marginal resources, leading to deforestation and soil erosion. Many studies recognize the environmental relevance of these factors, in the tradition of Hardin's (1968) discussion of the "tragedy of the commons." Examples include the study by Perrings and others (1988) on overgrazing in Botswana. That study, written with the Botswana National Conservation Strategy, shows that the lack of clearly defined property rights led individual herders to put as many cattle as possible on the range, causing overgrazing, bush encroachment, erosion, and desertification.

Because shifts in the pattern of resource use depend on the intervening institutional structure, there is no simple relationship between price-related policy reforms and the environment. For example, overfishing often results from the absence of property rights, which allows anyone to harvest the resource. Because individual resource users cannot benefit from conserving such resources, the rational choice is to harvest as long as marginal returns from fishing are positive. But even if fishing rights are secure, overfishing will result if discount rates on future income are extremely high. In this case, it would pay to treat fishing areas as a depletable rather than a renewable resource. The studies reviewed here show that the interplay among incentives and institutional factors can lead to different outcomes, depending on the combination of institutions and incentives.

- Barrett (1990) finds that although higher crop prices can lead to soil depletion, changes in pricing policy have had little effect on aggregate production and only a slight environmental impact in many low-income Sub-Saharan countries. He concludes that if enough incentives are provided to build up soil fertility, farmers might be more receptive to conservation and more willing to sacrifice current profits for bigger future harvests.

- Reed (1992) reports that government pricing policies for exports were believed to have led to deforestation in Côte d'Ivoire. But the lack of a consistent and secure land tenure system probably hastened deforestation even more.

- Lopez (1992) directly addresses the interaction between the effects of export crop price changes and the institutional factors governing resource ownership and management in Côte d'Ivoire. Using both household economic data and remote sensing information on agricultural and forest resources, Lopez finds that increased output prices can contribute to pressures for agricultural extensification. However, if producers have secure tenure and can internalize the implications of excessive resource exploitation, these pressures can be significantly reduced.

Institutional changes and policies that affect agricultural productivity and soil fertility interact in a complex way and have profound long-term effects on the environment in Sub-Saharan Africa. Cleaver and Schreiber (1993), discussing the links among rapid population change, agricultural stagnation, and environmental degradation in Africa, argue that traditional systems of land tenure and use were suited to people's survival needs when population densities and population growth rates were low. The population explosion over the past several decades has changed this. Moreover, inappropriate pricing, exchange rate, and fiscal policies—coupled with inadequate delivery of agricultural support services and research—undermined the possible gains in agricultural productivity and thus contributed to the persistence of rural poverty, rapid population growth, and environmental degradation.

Public Expenditure Rationalization: Little Is Known about Its Impact on the Environment

Paralleling the concern that public expenditure cuts for basic social services would harm the poor, the early adjustment-and-environment literature focused on what the rationalization of public spending meant for environmental protection services. The World Wildlife Fund study, for example, links expenditure reforms to reduced environmental infrastructure and agricultural extension (Reed 1992). Although it is reasonable to worry that fiscal austerity measures taken as part of an adjustment strategy might endanger the funding for environmental initiatives, very little empirical work addresses this subject. One study points out that government services aimed at environmental protection in semiarid regions of Sub-Saharan Africa have traditionally been very limited, so reducing government budgets would have negligible impact (Stryker and others 1989). Another study notes that forestry departments in West and Central African countries were weak, underfunded, and underequipped even before adjustment (Grut, Gray, and Egli 1991). The challenge for adjusting African countries, then, may not be merely to safeguard environmental protection services from budget cuts, but to strengthen those services and bring them up to an adequate level.

Notes

1. Sarris and van den Brink (1993) argue that in Tanzania it was the urban, middle-class households that bore the brunt of the crisis in terms of real income losses.

2. Shares are lower in savannah regions, where groundnuts are the major export (and considered in appendix table A.26 as a traded food crop).

3. It may take factor markets some time to adjust. Evidence from studies carried out in a couple of areas shows that the multiplier effects of growth on locally produced goods are lower in Africa than in Asia. Thus the transmission of growth throughout Africa's rural sector, though positive, may not be as strong as elsewhere.

4. To have a better idea of where to channel scarce public resources, we need to compare the returns to alternative public expenditures and their impact on the welfare of the poor.

5. Between 1965 and 1989, the proportion of school-age children in the total population fell from 43 to 26 percent in Korea, from 40 to 22 percent in Hong Kong, and from 44 to 24 percent in Singapore. In contrast, the proportion rose from 47 to 51 percent in Kenya and from 46 to 48 percent in Nigeria.

6. There are substantial incentives for timber smuggling or underreporting, and these practices may also be affected by reforms.

CHAPTER 7

The Road Ahead for Adjustment

MANY OF THE ADJUSTING COUNTRIES IN SUB-Saharan Africa have made progress in improving their macroeconomic, agricultural, and trade policies. Moreover, there is a consensus on the direction that further reforms in these areas should take.

- For macroeconomic stability, countries need to focus on establishing or maintaining realistic exchange rates, keeping budget deficits and inflation low, and increasing public sector savings.
- For agricultural growth, countries should further liberalize marketing systems and restructure marketing boards to reduce the taxation of farmers. They should also ensure that the regulatory framework is conducive to private sector marketing activity.
- In trade policy, the next steps are to move toward more automatic allocation of foreign exchange, to replace nontariff barriers with tariffs, and to offer exporters more support, including relief from import duties. Achieving a low, uniform tariff is a long-term objective.

Meanwhile, there has been little progress, if any, in reforming public enterprises, financial institutions, or public sector management. In these areas there is less consensus on what is needed to improve policies. There are also greater challenges, because improvement requires good governance and considerable institutional capacity, both of which are scarce.

- Reforming public enterprises is important if countries are to sustain their macroeconomic gains. As long as public enterprises are a drain on government finances and the banking sector, sound macroeconomic policy will be difficult. Governments have resisted privatization, but the alternatives—imposing hard budget constraints, granting the enterprises greater autonomy, and putting them on a commercial footing—seldom work. Governments elsewhere are getting around the political and institutional obstacles to privatization, and their experience might be useful in Africa.

■ Building effective financial systems is bound to take time, given the lack of institutional and regulatory capacity and the difficulty of reforming the public sector. A search for quick fixes is likely to move countries away from—not toward—sound financial institutions. Recapitalizing banks when their major clients have not been restructured—and when banks do not have strong incentives to avoid the accumulation of new bad loans—will most likely create new portfolio problems, adding to the fiscal demands and reducing the incentives for financial discipline. Downsizing publicly owned banks, privatizing them where possible, encouraging new entrants, and improving the financial infrastructure are slow fixes—but promising.

■ All aspects of public sector management require improvement, particularly budgeting, payroll management, investment planning and monitoring, and tax collection. Reallocating public spending toward basic services benefiting the poor is essential. The growing popular demands for more accountable and more transparent government will support progress in these areas.

The Guiding Principles for Adjustment

POLICY REFORM IS DIFFICULT IN AFRICA, AS THE REGION'S uneven record shows. Institutional capacity is weak, the reform agenda crowded, and the political commitment sometimes absent, increasing the need for clear principles to guide the design and implementation of adjustment programs. Drawing on successful experiences elsewhere, and taking Africa's circumstances into account, the following principles can guide the reform programs in Africa.

Keep Budget Deficits Low and the Exchange Rate Right

Strong fiscal discipline and realistic real exchange rates were keys to the success of the high-performing Asian economies. Keeping budget deficits small helps control inflation and avoid balance-of-payments problems. Keeping a realistic exchange rate pays off in foreign exchange and external competitiveness. What does this mean in practice? For trade reforms, the gains in efficiency should not be at the expense of lower tax revenues. For financial sector reform, the emphasis should be on protecting the solvency of the system to avoid costly public bailouts. For public sector enterprises, privatization is a double blessing—raising revenues and lowering subsidies. And to balance reforms that could weaken public finances—such as higher spending on health, education, and infrastructure—other expenditures must be reduced and the tax base broadened.

Foster Competition at Home and Abroad

An important lesson from the Asian economies is that competition in both foreign and domestic markets raises productivity growth. Those economies held large, state-promoted enterprises to rigorous performance standards based on success in international markets. And they typically exposed smaller enterprises to highly competitive domestic conditions. Their export-led strategies increased productivity growth by providing superior access to technology. Experience in Africa suggests that more competition leads to higher productivity, and that firms with privileged access to credit or foreign exchange are less efficient than those forced to compete. So a top priority for reform in Africa is to increase competition through domestic deregulation, trade reform, and the divestiture of public enterprises.

Use Scarce Government Resources Wisely

The capacity to govern well in Africa is developing but still limited. Technical capacity is weak. Accountability and transparency are lacking. And all too often, the power of the state is used to further narrow political objectives through favoritism toward one constituency or another. Given these handicaps, the state should not intervene where markets can work even moderately well. Markets may not work perfectly, but in many African countries it is not clear that governments can do better by intervening in them. Scarce public sector capacity should be devoted to activities that markets cannot perform alone: providing infrastructure and basic social services, running the legal and judicial institutions of a market economy, and protecting the environment. And even here, governments should devolve to the private sector the provision of as many subactivities as is practical, through competitive bidding and similar procedures. Reforms that reduce government intervention in areas where markets work, even imperfectly, should have high priority—for example, abolishing agricultural marketing boards rather than trying to make them work better, lowering tariffs across the board rather than granting special exemptions, and selling off public enterprises rather than pouring money and talent into them.

Moving Forward Where There Is Consensus

NO FORMULA EXISTS THAT WILL GUARANTEE SUB-SAHARAN Africa rapid economic growth and a prosperous future. However, most policymakers agree on a few key ingredients: macroeconomic policies that promote stability, agricultural policies that help farmers, and trade policies that boost exports and liberalize imports.

Getting Macroeconomic Policies Right

Better macroeconomic policies have already turned growth around in Africa. Avoiding overvalued exchange rates and keeping inflation and budget deficits low might sound like a boring recipe, but it works. It has worked well in East Asia, and it will work in Africa. Even so, more needs to be done to increase growth. Domestic savings are low relative to other developing countries, and private investment must pick up to sustain the current recovery. How should governments proceed on the macroeconomic policy front? They should focus on three things: keeping budget deficits and inflation low, establishing fully convertible currencies and competitive exchange rates, and increasing public savings.

After the early 1980s, the macroeconomic stance improved in most adjusting countries, though more than a third of them failed to increase external competitiveness. Despite the improvement, no adjusting country in Africa has what could be considered good macroeconomic policy. As of 1990–91, twelve of the twenty-nine adjusting countries in our study were not considered to be providing an adequate or fair macroeconomic environment. The prognosis for these countries is clear: higher rates of growth will not be possible until basic macroeconomic management improves. Countries should take the opportunity to bring down inflation and restore external competitiveness as quickly as possible.

Stability is still fragile even in countries closer to having good policies and enjoying a relatively stable macroeconomic environment—Ghana, Burundi, and The Gambia. And reversals of progress cannot be ruled out. Kenya, Madagascar, and Nigeria have resumed the administrative distribution of foreign exchange, even though foreign exchange allocations are in principle free of controls. Experience in other regions with large macroeconomic imbalances at the start of adjustment (primarily Latin America) indicates that the fiscal reforms necessary to consolidate stabilization can take five to ten years. Slippages can prolong the process by creating doubts about the government's commitment to the program. Many African countries that relaxed their demand management in response to domestic pressures—such as Congo, Ghana, Kenya, and Nigeria—have suffered adverse consequences. In Congo, increases in the wage bill gutted public investment. Inflation is surging in Nigeria, and the gap between the official and the parallel market exchange rates is widening in Kenya and Nigeria.

Most countries in the region need to cut budget deficits to avoid resorting to inflationary financing, domestic arrears, or additional external financing. Governments still rely too heavily on foreign grants as a source of revenue: deficits before grants continue to be large in most countries (more than 8 percent of GDP on average). Even in some relatively stable economies, grants cover a large share of government expenditure (55 percent in Burundi and 25 percent in Ghana). Although aid flows will probably continue in the near future, especially to countries adopting sound policies, it is in the interest of African governments to reduce their dependence on aid. Instead, governments should concentrate on increasing tax revenue, using broad-based taxes that do not unduly penalize businesses and curtailing exemptions that favor clients of the state. Tax reform is the most promising avenue for lowering deficits. Noninterest government spending has already been trimmed in many countries, so further cuts will yield only marginal benefits. But while there is limited scope for reducing the overall level of public spending, there is substantial opportunity for improving its composition and management. On the one hand, African countries underspend in the sectors that are a priority for development (such as health and education). On the other hand, they overspend on wages, the military, and subsidies to public enterprises.

Macroeconomic policies should also aim to raise domestic savings now. Experience elsewhere suggests that two aspects of the reform and development process will dictate the pace at which domestic savings respond to the gradual substitution of domestic funds for foreign financing. The first is the establishment of a tradition of macroeconomic stability. The second is the establishment of sound banking systems that provide the institutional basis for mobilizing household savings. Eliminating large negative real interest rates is crucial (see, for example, Giovannini 1983 and 1985; Gupta 1987; Corbo and Schmidt-Hebbel 1991). Positive interest rates are good, but the availability of reliable opportunities for deposit services is probably more important. Both were features of East Asia's success in mobilizing savings. African countries that were relatively successful in mobilizing domestic savings—Côte d'Ivoire in the 1970s, Kenya, and Zimbabwe—all had fairly good records of macroeconomic stability and financial sector development.

Given the complexity of devising additional policies to stimulate private savings, raising public savings is the most viable option in the short run. Public savings, negative in most of Sub-Saharan Africa, have generally not improved since countries began to adjust. Again, increasing tax revenues appears to be the best means of addressing this. However, the surest way to increase savings in the long term is to boost growth, since growth and savings are part of a virtuous circle, with high growth leading to high savings and thus to higher growth. Africa is still trapped in a vicious circle of low growth and low savings.

Getting the Incentives Right for Farmers

In tandem with macroeconomic reforms, adjustment programs should pursue agricultural reforms that reduce the taxation of farmers, facilitate their access to inputs, and ensure the timeliness of payments to them. Most countries are headed in this direction, but agriculture is still taxed too highly by overvalued exchange rates and government intervention in crop marketing and input distribution. Because the price distortions have been—and still are—large, tax reductions can induce a substantial output response.

The elimination of agricultural marketing parastatals is high on the adjustment agenda. Liberalizing the market so that private agents can compete with parastatals can be a useful transitional mechanism in the near term. But care must be taken not to undermine it with restrictive licensing procedures and other interventions that give marketing parastatals undue competitive advantages. Another potentially useful short-term transitional mechanism is linking producer prices to world market prices. This can make the inefficiencies of the parastatal apparent and provide greater impetus to reform. It is especially important to liberalize marketing (or at least link domestic producer prices to world prices) at the same time that real exchange rates are being depreciated. This will help to ensure that the benefits of depreciation are passed on to producers, instead of being used to shore up the financial position of the marketing board.

Removing price controls is an essential step in encouraging competitive private marketing of agricultural products, but the response has sometimes been disappointing. The biggest impediments to the development of greater private marketing channels are poor roads and transport services. Often there is also a lingering web of controls governing licensing, trading hours and locations, weights and measures, transportation services, the movement of goods, and so on. A comprehensive review of these regulations is needed to realize the gains in efficiency from increased competition. It is particularly important to reduce marketing costs arising from unnecessary regulations, because exchange rate depreciations add to marketing costs by increasing energy prices.

Reducing government intervention in the marketing system should be viewed as a complement to, not a substitute for, investments in infrastructure, farmer education, and agricultural research—essential elements of the long-term development agenda. The low aggregate supply response in agriculture in the short term and the larger impact of investments in services, infrastructure, and human capital have led some critics to argue that too much priority is put on prices and not enough on investments and institution building. But it would be misguided to see investments in infrastructure as a substitute for policy reform, because the payoff to investment is low if the policy environment is unfavorable. Furthermore, farmers are likely to respond more rapidly to improved investment incentives if rural infrastructure is good, if property rights are secure, if public and private institutions are strong, if appropriate technologies are available, and if input, factor, and product markets work well. Policy reforms and investments need to go hand in hand, and the investment agenda should not push the difficult tasks of reforming marketing systems and reducing taxation off center stage. Nor should countries wait until the basic adjustment reforms are completed before concentrating on improving the quality of public spending for agriculture and rural infrastructure—and for capacity-building invest-ments in research and other services.

Pushing Exports

Because exports are so beneficial, governments considering the se-quence of policy reforms should consider the needs of exporters care-fully; indeed, they would do well to apply an "exporters first" rule. A good start is to mitigate the adverse effects of policies that inadvertently hinder exports. These policies include marketing restrictions, import taxes, transport regulations, and limits on payments for services. In ad-dition, governments can encourage exports by passing back to exporters the full scarcity premiums of foreign exchange earnings—say, by adopt-ing full export retention schemes. For exporters to succeed in competi-tive international markets, however, governments will have to go further and use a broad range of direct and indirect measures to encourage ex-ports. Providing appropriate infrastructure, facilitating flexible labor markets and exporters' access to credit, ensuring the enforcement of contracts and the orderly formation and dissolution of businesses, as-sisting in marketing and promotion, and establishing special export zones with tax and infrastructure advantages—these are some of the mechanisms that have worked in other regions and that are beginning to be used with some success in Africa (box 7.1).

Getting more from traditional exports. Many Sub-Saharan countries rely for their export earnings on a handful of primary commodities. Cocoa, coffee, cotton, sugar, tea, and tobacco account for about two-thirds of the region's agricultural commodity exports (appendix table A.1). Because global demand for these commodities is limited, increased exports could flood the market, causing a drop in price. This situation—often called "the adding-up problem"—is particularly acute for countries that hold large world market shares for one or two such commodities (box 7.2). Since the commodities boom of the mid-1970s, world prices of Africa's major export crops have declined at about 4 percent a year, partly due to increased production in Asia and other regions.

How should the handful of countries that face a serious adding-up problem respond? Possibilities include export diversification, production quotas, and export taxes for the very few commodities most likely to suf-fer an adding-up problem. Of these, export taxes, if correctly calculated, are in theory the most effective way of maximizing welfare. By discour-

Box 7.1 Pushing Exports in Today's Global Marketplace

IN THE PAST TEN YEARS, SOUTHEAST ASIA'S newly industrializing economies—Indonesia, Malaysia, and Thailand—have charted a new and promising approach to selling in international markets. Adapting to the changed global trading environment and their own institutional constraints, these three countries have promoted exports by combining slow-but-sure liberalization of import restrictions with strengthened institutional and infrastructure support for exporters. Other East Asian economies are moving to similar trade regimes, shifting away from high domestic protection and offsetting export incentives. The new institutional frameworks include three mechanisms for encouraging exports:

- **Widely available export credit.** All these Asian economies provide export financing, often through an automatic rediscounting of export financing, sometimes at subsidized interest rates. In most cases, bridge financing is extended to *any* firm with a confirmed export order as evidenced by a letter of credit. For many small and medium-sized enterprises, bridge loans are their only access to formal-sector finance. The certainty of access to such credit encourages entrepreneurs to undertake new export ventures and helps them to penetrate foreign markets. The size of the subsidy is less important than the automatic access. Such credit schemes are based strictly on export performance because banks only collect payments on realized export sales, and they have proved more successful than subsidized credit directed to enterprises designated by the government.
- **Access to imports at world prices.** Because gradual reductions in protection of domestic

industry are slow to eliminate high-priced imports and the attendant negative impact on exports, East Asian governments have established a variety of institutions and mechanisms to give exporters access to imports at world market prices. These include large free-trade zones with their own extensive export-oriented infrastructure, smaller export processing zones, bonded warehouses, duty drawbacks, and tariff exemptions. Since the late 1980s, major exporters in Indonesia have had unrestricted duty-free access to imports.

- **Incentives for export-oriented foreign investors.** Southeast Asia's newly industrializing economies have been highly successful in wooing export-oriented direct foreign investment by waiving investment restrictions and offering special incentives. In Indonesia the proportion of approved investment going into export-producing enterprises increased from 38 percent in 1986 to 70 percent in 1991. In Thailand the proportion increased from 10 percent in 1971 to more than 50 percent in 1988. In these economies and in Malaysia, shifting the focus of foreign investment from import substitution to exports has generated substantially more exports *and* substantially more investment.

In each case, these export-push incentives have been designed to offset lingering distortions dating from import-substitution regimes. Combined with a strong commitment to a gradual but inexorable easing of import restrictions, they have demonstrated the governments' determination to prod firms and eventually the entire economy into becoming internationally competitive.

aging high-cost production, they can ensure that production stays within a level that the market will bear. They can also make incentives for diversification unnecessary, because market prices reflecting the taxes send a

Box 7.2 Africa's Adding-Up Problems: Not Serious in Most Cases

HOW CAN ONE EVALUATE THE SERIOUSNESS OF the adding-up problem for a country or region? Some analysts compare the elasticities of world demand with shares of world exports (see Godfrey 1985, for example). But a more appropriate way to measure the adding-up problem is to estimate the elasticity of export revenues with respect to changes in export volume: that is, the percentage of change in revenue when export volume increases by 1 percent. If an increase in exports has no effect on world prices, then a 1 percent increase in the volume of exports yields a 1 percent increase in revenue, or an elasticity of 1. If an increase in exports causes world prices to decline, the elasticity is less than 1. An elasticity of 0 means the country earns no additional revenue from an increase in production, while a negative elasticity means that increased production actually causes export revenue earnings from the commodity to decline. Obviously, elasticities are more likely to be small or negative for countries and regions that hold large shares of world markets than for exporters with very small market shares.

Based on Sub-Saharan Africa's share of world markets, long-term elasticities (calculated over a period of seven to ten years) are higher than short-term elasticities (calculated over two to three years) because of lags in the response of demand. Furthermore, individual countries would have higher elasticities than the figures shown in box table 7.1. Even so, regional elasticities are positive for all commodities except cocoa, which has a short-term elasticity of –0.19. This means that a 100 percent increase in Sub-Saharan Africa's export of cocoa would reduce export revenue by 19 percent in the short term. The long-term elasticity of 0.33 for cocoa means that a 100 percent increase in

Box Table 7.1 Production Levels and Revenue Elasticities for Sub-Saharan Africa's Major Commodities, 1989–90

| Commodity | Average production | | Revenue elasticity | |
	Thousands of tons	Percentage of world production	Short-term	Long-term
Cocoa	1,322	54.5	–0.19	0.33
Sisal	110	29.2	0.43	0.80
Coffee	1,258	20.7	0.64	0.80
Tea	299	16.3	0.68	0.83
Pineapples	1,242	12.3	0.84	0.92
Tobacco				
Burley	82	10.3	0.79	0.87
All	335	4.6	0.91	0.95
Vegetable oil	3,030	5.5	0.92	0.96
Cotton	957	5.4	0.88	0.95
Sugar	3,918	3.7	0.94	0.97
Oranges	725	1.2	0.98	0.99

Source: Akiyama and Larson (1993).

production would eventually boost revenue by 33 percent. This implies that it would be profitable for Sub-Saharan Africa to increase cocoa production over the long term only if the cost of the additional output was less than 33 percent of the world price. Similar adding-up problems are evident but less severe for coffee, sisal, tea, and tobacco. Export revenues from coffee, for example, would increase by 64 percent in the short term and 80 percent over the long term if production rose by 100 percent. So, it would be profitable to increase coffee exports if the cost of additional output were less than about 80 percent of the world price.

signal to farmers about the crops to grow and export. But effective implementation of export taxes is difficult. Because most commodities are already heavily taxed by a variety of implicit and explicit means, adding export taxes to an already complex and burdensome tax structure would likely reduce welfare, not enhance it. Furthermore, countries with a large share of the market are likely to face competition from producers from other countries, particularly over the long run, vitiating the benefits of export taxes. Another problem is that commodity export taxes are attractive to fiscally strapped governments and thus are difficult to remove when they are no longer welfare-enhancing——for example, when countries are threatened with supply increases from alternative sources. For these reasons, export taxes are probably best avoided in Sub-Saharan Africa at present.

Some analysts suggest that Africa and the international community should not fund research or agricultural extension efforts for commodities facing an adding-up problem. It certainly is not in the interest of producers to boost production if the increment would sharply suppress world prices. But producers can benefit—and do benefit elsewhere in the world—from research that lowers the marginal cost of additional production. Indeed, with appropriate productivity-enhancing technologies, traditional crops could well provide an important source of increased export earnings.

Sub-Saharan Africa could learn much from Malaysia, which has become a highly successful exporter of palm oil and cocoa. The estate sector in Malaysia worked hard to develop new high-yielding varieties and to improve horticultural practices, and the government's research and extension services helped diffuse the innovations to smallholders. Research and extension are vital for African countries to be competitive with other countries in producing primary commodities. But in most of Sub-Saharan Africa, except perhaps Kenya, research is often ignored or financed inadequately and with little accountability. One remedy might be to establish a committee of government representatives, farmers, private traders, and agricultural researchers who would decide what research and extension projects to fund and what concrete results to expect. The group would follow up on the approved projects and, if the projects were successful, ensure that researchers share in the rewards.

Breaking into other export markets. There is no argument about Africa's need to reduce its heavy dependence on a few agricultural commodities. But diversification does not have to mean rapid expansion into the manufacture and export of, say, computers or electronics or other goods for which demand is booming—expansion that could prove particularly difficult for Africa. Many of the world's most successful economies did not take off by moving quickly into high-growth exports. Chile increased its exports by about 15 percent a year in the

1980s while the share of agriculture in its exports held steady. The Republic of Korea and Taiwan, China, among others, rapidly expanded exports of traditional products—such as textiles, clothing, and footwear—even though markets for these goods were growing more slowly than world trade. Such successes came by cornering a greater share of existing markets rather than by venturing into newer markets.

In Africa, aside from the handful of agricultural commodities that face an adding-up problem, the region's tiny exports mean that even very modest success in world markets would translate into tremendous growth. For any Sub-Saharan country, capturing just 0.1 percent of the European market for textiles and clothing would imply at least a doubling of its manufactured exports, and for most, a tripling.

In promoting exports, governments should not try to pick "winners." Because most African countries are small, the market segments they succeed in will be narrow. That makes it unlikely that governments (or international agencies) can identify those segments in advance. Governments can best help entrepreneurs discover and develop competitive exports by getting out of the way—and sometimes by helping them along the way.

Removing obstacles to exports. Adjustment has made exporting more profitable for many countries, yet public sectors throughout Africa continue to inhibit exports. Although adjustment reforms will take years to complete, their eventual success may depend on strong export performance at an early stage. Therefore, removing regulatory and policy impediments to exporters—in such areas as the exchange rate, marketing, trade restrictions, domestic monopolies, and foreign investment—should be among the first targets of reform. It is also important to eliminate regulations in other sectors that impede export performance, or to at least reduce the negative impact on exporters. Government transport monopolies, for example, tend to hurt production for domestic use and production for imports more or less equally, since producers and importers face a similar handicap selling domestically. But the same monopolies penalize exports more, because exporters, competing in world markets, cannot pass on the higher costs. Financial services are similarly critical to exporters, who need credit and cheap, efficient international financial services. Here, too, shortcomings that are mostly a nuisance to domestic firms are a serious handicap for exporters. In such cases, government hindrances to efficient service should be dismantled, and if this is not possible, exporters should be allowed to contract for alternative service. Indeed, governments that are serious about facilitating exports must apply a similar analysis to their entire regulatory structure.

Another vital step is welcoming foreign participation. Penetrating foreign markets is never easy, and without foreign ties, few African firms will find it possible. Foreign firms bring contacts and knowledge about international production—crucial to export success. Initially, foreign participation should be primarily through joint ventures and marketing agreements rather than through large injections of capital.

Public sector support for exports. Governments should also seek ways to promote exports actively. In the long run, this means coordinating such development efforts as the education curriculum and the location of infrastructure with the needs of exporters. In the short run, governments can provide a helping hand in three areas: easier access to inputs, advantageous credit arrangements, and assistance in entering new markets.

For Sub-Saharan countries to expand manufactured exports with high import content, they must give exporters access to imports at world prices. Duty drawbacks—refunding import duties when imported goods are re-exported—have been a popular way of attempting this. But drawbacks have often entailed unacceptable delays in Africa, particularly when financially strapped governments have not refunded import duties. Limited institutional capacity has also undermined the success of drawback schemes. Efficient alternatives are reducing or maintaining low tariffs on inputs (to minimize the need for drawbacks) and establishing bonded warehouses where export-bound imports can enter duty-free.

The desirability of export processing zones (EPZs) is hotly contested. They appear to have been most successful where exports would have succeeded anyway—and not successful elsewhere. Interestingly, large EPZs with specialized infrastructure have not been noticeably more effective than simple free-trade zones and bonded production areas. So, governments should make the most of mechanisms other than EPZs to help exporters avoid administrative, regulatory, and tariff impediments.

Some governments, particularly in East Asia, have facilitated rapid export growth by providing exporters favorable credit terms, sometimes highly targeted. East Asian governments had the institutional strength to reward winners and withhold support from losers, in elaborate export contests with credit as the prize. Other governments with weaker institutional capacity have relied on more standard approaches, such as automatic rediscounting of letters of credit. African countries, because of the problems of governance and poor administrative skills, may likewise lack the capacity to use highly targeted tools. They should concentrate on helping the financial system fulfill basic functions, such as rediscounting export letters of credit. Limited government facilitation of automatic rediscounting may provide a useful and low-risk mechanism. Programs should encourage commercial banks to undertake such functions, rather than relying directly on central banks.

Governments often try to encourage exports by establishing export promotion agencies or by supporting private efforts to assist firms in design, marketing, and other services. The record of such assistance is poor to mixed. Where governments have their own agencies, the results have often been disappointing. But government support for privately organized promotion efforts, common in East Asia, has often succeeded. It can help firms overcome the fixed-cost barriers to entry, and it can hold the firms providing promotion services to standards of profitability. Before providing or supporting such services, governments should eliminate current-account service payment restrictions that hinder firms from hiring their own marketing personnel.

Regional trade integration has also been promoted as a way to induce export expansion. Some aspects of regional cooperation are unambiguously good, such as shared development of transport infrastructure and common monetary arrangements. Other aspects, such as the facilitation of trade within Africa, will help if they do not block integration with the rest of the world. The boost to exports will occur only if the region is outward-looking, joining the world economy.

Liberalizing Imports: How Much Further and How Fast?

Striking a balance between the desirability of reducing government restrictions on imports and the need to maintain adequate reserves of foreign exchange has been a challenge throughout the adjustment process. Most African policymakers have been unwilling to lift restrictions on imports and let the exchange rate float. They argue that because the supply of exports is very inelastic, the depreciation that would almost certainly result from such actions would increase the profitability of exports (in domestic currency) without increasing their volume. Exporters' profits thus increase at the expense of both intermediate users and final consumers of imported goods.

The solution to the problem of making key imports more accessible while not unduly benefiting exporters has generally been a dual exchange rate: foreign exchange is available for approved imports at a preferential rate, and available for other imports only at a premium. Under such schemes, exporters are required to surrender their foreign exchange for less than they could get in an open market, severing the cost of imports from the exchange rate for exports. Eliminating this distortion—so that exporters receive the most favorable exchange rate available—should have a high priority. But African governments must have an alternative mechanism for maintaining adequate reserves as they move toward exchange rate unification and import liberalization. Open general license schemes that progressively expand the list of eligible imports can serve as a valuable transition mechanism.

Replacing nontariff barriers with tariffs. Reducing the prevalence and severity of nontariff barriers (NTBs) is an important step toward rationalizing the trade environment. Indeed, the switch from NTBs to tariffs is such a high priority that the precise level of tariffs imposed should not be a major concern. Even very high tariffs, if imposed only for a clearly limited transition period, can be consistent with the long-term objectives of adjustment. The main concern with temporarily high tariffs is that they might distort investment. But this can be avoided if investors are persuaded that the government is committed to reform and the high rates are truly temporary. Furthermore, the anticipation of low tariffs in the future will persuade some consumers to delay high-tariff purchases, somewhat offsetting the advantage that domestic producers would otherwise obtain from elevated tariffs.

The details of switching from NTBs to tariffs—deciding how high tariff rates should be or how long they should last—must not be allowed to stall the process. Fine-tuning can be a major distraction from more fundamental aspects of reform, particularly if the process bogs down in industry-by-industry decisions. Similarly, time should not be lost on debating how best to tax luxury goods. High taxes on foreign luxury items that are not produced domestically are unlikely to result in costly distortions. Whether such taxes are tariffs or excise taxes is therefore inconsequential, and the issue should not be permitted to consume scarce administrative capacity.

This does not mean that switching from NTBs to tariffs can be unplanned. Ad hoc moves of unspecified duration make trade reform more difficult, and shifting rents from price differences to the treasury can create a powerful new lobby for retaining the tariff. Moreover, credibility can be undermined if the pace of tariff reduction is too slow—or if the tariff reductions are excessively backloaded, moving slowly at first and then very quickly in the final years of a long transition.

Low tariffs: not an urgent priority. Given the fiscal distress in Africa and the many years needed to upgrade taxation systems, African governments are correct to put revenue considerations ahead of any push to achieve a low (10 percent), uniform tariff rate—as long as they consider exporters' concerns and the need to eliminate NTBs. During the early phase of adjustment, tariffs in the moderate range are acceptable. But actions can still be undertaken in the short term to improve the tariff structure without sacrificing revenue. Most African countries have yet to achieve a modestly graduated tariff at a moderate level consistent with fiscal concerns. The first two steps—rationalization and a reduction in dispersion (discussed in chapter 3)—are priorities for creating a sensible tariff structure. Tariff reform carried out this way is likely to be much less costly fiscally than imagined. Improvements in collections at the high end (made possible by easier administration) and relatively large revenues from a minimum tax can easily offset a fairly substantial lowering of the overall tariff structure. A minimum tax can be instituted, however, only when effective systems are in place for giving exporters access to imported inputs at world prices.

Bringing Sub-Saharan Africa's tariffs from moderate, differentiated rates to low and completely uniform levels will take considerable time, and rightly so. Countries should attempt this final step only after a thoroughgoing reform of overall taxation, including the introduction of more efficient taxes to replace tariff revenues. Otherwise, lost tariff revenues will be replaced by even less efficient sources of income, like seigniorage, or matched instead by dangerous expenditure cuts. Further tariff reform might be needed, but other items on the trade reform agenda are more urgent than establishing a single low tariff.

Rethinking Adjustment Where There Is Less Success—And Less Consensus

WHILE ADJUSTING COUNTRIES ARE MAKING HEADWAY IN macroeconomic, agricultural, and trade policy reforms, they cannot afford to ignore the inadequacies in other sectors of the economy—particularly the public and financial sectors. Opinion is divided over how to proceed in these areas, and further research and debate are warranted. It is increasingly clear, however, that African countries need to explore more far-reaching ways of restructuring these sectors, similar to those being tried elsewhere with some success.

More generally, improving public sector management remains a major goal for the road ahead, and one that adjustment programs alone cannot be expected to accomplish. Perhaps the biggest challenge is to build a more effective civil service to provide the elements necessary for a well-functioning market economy, including a sound macroeconomic framework, well-managed public finances, an adequate legal frame-work, and a system for delivering essential services to the poor to promote growth with equity. There is increasing recognition that adjustment programs, with their focus on containing civil service costs, have had limited success in tackling more fundamental problems, such as the lack of public sector accountability and transparency in the public sector, civil service employment and pay practices that are unrelated to technical competence and productivity, regressive patterns of resource mobilization, expenditure priorities inconsistent with development objectives, and the limited capacity for policy analysis. Broader approaches that address the difficult tasks of building long-term institutional capacity and creating the conditions for improved governance are called for (Dia 1993; World Bank 1991a).

Selling Off Public Enterprises

How should Africa approach public enterprise reform? There are basically two schools of thought. The first contends that privatization is necessary to promote efficiency and to signal government's overall commitment to a development strategy led by the private sector. In this view, all commercially viable public enterprises—and those with the potential to become viable—should be privatized. Small enterprises could be sold off fairly quickly, while the sale of large enterprises would require more preparation. The major exception would be the "natural" monopolies (port handling and utilities), for which some form of nonasset divestiture—leasing, concessions, or incentive-based performance contracts—would likely be more appropriate. This school of thought argues that eliminating subsidies and exposing public enterprises to foreign and domestic competition may improve efficiency, but without privatization (or nonasset divestiture for the natural monopolies), vested bureaucratic and other interests may continue to subvert reform and undermine growth of the private sector.

The second school of thought favors enterprise rehabilitation through the use of hard budget constraints and deregulation. Its adherents contend that the benefits of privatization are overstated, or that privatization in Africa cannot succeed because it faces such large political, economic, and institutional obstacles. Given the lack of interest in privatization to date, they argue, there is little reason to expect that governments will be more committed to privatization programs or more capable of implementing them in the future. In this view, African governments would do better to impose hard budget constraints on public enterprises, lift restrictions on private sector entry, and let public enterprises in competitive sectors wither away. The public utilities would be put on a sounder commercial footing and subject to improved regulatory oversight by the government.

The two strategies are not mutually exclusive. Hard budget constraints and deregulation can, and must, be imposed as privatization is taking place in order for privatization to yield good results. A recent World Bank study argues that privatization of both competitive and noncompetitive enterprises will generate more immediate and greater benefits the more market-friendly the environment (Kikeri, Nellis, and Shirley 1992). But it is unlikely that Africa can accomplish the objectives of public enterprise reform—reducing public enterprise borrowing, improving economic efficiency, and generating private sector–led growth—without divesting. The same study found that shifts to private ownership, when correctly planned and executed, foster efficiency, encourage new investment, and free public resources for infrastructure and social programs. Evidence from Africa reinforces the conclusion that ownership does matter. In Kenya, total factor productivity in private enterprises increased 5.4 percent from 1986 to 1990, but only 1.2 percent in enterprises in which the government held a minority share. As for enterprises in which the government was the majority owner, total factor productivity fell 3 percent. A survey in Tanzania found that enterprises that were economically efficient, medium in scale, privately owned, and export-oriented tended to expand output significantly during the adjustment period, while firms that were economically inefficient in 1984, including the large parastatals, contracted.

Hard budgets: A soft option? Efforts to reform public enterprises through hard budget constraints without privatization tend to be undermined by the myriad of channels for soft budget support—and to result in no meaningful hardening of the budget. Soft subsidies are an example: they are negotiable and may be adjusted for past, present, or future cost overruns. They often come from sources that are difficult to monitor, such as social security funds or public holding companies. Soft enforcement of suppliers' contracts is another example: public enterprises do not pay for services they receive from other public enterprises or the private sector. Donor financing can also be soft, as when enterprises are not required to repay foreign exchange obtained through open general license schemes, or when donors finance public enterprise investment not recorded in the public expenditure program.

Some observers argue that subjecting protected state enterprises to sudden competitive shocks would force potentially viable firms into bankruptcy. They advocate helping these enterprises restructure to survive competitive pressure. But continuing government assistance often runs contrary to efforts to impose a hard budget and establish a competitive environment.

Limited evidence suggests that explicitly budgeted subsidies have declined. But there is much less evidence on the magnitude of implicit subsidies and other financial flows. The lack of data underscores the difficulty of relying on hard budgets to force public enterprise reform. Moreover, governments find it particularly difficult to impose hard budget constraints on public enterprises that provide strategic services (transport companies and banks) and on the natural monopolies. These enterprises are among the most inefficient and the most in need of reform, but because they provide essential services, they will not be left to founder if they encounter financial difficulties.

So, at best, the strategy of imposing hard budget constraints will probably work well only for the small public enterprises in retail service or manufacturing—most of which are either already starved for capital (and on the verge of folding) or prime candidates for privatization in any event. Outside Africa, hard budget constraints seem to have been most successful in countries that have been attractive to foreign investors or in those that suffered from a severe shortage of resources and had little choice but to enforce hard budget constraints. Neither of these conditions applies strongly to Africa.

Accelerating privatization: a test of political will. There is a perception that the major impediment to privatization in many African countries is the failure of political will. Why is political will lacking? Some contend that heavy aid inflows—with few penalties for poor performance—have reduced the appetite for fundamental reform (Berg 1993; Sherif 1993; Shaikh, Kikeri, and Swanson 1993). Public enterprises offer substantial scope for patronage and corruption, leading to strong resistance from those who have a lot to lose from reform. And public sector employees are well-placed to demonstrate their opposition to reforms in ways that can effectively bring economic activity to a halt. Privatization may be good economics, but it is bad politics.

Many African governments are now expressing interest in privatizing poorly performing public enterprises, so their political will may be growing. But even where governments profess their determination to proceed, privatization has often been hindered by an economic climate inhospitable to the private sector. Genuine institutional capacity limitations have also slowed privatization. Foreigners, nonindigenous residents (such as Asians), and even members of economically dynamic but politically out-of-favor African ethnic groups may be barred from acquiring public firms. The problem of finding buyers is exacerbated by weak capital markets and the disarray in the financial system. Governments are reluctant to sell profitable public enterprises, and the money-losers are rarely attractive to buyers at terms governments find acceptable. Markets to determine the value of assets up for sale are lacking, and the notion that the worth of state assets should be close to their book value has deep roots. Governments resist measures that would increase unemployment, a likely result of privatization because many public enterprises are heavily overstaffed. And governments have not persuaded the public that the benefits of privatization outweigh the costs.

Most of these problems are found in equal or greater intensity in the formerly socialist countries of Europe and Central Asia. Even so, in many of these countries outside Africa, privatization is proceeding rapidly. Five main lessons emerge from their experience.

- Establishing a stable, open environment favorable to the growth of new firms is essential to economic transformation.
- Foreign investment is an important part of the process.
- The privatization of small enterprises can proceed rapidly.

■ Large-scale privatization may take time, but determined fiscal and credit policies, along with more open markets, can force some restructuring of the state sector in the meantime. Extreme fiscal stress encourages action.

■ Specialized privatization agencies, useful in ameliorating the lack of administrative capacity, have narrower aims and stronger incentives for rapid sales than do government agencies.

The privatization agencies typically are joint ventures between a domestic agency and foreign financial institutions or services, with management contracted to private professionals. Strong incentives are built in for management to maximize the value of the portfolio. The agencies have the power—subject to the approval of their controlling boards—to make investments, to lend, and to acquire and divest holdings. In light of Africa's limited capacity to govern well, some of these techniques might be tried profitably in African countries.

A voucher system of privatization can be especially useful when the state needs to demonstrate fairness in selling valuable assets. Experiments in Mongolia and other formerly socialist countries to issue all citizens vouchers for shares in public firms have helped spread the benefits of privatization (box 7.3). There nevertheless are drawbacks. Designed to promote wide ownership, vouchers do little to put talented managers at the helm of privatized companies. They raise no capital, for either the state or the newly privatized firms. But for Africa, one of the biggest advantages is that vouchers might generate enough national interest to make privatization irreversible.

A few African countries have been experimenting with other mechanisms for assuring broad-based ownership. One approach is to reserve controlling shares for core investors (domestic, foreign, or joint-venture) who, with full management control, can improve performance. The remaining shares might be reserved for, say, employees, and sold to them at a discount or given away. Where a functioning stock exchange exists, some shares can be reserved for small investors—either for free giveaways or for direct sale on the stock exchange. Another option is a deferred public offering, where private investors acquire full ownership on the condition that a certain percentage of shares will be sold over time to small investors. But if such schemes are seen to jeopardize efficiency because of continuing government ownership, they may inhibit the private sector's interest in privatization.

Box 7.3 Using Vouchers to Privatize: Mongolia's Innovative Approach

GOVERNMENTS TYPICALLY BEGIN PRIVATIZING the public sector by offering companies for public sale. Not Mongolia. Mongolia came up with an ambitious plan to privatize 344 large enterprises and 1,601 small businesses by simply issuing vouchers for free shares to every citizen born before the Privatization Law of 1991. The system was designed to make the transfer of public assets speedy (the government originally announced its intention to privatize all 1,945 companies by the end of 1992) and to distribute assets to a private sector that lacked wealth.

The privatization plan entitled every citizen to three "red" vouchers and one "blue" voucher. Red vouchers, which carried a face value of Tugrik 1,000, were for the privatization of the 1,601 small businesses, all agricultural assets except livestock and land, and other small assets. Blue vouchers, which carried a face value of Tugrik 7,000, were for the privatization of the 344 large enterprises. Red vouchers were tradable on the secondary market. Blue vouchers were not tradable but could be assigned twice to nominees.

The face values of the vouchers, not set in stone, simply reflected the historical cost of the assets to be privatized. But because red vouchers were freely tradable, the market value of the coupon could diverge from its face value even before privatization. Although the blue vouchers were not tradable, they were for buying shares in enterprises that *were* tradable, at prices that would reflect their true market value.

Assets in the small privatization category have been transferred to the private sector through auctions organized by local authorities under the guidelines set by the Privatization Committee. Using red vouchers, agents or groups of agents bid on businesses, with the high bid winning the ownership certificate. But employees had the first right to acquire the business at the value determined by the Privatization Committee.

Assets in the large privatization category are being transferred through auctioning share blocks. After the Privatization Committee valued the assets, audited the balance sheets, and issued shares based on the net assets of companies approved to privatize, enterprises began being converted to joint-stock companies. Ten percent of the stock was immediately granted to employees. The remaining shares are being sold subsequently, in batches. Agents declare a price or price range for shares (in blue vouchers). Then brokers phone in bids to the stock market, with the highest bidder winning the batch of shares. After full privatization of a sufficient number of enterprises, share trading will begin and be open to foreigners.

Considerable progress has been made in the privatization schedule. A secondary market rapidly emerged for red vouchers, which valued the coupons at about 30 percent of their face value. By February 1992, some 80 percent of small enterprises were in private hands. The Mongolian Stock Exchange opened in February 1992, with the initial offering of large enterprises for vouchers. Within four months, thirty-four companies were listed on the exchange, and twenty-one of them—including such prominent ones as the Ulaanbaatar Hotel—had fully privatized. The vouchers have resulted in greater diffusion of share ownership than other privatization plans, where average citizens have narrow access to emerging private enterprises.

Source: Denizer and Gelb (1992).

The lack of capital and well-developed capital markets, often cited as an obstacle to privatization in Africa, may be more apparent than real. One way of minimizing financial constraints is to have partial sales, with full managerial control given to private investors. A second is attracting flight capital back home, as happened in a flood when several Latin American countries implemented reforms and lifted current account restrictions. Kenya's flight capital reached an estimated \$2.5 billion in 1991, and luring it back will require relaxing restrictions on the entry of foreign firms and foreign capital and moving vigorously ahead with other market-opening reforms. A third way to compensate for scarce capital is to sell in installments. But this strategy needs to be used carefully, as it has led to large defaults in Ghana, Guinea, and Mali.

Nonasset divestiture for the natural monopolies. The natural monopolies—essentially the public sector utilities—may not be suited to outright privatization, yet they are difficult to put on a sound commercial footing under public management. They are probably the most important enterprises to reform, because they provide strategic services necessary for private sector development. Government divestiture of management functions would strengthen the managers' ability to resist pressure from other parts of the public sector to use enterprise funds for off-budget spending. It would also help the government establish the credibility of its commitment to expanded private sector activity. Even if management of the entire enterprise is not privatized, certain services, such as billing, can be contracted to the private sector. To date, performance-based contracts have been used in Africa for power plant operation (in Côte d'Ivoire) and for the commercial aspects of operation, such as metering, billing, and collections (in Guinea and Guinea-Bissau) (Kessides 1993).

Often it is possible to split a utility into those parts that are natural monopolies and those in which competition is possible, permitting incremental privatization. In the case of an electric utility, for example, transmission and system control remain monopolies requiring appropriate regulation. But effective competition is frequently possible in electricity generation. A form of competition is also possible in distribution, whereby the operator competes with an "ideal" company and tariffs are set automatically according to an indexed formula, without further intervention by a regulatory agency. The operator's contract specifies whether he is paid directly by the government or whether he pays himself out of revenue collected. For enterprises that generate electricity, various approaches to remuneration are also possible. With a performance-based contract, the contractor is paid for services rendered; with leasing arrangements, the government leases the plant to the contractor, who recovers operating and maintenance costs and earns profits by selling power to the distribution network. The latter is easier to implement because the lines of responsibility can be defined clearly in the contract.

Given the limited regulatory capacity of most African countries, divestiture of public utility management poses special challenges. As the ultimate owner, the state will have to continue to set service goals, cost-minimization targets, and investment incentives. Designing good contracts and monitoring them requires sophisticated institutional capacity. This will be difficult in the African context, but it is unlikely to be any tougher than regulating a government-owned utility. Success depends on finding ways of designing contractual arrangements to reduce the government's regulatory burden while limiting the abuse of public assets. It may be preferable for the state to tolerate small losses in economic efficiency from simplified contracts if those contracts decrease the regulatory burden on government and considerably improve the delivery of key services to the public.

Financial Sector Reform: Haste Makes Waste

The most urgent challenge facing African financial systems is to get back to basics: operating a sound and efficient payment system, maintaining safe and sound banking, allocating credit efficiently, and enforcing financial discipline. Today's strategy of gradually removing financial repression, dismantling directed credit programs, introducing better accounting, legal, and supervisory frameworks, continuing with institution building, and deepening and developing capital and money markets is clearly headed in the right direction. But not everything is on track.

In designing reform programs, African governments and external donors have sometimes placed too much faith in quick fixes. Reform programs overestimated the benefits of restructuring balance sheets and recapitalizing banks—and underestimated the time it takes to improve financial infrastructure in an environment where the main borrowers (the government and the public enterprises) are financially distressed and institutionally weak. It was widely thought that banks could improve their performance simply by removing the bad loans from their balance sheets, replacing managers, and injecting new capital to bring their assets up to international standards. These measures were usually insufficient because incentives for managers remained largely unchanged, banks continued to suffer from political interference, and the main borrowers continued to face financial difficulties.

The dangers of premature balance-sheet restructuring. Restructured and well-capitalized banks are crucial in improving the banking system. What has so far eluded reformers in Africa is how to restructure in a way that minimizes losses, improves the accountability of banks and their clients, and sets the stage for a better-functioning system. Although bad loans can be readily removed from balance sheets, a mechanistic approach to cleaning balance sheets and recapitalizing banks does not break the link between bad clients and the banks, nor does it impose hard budget constraints on future losses. It is a shell game, not a solution.

African banks often began balance-sheet restructuring early, to improve their ability to provide the credit and basic financial services needed for an economic takeoff. Was this approach correct? Partly yes and partly no. Banks do play a role in financing working capital and in facilitating commercial transactions (such as opening letters of credit). But their role in financing long-term investment is usually small. Most firms finance investment by raising equity or retaining earnings, rather than by borrowing from banks. Perhaps more important for Africa, banks very rarely lend to new or small firms—the enterprises likely to invest more and grow faster in response to the new incentives.

A better sequence is to clean up bank balance sheets while simultaneously tackling difficult but key reforms such as privatizing and liquidating loss-making enterprises and reducing the dependence of the remaining parastatals on the financial sector. Without greater attention to these challenges and a credible government commitment to imposing market discipline on banks and borrowers, recapitalizing banks will not necessarily improve performance. Indeed, a cosmetic restructuring program that shifts bad debts from banks and borrowers to the national budget—without putting in place a system to ensure future accountability—sows the seeds for more irresponsible lending and future financial distress.

This does not mean that financial sector reform should begin late in an adjustment program. It means that governments should start with the problems of the real sector and continue to work on them in conjunction with balance-sheet cleanups. Furthermore, balance-sheet restructuring should not mean blanket forgiveness of bad debts. This reduces the incentive to banks to continue collection efforts, and it rewards borrowers who default. Where forgiveness is extended, it must be accompanied by credible signals to banks and borrowers that further portfolio losses will result in substantial penalties.

African governments' attempts to discipline banks have often been weak, particularly in small economies, where government threats to liquidate poorly run banks, especially large state banks, are not taken seriously. One alternative for governments is to downsize troubled banks as a way of penalizing bad lending and reducing the cost of restructuring. This will also foster greater competition. Another approach is to offer management and performance contracts to reputable private banks (foreign or domestic), letting them run the public banks until the investment environment improves enough that suitable buyers for the public banks come forward. Imposing hard budget constraints, removing inept managers, and prosecuting the more egregious cases of corruption would send a strong signal to managers and owners: they will not be bailed out if they run newly restructured banks back into the ground.

Some governments are simply not prepared to undertake such reforms. Yet the attitude and behavioral changes needed to reform the financial sector must come from within the political system to be credible and sustainable. Until governments show that they are moving on these issues—by cutting off credit to unviable clients and establishing fiscal control and macroeconomic stability—donors would do better not to fund cosmetic balance-sheet restructuring but to concentrate on laying the groundwork for future reform. This includes backing small, well-designed technical assistance projects that strengthen the legal, accounting, and supervisory frameworks, and providing advisers to the government and key financial institutions.

Balancing competition and solvency. Increasing competition, rather than shoring up balance sheets, is the key to improving the quality of financial services. Governments should thus encourage the development of small private institutions and the entry of secure private investors. Governments may also want to issue licenses to non-deposit-taking financial institutions. There are hazards, however, when entry policies are lax. Experience in Kenya, Madagascar, Nigeria, and West Africa shows that simply bringing in private investors will not result in stronger and more efficient financial institutions if the private sector believes that the government will always bail out distressed banks to protect the depositors. Unduly lax entry policies undermine the solvency and profitability of the banking system, particularly if banks compete for higher returns by taking on ever-riskier investments. Experiments with liberal entry into the financial system without adequate supervision have failed in Africa, just as in Argentina, Chile, and Uruguay. In Kenya many of the new bank or nonbank financial intermediaries licensed in the 1980s to speed up the "indigenization" of ownership have failed, or should be closed, because of weak management and inadequate capitalization.

The challenge is to strike a balance between the need to increase competition and the need to ensure the solvency of financial institutions. This is easier said than done. Most countries in the region lack the resources to regulate the banking system effectively. Given the high risks in the economic environment and the poor quality of management and information systems, a system that offers extra cushions against risk is desirable. Governments may want to consider requiring higher-than-normal capital-adequacy ratios (in excess of the recommended 8 percent risk-weighted capital regarded as sound by international standards). Alternatively, African countries can rely on foreign banks, which are necessarily more diversified, to handle much of the financial intermediation. Another way to minimize risks is to require domestic banks to invest part of their portfolio in diversified international mutual funds. The greater the diversification, the lower the capital requirement.[1]

In opening their financial sectors, governments need to tailor new entry provisions to suit market conditions. In countries with a reasonable number of private banks (such as Cameroon and Côte d'Ivoire), entry can be restricted, although the limited entry of sound, well-capitalized banks can be permitted to enhance competition. In countries with too many banks (such as Kenya and Nigeria), entry should be restricted and insolvent institutions should be closed or merged with more stable institutions. Countries with few banks, most of which are partially or fully state-owned, and few foreign bank branches (Burundi, Madagascar, Rwanda, Uganda, and some of the smaller members of the CFA franc zone) face a different challenge. They should strengthen supervision and privatize public banks while encouraging reputable foreign banks to enter the market. In countries with only one or two large publicly owned banks (such as Angola, Mozambique, and Tanzania), governments should pursue a strategy of downsizing the banks and admitting competitors, or break them into competing units that could then be sold to private domestic and foreign investors.

Eliminating directed credit. Directed credit programs in Africa have suffered from low repayment rates, which have in turn undermined bank profitability, increased government deficits (because both banks and borrowers tend to be state-owned), and hampered efforts to exercise fiscal discipline. Moreover, the targeting of directed credit has tended to be unduly influenced by political considerations. For these reasons, African governments should eliminate or significantly reduce directed credit.

Although directed credit in Africa has frequently been justified by the need to assist agriculture, providing subsidized loans to agricultural marketing boards has not been an effective way of doing this. Often the inputs financed have not reached the intended beneficiaries, and the record of loan repayments has been abysmal. Moreover, the need for agricultural credit can be reduced if prices and marketing are liberalized. Agricultural credit schemes run by the government or the commercial banks are an expensive way to reach farmers, and the informal sector may be able to reach them at lower social costs. Therefore, the funding of formal sector agricultural credit schemes should remain modest.

The role of informal financial markets. Africa's formal financial sectors are ill-equipped to undertake the broad expansion of retail operations needed to serve small savers and rural savers. Furthermore, banks lack the information and infrastructure to finance individual small enterprises and small farmers. Expanding branch networks to cater to these segments might cost far more than the benefits. If so, banks should concentrate on improving their current services, while allowing informal financial markets to handle areas where high transaction and information costs put the formal sector at a disadvantage. Some African banks are experimenting with links between the formal and informal sectors. Three-quarters of the market women in Ghana's principal cities save with revolving savings and credit organizations, about 500 of which are members of the Greater Accra Susu Collectors Cooperative Society (GASCCS). The Ghana Commercial Bank has a pilot study under way to open savings accounts with GASCCS members and possibly channel credit through them.

Donors may wish to provide financial nongovernmental organizations with limited funding, but they should not press informal financial institutions to become formal institutions. Nor should they encourage governments to begin taxing or regulating the informal financial sector. The strategy should be to reduce excessive taxation of the formal financial sector, improve the efficiency of its intermediation, and encourage it to cooperate with the informal sector.

Policy Reform and the Poor

THE LIKELIHOOD IS STRONG THAT COMPREHENSIVE ADJUST-ment programs have arrested significant deterioration in the incomes of African workers. Many, though not all, of the poor have probably benefited from the strong turnaround in growth in countries that have undertaken strong adjustment programs. But the growth rates attained thus far are still not enough to reduce the incidence of poverty, and public expenditure programs are far from focused on the basic services essential to improving the welfare of the poor.

Experience in other regions shows that broad-based growth can reduce poverty. Because poverty is primarily rural in Africa, African governments should strive to eliminate policy biases against agriculture. Where the real effective exchange rate is highly overvalued, reducing exchange rate distortions is probably one of the best things countries can do to increase growth rates and reduce poverty. To raise incomes of producers, macroeconomic reforms need to be accompanied by agricultural reforms so that farmers, rather than agricultural marketing boards, capture the benefits of real devaluation. Generating and disseminating new agricultural technologies and improving market links between the rural and urban sectors will also reduce consumer prices and raise farmers' incomes.

It is equally important to protect—and, where necessary, to strengthen—public expenditure programs benefiting the poor, particularly those for the delivery of basic services. Of course, not all social service spending merits protection; some of it is inefficient and regressive. Public expenditure programs should be analyzed to verify that the poor are actually benefiting and that investments are concentrated where the social returns are highest. And actual spending, as opposed to budgeted allocations, should be monitored to ensure that targeted needs are really being met.

More attention is now being given to shifting resources toward basic services, but a major change in government and donor priorities is still needed. There is a real threat that the more advantaged and articulate elite groups in African countries will forestall a redistribution of benefits accruing to the poor. In education, providing solid primary schooling to all children, especially girls, is crucial. In health, payoffs can come from spending less on tertiary facilities and spending more on primary care and cost-effective interventions (such as immunizations against infectious disease) to deal with health problems that have substantial externalities. As *World Development Report 1993* (World Bank 1993d) points out, countries that have been highly successful in improving the health of their people have emphasized access to an essential package of services. For example, part of the decline in infant mortality and the rise in life expectancy in Zimbabwe is attributed to the use of general tax revenues to finance an array of public health and clinical services.

The opportunity cost of using scarce funds to target narrow segments of the poor must be carefully considered, because there is a strong case for improving the delivery of basic social services instead. That may be not only more equitable but more efficient. It is difficult to target the poor through food subsidies or income subsidies, because they are not the dominant consumers of any food staple nor the dominant participants in any single income-producing agricultural activity. Programs that aim to benefit them by subsidizing specific goods or activities thus will have substantial leakage to the nonpoor. There are some exceptions: Zambia's adjustment program will maintain a transitional subsidy on a less refined type of maize that is consumed primarily by the poor. Civil works schemes appear promising for targeting impoverished urban dwellers, but they constitute only a small fraction of the poor.

The lack of data on changes in living standards over time hampers researchers from assessing more directly the effects of adjustment programs on the poor and distinguishing those effects more clearly from long-term economic and social trends. Using changes in social indicators as a way of assessing the impact of adjustment programs is analytically unsatisfactory, because the social indicators respond with considerable lag to changes in income and other factors such as literacy and female education. More empirical work is needed to find reliable indicators that distinguish between short-term and long-term economic trends and to provide the data that would help resolve the ongoing debate about whether adjustment helps or hurts the poor.

Adjustment Policies and the Environment

GROWTH-ORIENTED POLICIES THAT BENEFIT THE POOR CAN indirectly reduce pressure on the natural resource base by reducing the need to exploit fragile resources and by lowering fertility. They can also lessen distortions that lead to wasteful energy consumption or inefficient production. But growth-enhancing macro-economic and sectoral policies can also have a negative impact on the environment if other policy distortions exist or the regulatory framework is inadequate.

Incentive-related and institutional reforms in the trade, energy, and public enterprise sectors can play a role in protecting the environment. In many countries, industrial enterprises are given subsidies and protection from competition through trade barriers or other kinds of regulation. For polluting activities, this is detrimental to the environment, as it breeds excessive production levels and tends to conserve inefficient production processes. Structural adjustment reforms force these enterprises to face market conditions, which can enhance efficiency and protect the environment. Subsidizing petroleum products, as Nigeria does, promotes high and wasteful consumption, with ensuing air pollution problems. Adjustment measures to cut subsidies will therefore have beneficial impacts on air quality. This will, however, have to be balanced with pricing of biomass fuels that reflects the social costs as well as the costs of harvesting and transporting the fuels to market.

Although Sub-Saharan Africa is still basically rural, urbanization is proceeding rapidly. This will exacerbate problems related to contaminated water, poor sanitation, and pollution from motor vehicles. Public sector reform to make the delivery of water and sanitation services more efficient—by allowing private enterprises to compete in waste collection or water sales, for example—may combine efficiency gains with environmental improvements. This is yet another area where structural adjustment policies are quite compatible with environmental objectives.

Environmental damage can occur when macroeconomic incentives change but other distortions, such as underpricing of resources, persist. For example, reducing economywide distortions against the production of tradable commodities can have negative environmental impacts if the associated land or forestry resources continue to be underpriced. Grut, Gray, and Egli (1991) observe that low forest fees and low collection rates mean that forest revenues are generally very low compared with what they could be.[2] The very low cost to the timber industry of acquiring and holding large concession areas encourages acquisition rather than management of concessions. In areas targeted for limited exploitation, Grut, Gray, and Egli recommend that logging concessions be replaced by forest management concessions and that performance be evaluated by an independent inspection service, perhaps a private firm.

Policy reforms along these or similar lines could be implemented in conjunction with macroeconomic reforms to ensure that forest resources are priced appropriately—particularly important when changes in such policies alter the profitability of harvesting those resources.

Environmental damage also results sometimes from market failures. Even in economies that function well otherwise, environmental damage can be excessive without corrective policies and regulations. So, whatever the direction of macroeconomic policy, environmental protection through appropriately targeted policies and regulations should have high priority on its own merits.

The policy-induced distortions and institutional shortcomings are considerable, so there should be great opportunities for "no regrets" or "win-win" policy reforms, as *World Development Report 1992* (World Bank 1992d) proposed. But addressing environmental problems in ways that are in line with Africa's limited institutional and regulatory capacity will not be easy. As governments work to develop this capacity, they should consider offering firms and communities financial incentives to self-regulate. It is also prudent to expect that macroeconomic policy changes could occasionally, for some activities in some local areas, lead to unacceptable environmental damage. Where such consequences can be foreseen, they should be headed off by countervailing policies that directly address specific environmental problems. Because macroeconomic and broad sectoral policies are very general, they cannot possibly substitute for specific environmental interventions, and they should not be manipulated to serve environmental goals.

Identifying and maintaining key public expenditures to protect the environment will also be important in efforts to rationalize government spending. While very difficult to quantify, social expenditures—particularly those targeted at reducing poverty and indirectly at slowing population growth—could also be good for the environment, perhaps even more beneficial than funds explicitly earmarked for environmental protection. Further work needs to be done to weigh the implications of different public expenditure patterns, evaluate tradeoffs, and determine how they might best be rationalized to protect the environment while reducing poverty.

There is no shortage of criticism and debate on the environmental aspects of adjustment programs in Sub-Saharan Africa. But the empirical work needed to validate or correct the various propositions lags sorely behind. The challenge for policy-oriented research is to identify the direction and quantify the effects of various combinations of policy and institutional regimes—and to identify efficient ways of minimizing environmental damage without imposing a heavy administrative burden on the state.

Debt, Aid, and Adjustment

AFRICAN COUNTRIES ARE AMONG THE MOST INDEBTED economies in the world, although so far external debt has not been a cash-flow problem (except for Congo and Nigeria), thanks to new loans and frequent reschedulings. But the high external debt has costs: long negotiations occupy much of the time of policymakers, and the access to trade credit is limited (Helleiner 1992). As countries move toward better policies, the debt burden will become an obstacle, deterring investment. The sooner this obstacle is removed in countries undertaking major reform programs, the better.

The uncertainty associated with an unsustainable stock of external debt is costly for African countries. High debt stocks can discourage investment, both domestic and foreign. And if the debt is on the books, there is always some expectation that it will have to be serviced and that investors will be taxed to service it. There is little evidence, however, that the debt overhang alone has been the cause of low investment. In Latin America, debt reduction was associated with a recovery of investment only when it was accompanied by a strong change in incentives (both macroeconomic and sectoral).

The large stock of debt has probably also reduced access to trade credit in some African countries, as trade credit became more scarce and more expensive. Although information on short-term financing from commercial banks (measured by trade and interbank lines) is difficult to obtain, anecdotal information and rough estimates from stock data shed some light on the costs of the external debt burden. For example, Nigeria has experienced a marked decline in access to uninsured short-term financing from foreign commercial banks in the past few years. Central bank figures show that the public and publicly guaranteed short-term suppliers' credits fell from about $480 million in 1988 to $22 million at the end of 1991; they were still at roughly the same level at the end of 1992. These figures should be treated with caution, however, since new short-term credits may have been arranged directly from foreign banks in the form of "advances" on foreign currency-denominated deposits of developing country entities (importers and exporters) in foreign banks.

Another cost is the time and energy that finance ministers and other high-ranking government officials spend negotiating external debt issues with the Paris Club, multilateral organizations, and bilateral agencies—all at the expense of domestic policy issues. Moreover, governmental officials are concerned that potential new export earnings from policy reforms and new investment will be channeled into debt-service payments rather than growth-enhancing expenditures. Reducing Africa's external debt burden would provide clear signals to investors and governments that the debt burden will not unduly tax their efforts to promote economic recovery.

The Need for External Debt Reduction

The external debt burden continues to be large for many countries, and a sustainable solution to the debt problem is still elusive. Although debt restructuring is always done country by country, the general approach in practice has been to have across-the-board, fixed-percentage debt reductions, as offered in the enhanced Toronto terms and the proposed Trinidad terms.[3] But these move only a small number of countries to a sustainable position, using a present value of debt service of less than 200 percent of exports as a rough indicator of sustainability. As figure 7.1 shows, only six of the twenty-one severely indebted, low-income Sub-Saharan countries could achieve a sustainable position even with the Trinidad terms, while nine would still have a ratio in excess of 300 percent of exports.

Debt reduction alone will not restore private investment and commercial lending. But with strong policy reform efforts, it can contribute to establishing a climate favorable to new investment and growth, and it can free the energies of policymakers to tackle structural problems. Two points are worth emphasizing. First, it is important that debt reduction efforts aimed at restoring external viability be linked to comprehensive reform programs to make sure that debt reduction contributes to sustained growth and does not substitute for strong domestic policy reforms. Second, reducing the stock of debt is likely to have implications for the uniform treatment of creditors. The objective should be to lower the stock of debt to a viable level, in a way that maintains the access of adjusting countries to the concessional financ-

Figure 7.1 Debt Burdens of Severely Indebted, Low-Income African Countries under Alternative Rescheduling Terms, 1991

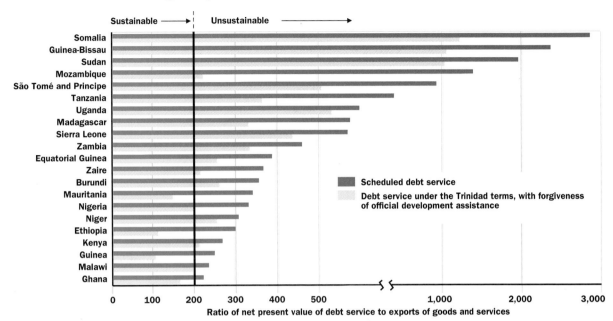

Note: Debt service is projected for 1992–2031 based on total external debt disbursed and outstanding at the end of 1991, assuming that no new disbursements are made and that amounts in arrears at the end of 1991 are payable in 1992. The present value of debt is calculated by discounting scheduled debt service over 1992–2031 at 8 percent a year. Debt reduction is 67 percent under the Trinidad terms.

Source: World Bank (1992c), figure 7.

Many countries face mounting debt, even under the Trinidad terms.

ing needed to supplement their own limited savings, even if that means different levels of debt reduction for different countries.

Aid and Adjustment: Promoting or Postponing Policy Reforms and Growth?

When aid accounts for 10 percent or more of GDP, as it does in Sub-Saharan Africa, it has powerful effects on many aspects of a country's economic life. At the macroeconomic level, it promotes growth and sustains consumption. But the large volume of aid can lead to soft budget constraints and distortions in the labor and capital markets (Younger 1992). In addition, managing complex aid programs funded by a variety of donors, each with special requirements, places a heavy burden on countries struggling to build their institutional capacity.

Donors are concerned that external transfers not crowd out domestic savings. The increases in net aggregate transfers—our measure of foreign savings—financed higher levels of investment as well as consumption (chapter 5). That some foreign savings financed higher consumption is neither surprising nor bad: in poor countries, donor resources are explicitly targeted at smoothing consumption over time, while the countries undertake the reforms and investments needed to put them on a sustainable growth path. Consumption-smoothing has clearly been a feature of successful adjustment in the past. For example, after the price of oil fell in the mid-1980s, Indonesia maintained consumption by borrowing and temporarily suspending investment, using the breathing space to implement policies that sparked growth in non-oil exports and investment. What clearly does not makes sense, under this rationale, is for external transfers to support consumption today when a country is not on the road to sustainable recovery.

That raises a related concern about whether higher levels of external transfers could lead to soft budget constraints. The argument often made is that external income flows enable governments to continue patterns of inefficient resource use that they would otherwise have to reform. External transfers may also impede real exchange rate adjustment if they make it possible for governments to maintain public sector salaries at above-market clearing rates where public sector wages play a major role in setting standards for collective wage agreements.

For the countries in our study sample, there was no clear relationship between change in net external transfers per capita and change in macroeconomic policies. Countries that benefited from increased transfers between 1981–86 and 1987–91 were almost equally split between those whose macroeconomic policies improved and those whose policies deteriorated, while countries that had declines in external transfers for the most part improved their macroeconomic policies (appendix table A.29).[4] This suggests that increases in external transfers do not necessarily forestall or retard reforms, while decreases may lead some countries to improve their policies. However, it is also possible that some countries, by improving policies, did not need increased transfers. The direction of causation between a decline in transfers and progress in policies is difficult to sort out. The key task is to design aid on a country-by-country basis so that it supports a policy and investment framework for high accumulation of capital and rising public savings.

Sub-Saharan Africa badly needs to maintain aid flows in the short to medium term if it is to avoid welfare declines that jeopardize the transition to sustainable growth. Sharp cuts in net transfers in the 1990s could undermine growth just as it is taking off. It is critical that aid be designed in a way that speeds rather than impedes growth. A prudent approach has three parts:

- A comprehensive development strategy and associated financial framework designed to support a gradual overall reduction in net transfers in the long term.
- A strong link to structural policy reforms that promote a shift away from large trade deficits and toward trade balance, as well as an increase in domestic savings, particularly public savings. Reforms that stimulate investment and improve public sector performance are especially necessary.
- A financing framework that tackles the unsustainable debt burden. It makes sense to clean up debt to achieve real sustainability, while simultaneously designing aid flows to ensure strong links between external transfers and sound policy.

A Broader Commitment to Reform

ONLY WITH STRONG GOVERNMENT COMMITMENT AND widespread public backing will policy reforms be sustained, a finding emphasized in the World Bank's recent review of its adjustment lending experience (OED 1993). When an adjustment program is launched, there must be a solid consensus on the need for change, as well as an increase in the power of the interest groups that will benefit from reforms in the course of the adjustment (World Bank 1992a). If government commitment is weak, opposition forces strong, or short-run costs high, the likelihood of stalls or reversals in policy reform is great. Zambia, for example, initiated an adjustment program in 1985, formally abandoned it two years later because of mounting opposition, and then returned to market-oriented economic policies in 1989 (Bates and Collier 1993). Ownership of an adjustment program starts with the government but does not end there.

Governments and donors alike are taking steps to expand national commitment to adjustment—for example, by launching broad public campaigns for help in the design of the program and by eliciting support from key opposition groups. The broader the identification with the program, the greater the chance of it succeeding. Creating strong ownership and commitment to reform is one of the major challenges on the road ahead for adjustment.

Where commitment is strong, it may be advantageous to design adjustment programs to minimize their vulnerability to derailment by those who stand to lose from the reforms, particularly in the initial phase of the program. Recent research on the political economy of adjustment (Haggard and Webb 1993) looks at three aspects of program design: speed, phasing, and compensation for losers.

- *Speed.* It appears preferable for a new administration to move quickly in putting reforms in place to foster the early emergence of new winners. Moving quickly can also enhance credibility, as delay only serves to raise questions about the government's resolve. Nonetheless, gradual reform seems to have worked well in a few cases where macroeconomic imbalances were not severe.
- *Phasing.* Bundling reforms together may be preferable to phasing them in one at a time. By bundling reforms, people may lose from some but gain from others. This can quell opposition to the overall reform program. For example, replacing nontariff barriers with tariffs may be more palatable if it is accompanied by reforms improving external competitiveness. But bundling does not mean overloading an adjustment program with reforms of secondary importance, nor pursuing reforms out of sequence.
- *Compensating losers.* There is general agreement that social safety nets should exist for the truly poor or those likely to become impoverished. The question is whether it makes sense to "buy off" politically powerful losers through direct compensation schemes. The political benefits of direct compensation schemes are mixed, and they sometimes undermine the overall goals of the reform programs. A better approach may be to undertake complementary reforms that allow the losers under certain reforms to become the winners under other reforms.

Conclusion

A DJUSTMENT IS NOT AN END IN ITSELF FOR AFRICA, BUT AS
other developing regions have discovered, it is an essential step
to getting on a poverty-reducing growth path. In Sub-Saharan
Africa the road ahead for adjustment is clear: continue with the macroeconomic reforms, complete the trade and agricultural sector reforms,
restructure public finances, and provide an environment conducive to
private production and provision of goods and services. Successful
implementation of these reforms implies a fundamental transformation in the role of the state, not easy in the African context of weak
institutions and often intense political opposition.

Even if the necessary policy reforms can be carried out, adjustment
programs will not solve all of Africa's problems. Adjustment can only
create the necessary foundation for the resumption of growth. Reducing
poverty and improving standards of living will require continuing investments in human capital and infrastructure and improvement in institutional capacity. Strong leadership and good governance are needed
above all, perhaps, to ensure that resources are used to achieve development goals.

Daunting? Yes. Impossible? No. The following passage aptly de-
scribes the economic situation in a typical African economy before it
started to adjust:

> The trade regime was characterized by import substitution, in-
> cluding the familiar set of complex multiple exchange rates, im-
> port licensing, and overvaluation. The economy was heavily re-
> liant on foreign aid, with exports accounting for 3 percent of
> output, while imports amounted to over 10 percent. While infla-
> tion had been brought under control, output growth rates were
> stagnant. Furthermore, manufacturing accounted for just 11 per-
> cent of GNP, with over 45 percent of output concentrated in the
> primary sector. (Collins and Park 1989, pp. 169–70)

The description is not for an African country, however—it is for the
Republic of Korea in 1960. Korea's rapid development since then is well
known; indeed, Korea and seven of its neighbors have dazzled the world
by growing faster than any other region over the past fifteen years. *The
East Asian Miracle: Economic Growth and Public Policy* (World Bank
1993a) analyzes in detail the success of these remarkably high-perform-

ing economies. One valuable and hopeful lesson for Africa is that spectacular increases in growth are indeed possible—if the right policies are in place. By embracing structural adjustment, Africa is now taking the crucial first step in creating a favorable economic environment for sustainable growth and development.

Notes

The discussion of privatization of public enterprises in this chapter draws heavily on Berg (1993) and Shaikh, Kikeri, and Swanson (1993).

1. A similar diversification gain could be obtained if the central bank invested its reserves in a diversified basket of assets, but it would have difficulty modulating its position with the expansion and contraction of domestic banking.

2. Forest fees cover the sale of standing timber and other wood and nonwood forest outputs to the timber industry and other users. The fees include volume-based stumpage charges, concession fees, stamp fees, area-based silvicultural fees, and so on.

3. The enhanced Toronto terms, adopted by the Paris Club in December 1991, provide concessional and non-concessional options for debt reduction. The concessional options amount to 50 percent forgiveness in present value terms on debt service payments falling due during the consolidation period; the nonconcessional option offers long-term rescheduling. The Trinidad terms, proposed in September 1990 but not adopted, would reduce the debt burden of the poorest heavily indebted countries by (a) rescheduling the whole stock of eligible Paris Club debt in one effort rather than in tranches; (b) significantly increasing debt relief, with two-thirds forgiveness as a benchmark; (c) capitalizing interest and requiring no payments during the first five years; and (d) setting repayment periods in the rescheduling packages at twenty-five years, with a flexible repayment schedule.

4. The same result is obtained using the *level* of net transfers per capita instead of the *change* in net transfers per capita.

Appendix A
Statistical Tables

Table A.1 Share of Sub-Saharan Africa's Agricultural Export Earnings, by Major Crop *(percent)*

Crop	1961–69	1970–79	1980–89	1989–90
Bananas	1.3	0.7	0.5	0.7
Cocoa	16.1	20.6	21.9	19.5
Coffee	19.2	25.9	26.7	20.5
Cotton	10.0	9.1	8.5	12.0
Groundnuts	10.9	5.5	2.1	2.5
Rubber	2.6	1.7	2.1	3.0
Sugar	4.0	4.7	5.8	7.0
Tea	2.1	2.6	3.7	4.2
Tobacco	3.9	3.2	4.8	6.4
All nine crops	70.0	74.1	76.0	75.9

Note: Data may not add up to totals because of rounding.
Source: FAO data.

ADJUSTMENT IN AFRICA

Table A.2 Fiscal Indicators

Country	Overall fiscal balance including grants — Percentage of GDP[a] 1981–86	1990–91	Difference between 1981–86 and 1990–91 (percentage points)	Overall fiscal balance excluding grants — Percentage of GDP[a] 1981–86	1990–91	Difference between 1981–86 and 1990–91 (percentage points)	Primary fiscal balance including grants — Percentage of GDP[a] 1981–86	1990–91	Difference between 1981–86 and 1990–91 (percentage points)	Total revenue — Percentage of GDP 1981–86	1990–91	Difference between 1981–86 and 1990–91 (percentage points)
Surplus or small overall deficit (including grants) in 1990–91												
The Gambia	-4.7	2.7	7.4	-13.9	-6.2	7.7	-2.4	6.7	9.1	18.8	20.8	2.0
Ghana[b]	-3.1	0.8	4.0	-3.4	-0.7	2.8	-1.5	2.4	3.9	8.1	13.8	5.7
Mauritania	-4.3	-0.9	3.4	-5.2	-2.7	2.5	-2.1	1.7	3.8	22.1	23.5	1.4
Tanzania	-8.5	-0.9	7.6	-11.0	-5.1	6.0	-6.1	2.6	8.7	18.4	22.1	3.6
Senegal	-6.0	-1.1	4.8	-7.0	-2.6	4.5	-3.0	1.4	4.4	18.4	18.0	-0.4
Moderate deficit												
Gabon	-0.4	-1.7	-1.4	-0.7	-2.2	-1.5	2.3	4.0	1.7	33.2	25.9	-7.3
Malawi	-8.4	-2.5	6.0	-11.4	-5.8	5.7	-3.1	0.5	3.7	20.0	19.0	-1.0
Burundi	-8.5	-3.3	5.2	-12.3	-11.4	0.9	-7.5	-1.5	6.0	13.9	16.3	2.4
Togo	-3.6	-3.3	0.3	-7.0	-5.7	1.4	1.5	0.5	-1.0	28.1	19.8	-8.3
Burkina Faso	-9.4	-3.4	6.0	-16.8	-6.5	10.3	-8.5	-2.1	6.4	13.3	13.7	0.4
Large deficit												
Uganda	-5.2	-4.1	1.1	-6.0	-7.0	-1.0	-3.8	-3.1	0.7	9.1	7.3	-1.8
Nigeria	-5.8	-4.5	1.4	-5.8	-4.5	1.4	-2.7	5.8	8.5	13.1	19.7	6.6
Madagascar	-5.8	-5.1	0.7	-6.3	-6.5	-0.1	-4.6	-3.3	1.3	12.5	10.2	-2.4
Mali	-7.7	-5.3	2.4	-12.8	-10.3	2.5	-7.3	-3.9	3.4	13.8	16.3	2.5
Kenya	-7.3	-5.6	1.7	-7.3	-7.8	-0.5	-3.4	5.8	9.2	23.3	22.7	-0.7
Benin	-8.5	-6.3	2.2	-13.7	-8.6	5.0	-6.5	-3.5	3.1	14.9	10.7	-4.2
Central African Republic	-4.3	-6.5	-2.2	-7.5	-12.7	-5.1	-3.3	-5.2	-2.0	13.6	11.2	-2.4
Rwanda	-3.7	-7.0	-3.3	-7.1	-12.5	-5.3	-3.2	-5.4	-2.2	12.0	11.7	-0.4

Very large deficit												
Niger	-4.9	-7.2	-2.4	-8.5	-11.7	-3.3	-2.5	-5.1	-2.6	11.0	9.4	-1.6
Sierra Leone	-12.0	-7.7	4.3	-13.2	-10.5	2.7	-9.9	-1.3	8.6	9.4	10.4	1.0
Congo	-7.3	-7.7	-0.5	-7.6	-8.2	-0.6	-3.0	0.2	3.2	35.1	25.3	-9.8
Zimbabwe	-8.2	-8.3	-0.1	-9.7	-9.8	-0.1	-4.0	-1.6	2.4	30.3	37.3	6.9
Zambia	-14.4	-8.5	5.9	-15.2	-14.7	0.5	-7.1	-1.0	6.1	23.1	20.4	-2.7
Cameroon	-0.1	-8.6	-8.5	-0.1	-8.6	-8.5	0.7	-5.0	-5.6	23.0	15.4	-7.7
Mozambique	-13.7	-8.9	4.7	-16.2	-28.5	-12.3	-13.4	-6.0	7.4	21.7	23.1	1.5
Côte d'Ivoire	-6.8	-13.0	-6.2	-6.8	-13.0	-6.2	0.6	-1.5	-2.1	30.1	23.2	-7.0
Medians												
All countries	-6.4	-5.2	1.9	-7.6	-8.0	0.7	-3.2	-1.4	3.5	18.4	18.5	-0.5
Low-income countries	-6.6	-4.8	2.9	-9.7	-7.4	1.4	-3.6	-1.4	3.8	13.9	16.3	0.0
Middle-income countries	-6.4	-8.0	-0.9	-6.9	-8.4	-1.0	-1.2	-0.6	2.0	30.2	24.2	-7.1
Countries with fixed exchange rates	-6.0	-6.3	-0.5	-7.5	-8.6	-0.6	-3.0	-2.1	1.7	18.4	16.3	-4.2
Countries with flexible exchange rates	-7.3	-4.5	4.0	-9.7	-7.0	0.9	-3.8	-1.0	6.0	18.4	19.7	1.4
Oil-exporting countries	-3.1	-6.1	-0.9	-3.3	-6.3	-1.0	-1.0	2.1	2.5	28.1	22.5	-7.5

Note: Chad, Guinea, and Guinea–Bissau are excluded because of insufficient data.

a. A negative number indicates a deficit; a positive number indicates a surplus.

b. Fiscal data for Ghana are based on the "narrow coverage" definition, which excludes capital expenditure financed through external project aid and the corresponding grants and loans.

(Table continues on the following page.)

Table A.2 (continued)

Country	Total expenditure Percentage of GDP 1981–86	1990–91	Difference between 1981–86 and 1990–91 (percentage points)	Capital expenditure Percentage of GDP 1981–86	1990–91	Difference between 1981–86 and 1990–91 (percentage points)	Interest payments Percentage of GDP 1981–86	1990–91	Difference between 1981–86 and 1990–91 (percentage points)	Public wages and salaries Percentage of GDP 1981–86	1990–91	Difference between 1981–86 and 1990–91 (percentage points)
Surplus or small overall deficit (including grants) in 1990–91												
The Gambia	32.6	27.0	-5.7	12.4	9.2	-3.2	2.3	4.0	1.7	8.1	5.6	-2.5
Ghana[b]	11.5	14.4	2.9	1.7	3.2	1.4	1.7	1.6	0.0	3.2	4.4	1.2
Mauritania	27.3	26.2	-1.2	2.5	5.4	3.0	2.3	2.6	0.4	11.8	6.1	-5.7
Tanzania	29.4	27.1	-2.3	6.8	3.9	-2.9	2.4	3.6	1.1	6.5	5.6	-0.9
Senegal	25.4	20.6	-4.8	3.8	2.7	-1.1	3.0	2.6	-0.4	10.0	8.3	-1.8
Moderate deficit												
Gabon	33.9	28.1	-5.8	16.7	4.9	-11.9	2.7	5.7	3.0	5.6	8.2	2.6
Malawi	31.4	24.8	-6.7	8.7	6.1	-2.6	5.3	3.0	-2.3	5.3	4.2	-1.1
Burundi	26.2	27.7	1.5	13.7	13.3	-0.4	1.0	1.8	0.8	5.9	6.6	0.7
Togo	35.1	25.5	-9.6	10.7	6.2	-4.6	5.2	3.9	-1.3	9.2	9.0	-0.2
Burkina Faso	30.0	20.1	-9.9	15.7	7.5	-8.3	0.9	1.3	0.4	7.8	9.2	1.4
Large deficit												
Uganda	15.1	14.3	-0.8	2.2	6.4	4.3	1.4	1.0	-0.4	2.3	1.2	-1.1
Nigeria	18.9	24.2	5.2	9.5	4.8	-4.7	3.2	10.3	7.1	1.9	1.7	-0.2
Madagascar	18.9	16.6	-2.3	6.6	7.1	0.5	1.2	1.8	0.6	6.2	4.5	-1.8
Mali	26.6	26.6	0.0	10.5	11.5	1.0	0.4	1.5	1.0	7.4	5.9	-1.5
Kenya	30.6	30.5	-0.1	7.1	6.0	-1.2	3.9	11.4	7.5	8.7	5.9	-2.9
Benin	28.5	19.3	-9.3	11.0	5.6	-5.4	2.0	2.8	0.9	9.0	8.6	-0.4
Central African Republic	21.1	23.8	2.7	6.9	11.2	4.4	1.1	1.3	0.2	9.0	6.9	-2.2
Rwanda	19.1	24.1	5.0	8.2	7.5	-0.7	0.6	1.7	1.1	5.5	6.3	0.8

Very large deficit

Niger	19.4	21.1	1.6	8.7	8.3	-0.4	2.4	2.2	-0.2	3.8	5.7	1.9
Sierra Leone	22.5	20.9	-1.7	4.3	3.8	-0.5	2.1	6.4	4.3	6.0	3.7	-2.3
Congo	42.7	33.5	-9.2	18.7	3.2	-15.6	4.2	8.0	3.7	8.4	12.8	4.5
Zimbabwe	40.0	47.1	7.1	6.0	8.5	2.5	4.1	6.7	2.5	10.2	16.1	5.9
Zambia	38.3	35.0	-3.3	4.9	7.5	2.6	7.3	7.5	0.2	8.5	4.6	-3.9
Cameroon	23.1	23.9	0.8	10.6	5.8	-4.8	0.7	3.6	2.9	5.4	9.2	3.7
Mozambique	37.9	51.6	13.7	13.8	26.6	12.8	0.2	2.9	2.7	6.8	5.2	-1.6
Côte d'Ivoire	36.9	36.1	-0.8	10.0	2.8	-7.2	7.4	11.5	4.1	8.9	12.5	3.6

Medians

All countries	27.9	25.1	-1.0	8.7	6.1	-0.9	2.3	3.0	0.9	7.1	6.0	-0.7
Low-income countries	27.0	24.5	-1.0	8.5	6.8	-0.5	2.0	2.7	0.7	6.6	5.7	-1.1
Middle-income countries	35.4	30.8	-2.8	10.3	4.0	-6.0	3.6	6.2	3.0	8.6	10.8	3.7
Countries with fixed exchange rates	28.5	23.9	-4.8	10.6	5.8	-4.8	2.4	2.8	0.9	8.4	8.6	1.4
Countries with flexible exchange rates	27.3	26.2	-0.8	6.8	6.4	-0.4	2.3	3.0	1.1	6.2	5.2	-1.1
Oil-exporting countries	28.5	26.1	-2.5	13.7	4.8	-8.3	2.9	6.8	3.4	5.5	8.7	3.2

Sources: IMF and World Bank data.

Table A.3 Seigniorage and Inflation (*percent*)

Country	Seigniorage[a] 1981–86	Seigniorage[a] 1990–91	Inflation[b] 1981–86	Inflation[b] 1990–91
Extremely high seigniorage in 1990–91				
Tanzania	3.8	7.6[c]	30.6	21.0
Sierra Leone	6.2	6.2	57.1	106.8
Zambia	3.6	4.0	26.2	101.8
Mean	**4.5**	**5.9**	**38.0**	**76.5**
Median	**3.8**	**6.2**	**30.6**	**101.8**
High seigniorage				
Nigeria	1.1	2.9	17.4	10.2
Benin	−2.4	2.7	4.3[d]	0.1[d]
Zimbabwe	0.8	2.5	15.0	20.8
The Gambia	1.8	1.8	20.7	10.4
Kenya	1.2	1.8	11.8	13.3
Mean	**0.5**	**2.3**	**13.9**	**11.0**
Median	**1.1**	**2.5**	**15.0**	**10.4**
Moderate seigniorage				
Madagascar	1.6	1.5	19.4	6.5
Togo	1.9	1.4	6.5	1.0
Mauritania	1.7	1.1	10.3[e]	6.6[e]
Malawi	1.0	1.0	13.3[e]	12.2[e]
Rwanda	0.2	0.8	5.3	11.9
Congo	0.1	0.8	9.8[e]	−0.3[e]
Mean	**1.1**	**1.1**	**10.8**	**6.3**
Median	**1.3**	**1.1**	**10.0**	**6.5**
Low seigniorage				
Ghana	3.3	0.4	56.0	27.6
Côte d'Ivoire	1.1	0.4	5.9	0.6
Gabon	0.6	0.2	9.2	5.2
Cameroon	0.7	0.0	10.2	0.5
Burkina Faso	1.0	−0.1	6.2	1.9
Mali	1.7	−0.6	6.0[d]	3.3[d]
Central African Republic	1.1	−0.6	9.6[e]	0.3[e]
Niger	0.6	−0.7	6.0	−4.3
Low seigniorage (continued)				
Senegal	1.0	−0.8	11.0	−0.7
Chad	1.8	−0.8	5.0[e]	0.6[e]
Mean	**1.3**	**−0.3**	**12.5**	**3.5**
Median	**1.1**	**−0.3**	**7.7**	**0.6**
Unclassified				
Burundi	1.0	—	7.7	8.0
Guinea-Bissau	—	—	40.5[e]	35.0[e]
Guinea	—	—	—	24.2[e]
Mozambique	—	—	18.5[e]	35.9[e]
Uganda	—	—	87.6[e]	32.2[e]
Mean	**—**	**—**	**38.6**	**27.1**
Median	**—**	**—**	**29.5**	**32.2**
Medians				
All countries	1.1	0.9	10.6	8.0
Low-income countries	1.6	1.3	12.6	10.4
Middle-income countries	0.8	0.3	10.0	0.5
Countries with fixed exchange rates	1.0	0.0	6.3	0.5
Countries with flexible exchange rates	1.6	1.8	19.0	20.8

— Not available.

a. Seigniorage was calculated as $(M1_t - M1_{t-1})/GDP_t - g_t(M1/GDP)_t$, where $M1_t$ is the stock of money at the end of period t, GDP_t is gross domestic product at time t, and g_t is real GDP growth.

b. Inflation was calculated as the percentage change in the consumer price index.

c. Based on M2.

d. The private consumption deflator was used when the consumer price index was not available.

e. The GDP deflator was used when the consumer price index was not available.

Sources: IMF and World Bank data.

Table A.4 Real Interest Rate for Deposits *(percent)*

Country	1981–86	1990–91	Country	1981–86	1990–91
Highly positive interest rate in 1990–91			*Highly negative*		
Niger	6.3	16.0[a]	Rwanda	1.5	−9.9
Senegal	−1.7	8.9[a]	Zimbabwe	−3.3	−12.5
Congo	0.2	8.7[a]	Sierra Leone	−36.0	−30.7
Cameroon	−1.5	8.7[a]	**Mean**	**−12.6**	**−17.7**
Central African Republic	1.9	6.8[a]	**Median**	**−3.3**	**−12.5**
Gabon	0.3	6.7[a]			
Benin	4.8	6.6[a]	*Unclassified*		
Togo	4.0	5.9[b]	Burundi	−1.8	—
Côte d'Ivoire	2.5	5.4[a]	Guinea	—	—
Chad	3.9	5.2[b]	Guinea-Bissau	—	—
The Gambia	−9.8	3.2[a]	Madagascar	−4.8	—
Mean	**1.0**	**7.5**	Mauritania	−4.0	—
Median	**1.9**	**6.7**	Mozambique	—	—
			Tanzania	−20.1	—[d]
"Acceptable" range			Zambia	−15.8	—
Mali	2.4	2.8[a]			
Ghana	−16.4	2.8[a]			
Burkina Faso	2.7	2.6[a]			
Nigeria	−5.9	1.7[a]			
Malawi	−3.7	−0.3[a]			
Kenya	0.9	−1.0			
Uganda	−38.6	−2.9[a, c]			
Mean	**−8.4**	**0.8**			
Median	**−3.7**	**1.7**			

— Not available.

Note: The real interest rate is calculated as $[(1+R) \div (1+\pi) -1] \cdot 100$, where R is the nominal interest rate and π is the inflation rate.

a. The real interest rate for 1991 was calculated using the 1991 inflation rate.

b. The real interest rate for 1990 and 1991 was calculated using the 1990 inflation rate.

c. The inflation rate was based on the annual change in the consumer price index and on the implicit GDP deflator.

d. Precise data were not available for Tanzania in 1990–91, but World Bank staff estimate the real interest rate to have been about 5 percent.

Source: IMF data.

Table A.5 Parallel Market Exchange Rate Premium *(percent)*

Country	1981–86	1990–91
Sub-Saharan adjusters[a]		
Extremely high premium in 1990–91		
Mauritania	121.5	166.6
Mozambique	2,110.8	62.6
Sierra Leone	49.4	104.4
Tanzania	248.8	74.5
Zambia	46.3	149.7
High premium		
Rwanda	43.7	47.5
Moderate premium		
Burundi	24.1	20.9
The Gambia	13.8	21.3[b]
Malawi	53.6	29.4
Nigeria	232.7	25.1
Uganda	190.0	24.6
Zimbabwe	81.3	23.5
Low premium		
Ghana	1,098.2	3.4
Guinea	655.2	7.6
Guinea-Bissau	59.7	−2.3[b]
Kenya	15.1	7.3
Madagascar	42.0	7.1[b]
Mean	**299.2**	**45.5**
Excluding Mozambique	**186.0**	**44.4**
Median	**59.7**	**24.6**
Other adjusting countries		
Argentina	32.8	42.4[b]
Bolivia	136.2	1.5[b]
Costa Rica	204.7	15.9[b]
Indonesia	4.2	2.6[b]
Mexico	13.9	6.8[b]
Morocco	6.0	13.1[b]
Philippines	12.3	7.1[b]
Thailand	−2.2	2.0[b]
Turkey	9.6	2.4[b]
Venezuela	110.3	5.2[b]
Mean	**52.8**	**9.9**
Median	**13.1**	**6.0**

Note: The parallel market exchange rate premium is calculated as the percentage difference between the parallel market exchange rate and the official exchange rate (in domestic currency at the end of the period).

a. Data are only for countries with flexible exchange rates.

b. Data are for 1990.

Sources: International Currency Analysis, Inc. (various years); IMF data.

Table A.6 Change in the Real Effective Exchange Rate, 1980 to 1990–91 *(percent)*

Countries with fixed exchange rates	
Benin	10.8
Burkina Faso	10.3
Cameroon	−18.4
Central African Republic	9.1
Chad	18.7
Congo	−9.2
Côte d'Ivoire	2.8
Gabon	7.8
Mali	10.8
Niger	28.6
Senegal	−4.0
Togo	9.7
Countries with flexible exchange rates	
Burundi	37.3
The Gambia	−26.0
Ghana	471.0
Kenya	64.2
Madagascar	109.9
Malawi	6.8
Mauritania	26.7
Mozambique	39.7
Nigeria	355.5
Rwanda	−11.5
Sierra Leone	−11.7
Tanzania	182.2
Uganda	945.3
Zambia	132.2
Zimbabwe	74.6

Note: An increase in the real effective exchange rate constitutes a depreciation; a decrease constitutes an appreciation. Guinea and Guinea-Bissau are excluded because of insufficient data.

Source: World Bank data.

Table A.7 Foreign Exchange Allocation and Import Controls for Selected Countries

Country	Controls on foreign exchange allocation		Parallel market exchange rate premium (percent)		Implied import restrictiveness (index scores)[a]	
	Before reforms	Late 1992	1985–86	1990–91	Before reforms	After reforms
Severe overvaluation followed by lowering of trade barriers						
Ghana	●	○	142	3	217	29
Severe overvaluation followed by substantial progress						
The Gambia	●	○	96	21	—	—
Guinea-Bissau	●	●	66	–2	—	—
Madagascar	●	✪	7	7	37	11
Mozambique	●	✪	4,457	63	—	—
Nigeria	●	○	235	25	34	1
Tanzania	●	⊗	253	75	103	39
Uganda	●	○	337	24	—	—
Zambia	●	⊗	36	150	65	57
No overvaluation, ongoing liberalization						
Burundi	●	○	22	21	12	7
Kenya	●	○	2	7	45	60
Malawi	●	⊗	26	29	—	—
Rwanda	●	○	39	47	—	—
Zimbabwe	●	✪	56	23	–9	–15

● All foreign exchange allocation is controlled.
✪ 25–50 percent is controlled.
⊗ Less than 25 percent is controlled.
○ Almost no controls.
— Not available.

a. The index measures the percentage of deviation of actual imports from their notional demanded level. Notional import demand is defined as $\alpha + \beta GDP + \gamma REER$, where α is a constant calculated to equalize actual and notional imports in the 1970s, β is an income elasticity equal to 1.25, γ is an exchange rate elasticity equal to 1, and REER is the real effective exchange rate.

Sources: World Bank staff; International Currency Analysis, Inc. (various years); IMF data; Narasimhan and Pritchett (1993).

Table A.8 Import Items Subject to Nontariff Barriers

Country	Before reforms	Late 1992
Benin	All	0
Burkina Faso	Hundreds	19[a]
Burundi	Nearly all	0
Cameroon	Hundreds	Hundreds
Central African Republic	—	—
Chad	—	—
Congo	33 categories	13 categories
Côte d'Ivoire	37 percent	Little change
Gabon	30	4
The Gambia[b]	—	—
Ghana	All	2
Guinea	—	—
Guinea-Bissau	—	—
Kenya	24 percent	0
Madagascar	All	0[c]
Malawi	All	Few
Mali	58	0
Mauritania	Hundreds	0
Mozambique	—	0
Niger	Hundreds	9
Nigeria	All	19 categories
Rwanda	Nearly all	0
Senegal	Hundreds	About 15
Sierra Leone	—	—
Tanzania	Nearly all	About 100
Togo	20	2
Uganda	—	5
Zambia	Nearly all	0
Zimbabwe	All	Few

— Not available.

Note: Nontariff barriers include quantitative restrictions and special licensing requirements other than for health and safety reasons.

a. As of early 1993.

b. The Gambia has undertaken a trade reform, but precise data are not available.

c. Substantial intervention exists through the control of foreign exchange.

Source: World Bank staff.

Table A.9 Marketing Controls on Major Agricultural Exports

Country	Crop	Export sales		Domestic purchasing from producers		Producer pricing	
		Before reforms	Late 1992	Before reforms	Late 1992	Before reforms	Late 1992
Benin	Cotton	●	●	●	●	■	◧
Burkina Faso	Cotton	●	●	●	●	■	■
Burundi	Coffee	●	◐	●	◐	■	■
	Tea	●	●	●	●	■	■
Cameroon	Coffee	●	⊗	●	◐	■	■
	Cocoa	●	⊗	●	⊗	■	■
Central African Rep.	Coffee	●	●	●	◐	■	■
	Cotton	●	●	●	●	■	■
Chad	Cotton	●	●	●	●	■	◧
Congo	Coffee	●	●	●	●	■	□
	Cocoa	●	●	●	●	■	□
Côte d'Ivoire	Cocoa	⊗	⊗	○	○	■	⊠
	Coffee	⊗	⊗	○	○	■	⊠
Gabon	Cocoa	●	●	●	●	■	■
	Coffee	●	●	●	●	■	■
The Gambia	Groundnuts	●	◐	●	◐	■	◇
Ghana	Cocoa	●	●	●	●	■	■
Guinea	Coffee	●	○	●	○	■	◇
Guinea-Bissau	Cashews	●	⊗	●	⊗	■	◇
Kenya	Coffee	●	●	●	●	◧	◧
	Tea	◐	◐	●	●	◧	◧
Madagascar	Vanilla	⊗	⊗	⊗	⊗	■	■
	Coffee	⊗	○	⊗	○	■	◇
Malawi	Tobacco (smallholdings)	●	◐	●	◐	■	◧
	Tea	○	○	○	○	◇	◇
Mali	Cotton	●	●	●	●	■	◧

Country	Crop	Export sales		Domestic purchasing from producers		Producer pricing	
		Before reforms	Late 1992	Before reforms	Late 1992	Before reforms	Late 1992
Mozambique	Cashews	●	◑	●	⊗	■	□
Niger	Cowpeas	●	⊗	●	○	■	◇
Nigeria	Cocoa	●	⊗	●	⊗	■	◇
	Palm oil	●	○	●	○	■	◇
Rwanda	Coffee	●	●	●	●	■	■
	Tea	●	●	●	●	■	■
Senegal	Groundnuts	●	●	●	●	■	■
	Cotton	●	●	●	●	■	■
Sierra Leone	Cocoa	●	○	●	○	■	◇
	Coffee	●	○	●	○	■	◇
Tanzania	Coffee	●	◑	●	●	■	□
	Cotton	●	●	●	●	■	□
Togo	Cotton	●	●	●	⊗	■	■
	Coffee	●	●	●	●	■	■
Uganda	Coffee	●	◑	●	◑	■	□
	Cotton	●	●	●	●	■	□
Zambia	Cotton	●	●	●	●	■	■
	Tobacco	●	○	●	⊗	■	◇
Zimbabwe	Tobacco	○	○	○	○	◇	◇
	Cotton	●	●	●	●	◇	◇

● Public sector monopoly (including cooperatives and de facto monopolies).
◑ Parastatals and private traders in competition.
⊗ Exporters/private purchasing agents licensed by government or parastatals.
○ Private sector competition.
Note: Mauritania is excluded because it has no major export crops.
Source: World Bank staff.

■ Price set at government's discretion.
◧ Price set but linked to world prices.
⊠ Indicative producer price recommended; export price linked to world market prices.
□ Indicative producer price recommended.
◇ No prices set.

Table A.10 Monopoly Activities before Reforms

Country	Petroleum: Imports/wholesale supply	Petroleum: Distribution	Fertilizer: Imports	Fertilizer: Distribution	Exports: Crop 1ᵃ	Exports: Crop 2ᵃ	Wheat flour milling	Maize milling	Sugar production	Vegetable oil production	Textile production	Cement production	Mineral extraction
Benin	●	●	●	●	●	n.a.	□	□	●	●	●	●	●
Burkina Faso	●	□	□	□	●	n.a.	●	n.a.	●	□	□	n.a.	□
Burundi	□	□	●	●	●	●	●	n.a.	●	●	●	n.a.	□
Cameroon	●	●	●	●	●	●	●	□	—	—	—	●	n.a.
Central African Republic	●	●	●	●	●	●	n.a.	n.a.	●	n.a.	—	n.a.	□
Chad	□	□	□	□	●	n.a.	n.a.	n.a.	●	□	●	n.a.	n.a.
Congo	●	●	—	—	●	●	●	●	●	●	□	●	●
Côte d'Ivoire	●	□	□	□	●	●	▲	n.a.	●	●	□	□	n.a.
Gabon	●	□	—	—	●	●	●	—	●	—	—	—	—
The Gambia	●	□	●	●	●	n.a.	●	●	n.a.	●	n.a.	▲	n.a.
Ghana	●	□	●	□	●	n.a.	□	□	□	□	□	□	—
Guinea	●	●	●	●	●	n.a.	●	●	●	●	●	●	●
Guinea-Bissau	●	●	●	□	●	n.a.	—	●	●	●	●	—	—
Kenya	●	□	●	●	●	□	●	●	●	□	●	●	n.a.
Madagascar	●	●	●	●	●	●	●	□	●	●	●	●	□
Malawi	●	●	●	●	●	□	□	□	▲	□	□	□	●
Mali	●	□	●	●	●	n.a.	—	□	●	□	□	□	□
Mauritania	●	●	□	□	n.a.	n.a.	□	n.a.	n.a.	□	□	□	●
Mozambique	●	□	n.a.	n.a.	●	n.a.	□	□	—	□	□	—	●
Niger	●	●	●	●	●	n.a.	●	n.a.	n.a.	—	●	●	●
Nigeria	●	●	●	●	●	●	—	—	●	—	—	●	—
Rwanda	□	□	□	□	●	●	—	—	—	—	—	—	—
Senegal	▲	□	●	●	●	●	▲	n.a.	▲	●	▲	▲	●
Sierra Leone	●	●	●	●	●	●	—	—	—	—	—	—	—
Tanzania	●	●	●	●	●	●	●	●	●	●	□	●	●
Togo	●	●	●	●	●	●	●	●	●	●	□	●	●
Uganda	□	□	●	●	●	●	—	—	—	—	—	—	—
Zambia	●	●	●	●	●	●	—	—	—	—	—	●	—
Zimbabwe	●	□	●	▲	□	●	□	□	▲	□	□	▲	□

● Public monopoly.   ▲ Private monopoly.   □ No monopoly.   n.a. Not applicable.   — Data not available.

a. See table A.9 for specific crops for each country.

Source: World Bank staff.

	Imports								Services							
Wheat	Rice	Sugar	Other staple foods	Vegetable oil	Drugs	Textiles	Cement	Banking	Telecommunications	Hiring of labor	Personal insurance (life, automobile, etc.)	Import insurance	International shipping	Urban bus transportation	Country
□	□	□	□	□	●	□	□	●	●	●	●	●	●	□	Benin
●	●	●	□	●	●	□	●	□	●	●	●	□	□	●	Burkina Faso
●	—	●	—	—	●	—	—	□	●	●	●	●	n.a.	●	Burundi
□	●	●	●	●	—	□	□	□	●	□	—	—	●	●	Cameroon
□	□	—	□	□	—	□	□	□	●	●	●	●	n.a.	—	Central African Republic
□	□	□	□	□	●	●	●	—	—	—	●	●	□	□	Chad
●	●	●	□	●	●	—	●	□	●	●	●	●	□	●	Congo
▲	●	□	□	□	□	□	□	□	●	□	□	□	□	□	Côte d'Ivoire
—	—	—	—	—	—	—	—	●	●	●	●	●	—	—	Gabon
—	●	▲	●	●	●	□	●	●	●	●	●	●	□	●	The Gambia
●	□	□	□	□	●	□	□	●	●	□	●	●	●	□	Ghana
●	●	●	●	●	●	●	●	●	●	●	●	●	●	●	Guinea
—	●	□	□	□	□	□	●	●	●	□	●	●	—	—	Guinea-Bissau
●	●	●	—	●	□	□	□	□	●	□	●	●	□	□	Kenya
●	—	●	—	●	□	□	□	●	—	□	—	—	—	—	Madagascar
□	□	▲	n.a.	□	—	□	□	—	□	□	□	□	n.a.	□	Malawi
●	●	□	●	●	●	—	●	□	●	●	□	□	n.a.	□	Mali
□	●	●	●	●	●	□	□	●	●	●	●	●	●	●	Mauritania
●	●	●	●	●	●	●	●	●	●	□	n.a.	n.a.	●	●	Mozambique
●	●	—	—	—	—	—	—	—	●	●	●	●	—	●	Niger
n.a.	n.a.	□	—	—	—	—	—	—	—	□	—	—	—	—	Nigeria
—	—	—	—	—	—	—	—	—	—	—	—	—	—	—	Rwanda
●	●	▲	□	□	□	□	●	□	●	□	□	□	□	●	Senegal
—	●	□	—	—	—	—	—	□	●	□	□	—	—	—	Sierra Leone
●	●	●	●	●	●	□	—	●	●	□	●	●	□	●	Tanzania
●	●	●	●	●	●	□	—	●	●	□	●	□	□	●	Togo
—	—	●	●	—	—	—	—	●	●	□	—	—	—	—	Uganda
—	—	—	—	—	—	—	—	□	●	—	●	●	—	—	Zambia
●	●	—	□	—	—	□	▲	□	●	□	□	□	□	●	Zimbabwe

235

Table A.11 Monopoly Activities, Late 1992

Country	Petroleum Imports/wholesale supply	Petroleum Distribution	Fertilizer Imports	Fertilizer Distribution	Exports Crop 1[a]	Exports Crop 2[a]	Wheat flour milling	Maize milling	Sugar production	Vegetable oil production	Textile production	Cement production	Mineral extraction
Benin	●	●	●	●	●	n.a.	□	□	●	●	□	□	●
Burkina Faso	●	□	□	□	●	n.a.	●	n.a.	●	□	□	●	□
Burundi	□	□	□	□	□	●	□	n.a.	●	●	●	n.a.	□
Cameroon	●	□	□	□	●	●	□	□	—	—	—	●	n.a.
Central African Republic	●	●	●	●	●	●	n.a.	n.a.	●	□	—	n.a.	□
Chad	□	□	□	□	●	n.a.	n.a.	n.a.	●	□	●	n.a.	n.a.
Congo	●	●	—	—	●	●	●	●	▲	●	●	●	n.a.
Côte d'Ivoire	●	□	□	□	●	●	▲	n.a.	●	●	□	□	n.a.
Gabon	●	□	—	—	●	●	□	□	□	●	□	●	—
The Gambia	□	□	□	□	□	n.a.	□	□	n.a.	●	□	▲	n.a.
Ghana	●	□	□	□	●	n.a.	□	□	□	□	□	□	□
Guinea	□	□	□	—	□	n.a.	—	—	—	●	—	—	—
Guinea-Bissau	●	□	□	□	□	n.a.	—	—	●	□	●	—	—
Kenya	●	□	□	□	□	□	□	□	●	□	□	●	□
Madagascar	●	●	●	□	●	□	●	□	●	●	▲	●	□
Malawi	●	□	□	□	□	□	□	□	▲	□	□	▲	●
Mali	●	□	□	□	●	n.a.	□	□	□	●	□	□	□
Mauritania	▲	▲	□	□	n.a.	n.a.	n.a.	n.a.	□	n.a.	□	□	●
Mozambique	●	□	□	□	□	n.a.	□	□	●	□	□	—	●
Niger	●	●	□	●	□	n.a.	●	n.a.	n.a.	—	●	—	●
Nigeria	●	□	●	●	□	□	□	□	□	□	□	□	□
Rwanda	□	□	□	□	●	●	—	—	—	—	—	—	—
Senegal	▲	□	□	□	●	●	▲	n.a.	▲	●	▲	▲	●
Sierra Leone	□	□	□	●	□	□	—	—	—	—	—	—	□
Tanzania	●	□	●	□	●	●	□	□	●	□	□	●	□
Togo	□	□	□	□	●	●	□	□	□	□	□	▲	●
Uganda	□	□	□	□	●	●	□	□	□	□	□	□	□
Zambia	●	●	□	□	●	□	—	—	—	—	—	●	—
Zimbabwe	●	□	●	□	□	●	□	□	▲	□	□	▲	□

● Public monopoly. ▲ Private monopoly. □ No monopoly. n.a. Not applicable. — Data not available.

a. See table A.9 for specific crops for each country.
Source: World Bank staff.

	Imports								Services							
Wheat	Rice	Sugar	Other staple foods	Vegetable oil	Drugs	Textiles	Cement	Banking	Telecommunications	Hiring of labor	Personal insurance (life, automobile, etc.)	Import insurance	International shipping	Urban bus transportation	Country
---	---	---	---	---	---	---	---	---	---	---	---	---	---	---	---
□	□	□	□	□	●	□	□	□	●	□	□	□	●	□	Benin
●	●	●	□	□	□	□	□	□	●	□	□	□	□	●	Burkina Faso
□	□	□	□	□	□	□	□	□	●	□	●	●	n.a.	□	Burundi
□	□	□	□	□	—	□	□	□	●	□	□	□	●	●	Cameroon
□	□	▲	□	□	□	□	□	□	●	□	—	□	n.a.	—	Central African Republic
□	□	●	□	□	□	□	□	□	●	□	●	□	□	□	Chad
●	▲	●	▲	●	—	—	●	□	●	□	●	●	●	□	Congo
▲	●	—	□	□	□	□	□	□	●	□	□	□	□	□	Côte d'Ivoire
—	—	—	—	—	—	—	—	□	●	□	—	—	—	—	Gabon
□	□	□	□	□	□	□	□	□	▲	□	□	□	□	□	The Gambia
●	□	□	□	□	□	□	□	□	●	□	—	□	●	□	Ghana
—	□	—	□	□	□	□	□	□	●	●	□	□	—	●	Guinea
—	□	—	□	□	□	□	□	□	—	□	●	●	—	—	Guinea-Bissau
●	□	□	□	▲	□	□	□	□	●	□	□	□	□	□	Kenya
●	□	●	□	●	□	□	□	□	●	□	●	●	□	□	Madagascar
□	□	□	n.a.	□	□	□	▲	□	□	□	□	□	□	□	Malawi
□	□	□	□	□	□	□	□	□	□	□	□	□	n.a.	□	Mali
□	□	●	□	□	□	□	□	□	●	□	●	●	□	●	Mauritania
□	□	□	□	□	●	□	□	□	●	□	n.a.	n.a.	□	□	Mozambique
●	●	—	□	—	□	□	□	—	●	●	□	□	—	—	Niger
●	n.a.	□	—	n.a.	—	—	—	□	□	□	□	□	□	□	Nigeria
—	—	—	□	—	□	□	□	□	□	□	□	□	□	—	Rwanda
●	●	▲	□	□	□	□	□	□	●	□	□	□	□	□	Senegal
—	□	—	—	—	—	—	—	□	□	□	□	—	□	—	Sierra Leone
□	□	□	□	□	□	□	n.a.	●	●	□	●	□	□	□	Tanzania
□	□	□	□	●	▲	□	□	□	●	□	□	□	—	□	Togo
□	□	□	□	□	□	□	□	□	●	□	□	□	□	□	Uganda
●	□	—	□	□	□	□	□	□	●	—	□	□	—	—	Zambia
●	□	□	□	□	□	□	□	□	●	□	□	□	□	●	Zimbabwe

Table A.12 Government Intervention in Selected Markets before Reforms

Country	Export crop marketing score[a]	Monopoly Ratio[b]	Monopoly Score[c]	Price control score[d]	Overall score[e]
Medium market intervention					
Chad	4	0/5	0	2	14
Zimbabwe	1	4/5	4	4	15
Rwanda	4	0/4	0	4	16
Uganda	4	1/4	1	4	18
Heavy market intervention					
Gabon	4	1/3	2	4	19
Burundi	4	2/5	2	4	20
Côte d'Ivoire	4	2/5	2	4	20
Kenya	3	4/5	4	4	21
Burkina Faso	4	3/5	3	4	22
Ghana	4	3/5	3	4	22
Mauritania	4	3/5	3	4	22
Senegal	4	3/5	3	4	22
The Gambia	4	4/5	4	3	23
Malawi	4	4/5	4	3	23
Benin	4	4/5	4	4	24
Cameroon	4	4/5	4	4	24
Central African Republic	4	4/5	4	4	24
Congo	4	3/4	4	4	24
Mali	4	4/5	4	4	24
Nigeria	4	3/4	4	4	24
Sierra Leone	4	4/5	4	4	24
Togo	4	4/5	4	4	24
Guinea	4	5/5	5	4	26
Guinea-Bissau	4	5/5	5	4	26
Madagascar	4	5/5	5	4	26
Mozambique	4	4/4	5	4	26
Niger	4	5/5	5	4	26
Tanzania	4	5/5	5	4	26
Zambia	4	4/4	5	4	26

a. The scoring system was as follows: 1—No government involvement in domestic purchasing or exporting of major export crop. 2—Public and private sectors in competition; no official price setting for private traders. 3—Public sector monopoly but prices linked to world market prices. 4—Public sector monopoly in purchasing/exporting; prices not linked to world market prices.

b. The numerator is the number of monopolized sectors; the denominator is the total number of sectors with data available. Five sectors were considered: petroleum importing and wholesale supply, retail distribution of refined petroleum products, fertilizer importing and/or distribution, wheat and/or rice importing, and domestic marketing of food crops.

c. Computed by multiplying the monopoly ratio by 5 (the total number of subsectors) and rounding to the nearest whole number.

d. The scoring system was as follows: 1—No price controls (other than on refined petroleum products). 2—Prices controlled for fewer than ten goods. 3—Prices controlled for ten to twenty-five goods. 4—Prices controlled for more than twenty-five goods.

e. Computed by weighting the marketing, monopoly, and price control scores by 3, 2, and 1, respectively. Overall scores of 4–11 were classified as little intervention, 12–18 as medium, and 19 and above as heavy.

Source: World Bank staff.

Table A.13 Government Intervention in Selected Markets, Late 1992

Country	Export crop marketing score[a]	Monopoly Ratio[b]	Monopoly Score[c]	Price control score[d]	Overall score[e]
Little market intervention					
Guinea	1	0/4	0	2	5
The Gambia	2	0/5	0	1	7
Uganda	2	0/5	0	1	7
Guinea-Bissau	1	2/5	2	1	8
Sierra Leone	2	1/5	1	1	10
Chad	3	0/5	0	2	11
Nigeria	1	3/5	3	2	11
Medium market intervention					
Mali	3	1/5	1	1	12
Mozambique	2	1/5	1	4	12
Burundi	4	0/5	0	1	13
Malawi	3	1/5	1	2	13
Niger	1	4/5	4	2	13
Zimbabwe	1	4/5	4	2	13
Rwanda	4	0/4	0	2	14
Togo	4	0/5	0	2	14
Mauritania	4	1/5	1	1	15
Côte d'Ivoire	3	2/5	2	3	16
Benin	3	3/5	3	2	17
Cameroon	4	1/5	1	3	17
Gabon	4	1/3	2	2	17
Ghana	4	2/5	2	1	17
Kenya	3	3/5	3	3	18
Senegal	4	2/5	2	2	18
Tanzania	4	2/5	2	2	18
Zambia	4	2/4	3	1	18
Heavy market intervention					
Burkina Faso	4	2/5	2	4	20
Central African Republic	4	3/5	3	2	20
Congo	4	3/4	4	2	22
Madagascar	4	4/5	4	3	23

a. The scoring system was as follows: 1—No government involvement in domestic purchasing or exporting of major export crop. 2—Public and private sectors in competition; no official price setting for private traders. 3—Public sector monopoly but prices linked to world market prices. 4—Public sector monopoly in purchasing/exporting; prices not linked to world market prices.

b. The numerator is the number of monopolized sectors; the denominator is the total number of sectors with data available. Five sectors were considered: petroleum importing and wholesale supply, retail distribution of refined petroleum products, fertilizer importing and/or distribution, wheat and/or rice importing, and domestic marketing of food crops.

c. Computed by multiplying the monopoly ratio by 5 (the total number of subsectors) and rounding to the nearest whole number.

d. The scoring system was as follows: 1—No price controls (other than on refined petroleum products). 2—Prices controlled for fewer than ten goods. 3—Prices controlled for ten to twenty-five goods. 4—Prices controlled for more than twenty-five goods.

e. Computed by weighting the marketing, monopoly, and price control scores by 3, 2, and 1, respectively. Overall scores of 4–11 were classified as little intervention, 12–18 as medium, and 19 and above as heavy.

Source: World Bank staff.

Table A.14 Tax Revenue in Selected Countries *(percentage of GDP)*

Country	Total tax revenue		Revenue by type of tax					
			Income and profits		Goods and services		International trade	
	1986	1992	1986	1992	1986	1992	1986	1992
Burundi	14.4	15.8	3.3	3.9	4.2	6.8	6.5	5.0
The Gambia	17.6	19.5	2.9	2.7	1.0	7.6	13.7	9.2
Ghana	12.2	10.0	2.8	2.1	3.8	4.3	5.6	3.6
Kenya	19.6	19.1	6.3	6.7	8.2	10.2	5.1	2.2
Madagascar	8.6	8.6	1.5	1.3	2.5	2.7	4.4	4.4
Malawi	14.8	16.9	6.3	6.9	5.1	6.3	3.2	3.6
Mauritania	19.9	16.5	6.3	5.9	3.2	2.9	9.0	7.9
Mozambique	9.4	21.7	2.6	3.7	5.4	9.3	0.9	8.0
Niger	9.1	9.0	2.4	3.2	2.3	1.3	4.1	3.9
Senegal	14.6	14.5	3.4	3.9	4.5	3.7	5.9	6.8
Tanzania	15.3	17.6	4.1	4.7	7.1	6.3	3.3	4.2
Uganda	6.0	6.1	0.4	0.8	1.4	2.3	3.8	2.8

Note: This table includes only those study-sample countries that benefited from the IMF's Structural Adjustment Facility and the Enhanced Structural Adjustment Facility in Sub-Saharan Africa during 1986–92. Data are averaged for calendar years and may not add up to totals because minor taxes are excluded.

Source: IMF staff.

Table A.15 Changes in External Income and in GDP per Capita Growth between 1981–86 and 1987–91

Country	Annualized change in external income (percentage points)			Difference in average annual GDP per capita growth (percentage points)
	Due to changes in the terms of trade	Due to changes in net transfers	Total	
Increases in external income				
Mozambique	—	6.6	6.6	7.6
Tanzania	-0.1	3.3	3.2	2.9
Zambia	1.5	0.1	1.6	0.9
Sierra Leone	0.4	0.5	0.9	2.9
Madagascar	0.0	0.8	0.8	1.6
Chad	-0.1	0.9	0.8	-1.9
Malawi	-0.7	1.5	0.7	2.2
Uganda	-0.2	0.8	0.6	4.3
Central African Republic	-0.1	0.5	0.4	-2.6
Benin	-0.1	0.4	0.4	-3.1
Ghana	-0.2	0.5	0.3	3.7
Kenya	-0.6	0.8	0.2	1.5
Burundi	-0.6	0.7	0.1	-0.9
Rwanda	-0.3	0.3	0.0	-5.5
Mean	**-0.1**	**1.3**	**1.2**	**1.0**
Median	**-0.1**	**0.7**	**0.7**	**1.5**
Declines in external income				
Mali	0.0	-1.2	-1.1	-1.6
Côte d'Ivoire	-1.0	-0.2	-1.2	-2.6
The Gambia	-0.2	-1.0	-1.3	-0.8
Togo	-1.3	-0.1	-1.4	1.4
Niger	-1.3	-0.1	-1.5	2.5
Declines in external income (continued)				
Mauritania	0.0	-2.3	-2.4	-0.1
Gabon	-3.2	0.5	-2.7	0.9
Nigeria	-2.3	-0.6	-2.9	7.0
Congo	-3.6	-1.7	-5.3	-4.9
Burkina Faso	-0.1	-0.3	-0.5	-1.7
Zimbabwe	-0.1	-0.5	-0.5	0.7
Cameroon	-1.2	0.5	-0.7	-12.5
Senegal	0.0	-0.8	-0.8	-0.6
Mean	**-1.1**	**-0.6**	**-1.7**	**-1.0**
Median	**-1.0**	**-0.5**	**-1.3**	**-0.6**
Medians				
All countries	-0.4	0.4	-0.2	0.7
Low-income countries	-0.2	0.5	0.3	0.9
Middle-income countries	-0.8	-0.4	-0.9	-1.6
Countries with fixed exchange rates	-0.5	-0.1	-0.8	-1.8
Countries with flexible exchange rates	-0.4	0.5	0.2	1.6
Oil-exporting countries	-2.9	-0.1	-2.9	-2.0

— Not available.

Note: Guinea and Guinea-Bissau are excluded because of insufficient data.

Sources: IMF and World Bank data.

Table A.16 Changes in the Real Effective Exchange Rate (REER) and in GDP per Capita Growth between 1981–86 and 1987–91

Country	Change in the average REER (percent)[a]	Difference in average annual GDP per capita growth (percentage points)
Large depreciation of the REER		
Nigeria	404.4	7.0
Ghana	283.7	3.7
Tanzania	255.4	2.9
Madagascar	99.2	1.6
Mozambique	86.9	7.6
Zambia	65.0	0.9
Burundi	56.7	-0.9
Zimbabwe	49.9	0.7
Uganda	46.5	4.3
Kenya	42.7	1.5
Mean	**139.1**	**2.9**
Median	**76.0**	**2.3**
Moderate depreciation of the REER		
Sierra Leone	34.6	2.9
Mauritania	31.7	-0.1
The Gambia	16.7	-0.8
Malawi	8.4	2.2
Rwanda	8.1	-5.5
Chad	5.6	-1.9
Niger	4.3	2.5
Central African Republic	1.4	-2.6
Mean	**13.9**	**-0.4**
Median	**8.3**	**-0.5**
Appreciation of the REER		
Togo	-4.7	1.4
Burkina Faso	-5.7	-1.7
Congo	-6.7	-4.9
Mali	-9.2	-1.6
Benin	-12.2	-3.1
Senegal	-14.0	-0.6
Gabon	-19.2	0.9
Côte d'Ivoire	-20.8	-2.6
Cameroon	-27.1	-12.5
Mean	**-13.3**	**-2.7**
Median	**-12.2**	**-1.7**
Medians		
All countries	8.4	0.7
Low-income countries	31.7	1.4
Middle-income countries	-16.6	-1.6
Countries with fixed exchange rates	-8.0	-1.8
Countries with flexible exchange rates	49.9	1.6
Oil-exporting countries	-13.0	-2.0

Note: Guinea and Guinea-Bissau are excluded because of insufficient data.

a. An increase in the real effective exchange rate constitutes a depreciation; a decrease constitutes an appreciation.

Source: World Bank data.

Table A.17 Average Annual GDP per Capita Growth for Countries Classified by Macroeconomic and Market Intervention Policies
(percent)

MARKET INTERVENTION, LATE 1992

MACROECONOMIC POLICY STANCE, 1990–91		Limited 1981–86	Limited 1987–91	Medium 1981–86	Medium 1987–91	Heavy 1981–86	Heavy 1987–91	All countries 1981–86	All countries 1987–91
Adequate or fair	Gambia	1.2	0.3						
	Nigeria	−4.6	2.4						
	Uganda	−1.5	2.8						
	Burundi			2.1	1.2				
	Gabon			−2.7	−1.9				
	Ghana			−2.4	1.3				
	Kenya			−0.5	0.9				
	Malawi			−1.4	0.7				
	Mali			0.4	−1.2				
	Mauritania			−0.9	−1.0				
	Senegal			0.4	−0.2				
	Togo			−2.8	−1.4				
	Burkina Faso					2.2	0.4		
	Madagascar					−3.7	−2.1		
	Median	**−1.5**	**2.4**	**−0.9**	**−0.2**	**−0.8**	**−0.8**	**−1.2**	**0.4**
Poor or very poor	Sierra Leone	−2.1	0.8						
	Benin			1.1	−2.0				
	Cameroon			4.6	−7.9				
	Côte d'Ivoire			−4.2	−6.8				
	Mozambique			−5.9	1.7				
	Niger			−4.9	−2.4				
	Rwanda			0.4	−5.0				
	Tanzania			−1.7	1.3				
	Zambia			−3.2	−2.3				
	Zimbabwe			0.3	1.0				
	Central African Republic					−0.1	−2.8		
	Congo					4.1	−0.7		
	Median	**−2.1**	**0.8**	**−1.7**	**−2.3**	**2.0**	**−1.8**	**−0.9**	**−2.1**
Unclassified	Chad	4.5	2.6						
	Guinea-Bissau	2.9	1.5						
	Guinea	—	—						
	Median	**3.7**	**2.1**						
All countries	Median	**−0.2**	**1.9**	**−1.2**	**−1.1**	**1.0**	**−1.4**	**−0.7**	**0.1**

— Not available.
Sources: Tables 5.1 and A.13.

Table A.18 Changes in Producer Prices of Export Crops and in Agricultural Growth

Country	Change in the real producer price of export crops, 1981–83 to 1989–91 (percent)	Difference in average annual agricultural growth rate between 1981–86 and 1987–91 (percentage points)
Improvement in producer prices		
Ghana	96.5	2.2
Nigeria	46.5	2.7
Burkina Faso	30.6	−2.3
Benin	21.7	−0.1
Mozambique	16.2	5.2
Togo	15.8	−1.8
Tanzania	8.3	1.9
Mali	5.8	2.5
Madagascar	5.3	0.9
Niger	2.6	—
Mean	**24.9**	**1.3**
Median	**16.0**	**1.9**
Deterioration in producer prices		
Central African Republic	−1.8	−2.9
Zimbabwe	−4.8	−4.7
Malawi	−8.8	2.3
Senegal	−11.7	−2.2
Chad	−12.9	6.9
Burundi	−18.1	−1.6
Rwanda	−23.3	−0.1
The Gambia	−25.0	−10.0
Kenya	−26.1	−0.3
Gabon	−29.4	1.5
Congo	−31.3	1.9
Uganda	−36.8	6.4
Zambia	−42.7	−1.6
Cameroon	−44.3	−4.7
Côte d'Ivoire	−49.6	8.2
Guinea-Bissau	−52.1	−5.0
Sierra Leone	−62.0	1.4
Mean	**−28.3**	**−0.3**
Median	**−26.1**	**−0.3**

— Not available.

Note: Guinea is excluded because of insufficient data; Mauritania is excluded because it has no major export crops.

Source: World Bank data.

Table A.19 Changes in Agricultural Taxation and Agricultural Growth

Country	Change in the real protection coefficient, 1981–83 to 1989–91 (percent)[a]	Difference in average annual agricultural growth rate between 1981–86 and 1987–91 (percentage points)
Large decrease in overall taxation of export crop producers		
Ghana	341.0	2.2
Guinea	325.8	—
Madagascar	117.1	0.9
Malawi	78.3	2.3
Uganda	33.9	6.4
Central African Republic	31.5	−2.9
Tanzania	30.6	1.9
Mean	**136.9**	**1.8**
Median	**78.3**	**2.0**
Small decrease in overall taxation		
Burkina Faso	17.9	−2.3
Rwanda	15.2	−0.1
Burundi	15.0	−1.6
Togo	10.9	−1.8
Gabon	10.7	1.5
Mali	9.4	2.5
Kenya	8.9	−0.3
Congo	4.5	1.9
Nigeria	1.3	2.7
Niger	1.1	—
Mean	**9.5**	**0.3**
Median	**10.0**	**−0.1**
Increase in overall taxation		
Mozambique	−2.0	5.2
Zimbabwe	−3.1	−4.7
The Gambia	−10.3	−10.0
Côte d'Ivoire	−23.2	8.2
Chad	−27.4	6.9
Benin	−27.6	−0.1
Senegal	−28.3	−2.2
Sierra Leone	−33.4	1.4
Cameroon	−34.7	−4.7
Guinea-Bissau	−70.3	−5.0
Zambia	−76.0	−1.6
Mean	**−30.6**	**−0.6**
Median	**−27.6**	**−1.6**

— Not available.

Note: Mauritania is excluded because it has no major export crops.

a. An increase in the real protection coefficient constitutes a decrease in agricultural taxation.

Source: World Bank data.

Table A.20 Agricultural Growth

Country	Average annual growth rate (percent) 1981–86	Average annual growth rate (percent) 1987–91	Difference between 1981–86 and 1987–91 (percentage points)
Large improvement in macroeconomic policies[a]			
Ghana	-0.2	2.0	2.2
Tanzania	3.4	5.3	1.9
The Gambia	7.4	-2.6[b]	-10.0
Burkina Faso	5.0	2.7	-2.3
Nigeria	1.2	3.9	2.7
Zimbabwe	5.3	0.6	-4.7
Mean	**3.7**	**2.0**	**-1.7**
Median	**4.2**	**2.4**	**-0.2**
Small improvement[a]			
Madagascar	1.6	2.5	0.9
Malawi	1.6	3.9	2.3
Burundi	4.1	2.5	-1.6
Kenya	3.4	3.1	-0.3
Mali	0.5	3.0	2.5
Mauritania	3.1	0.4[b]	-2.7
Senegal	4.1	1.9	-2.2
Niger	3.4	—	—
Uganda	-1.8	4.7	6.4
Mean	**2.2**	**2.7[c]**	**0.7**
Median	**3.1**	**2.8**	**0.3**
Deterioration[a]			
Benin	4.7	4.6	-0.1
Central African Rep.	3.0	0.1	-2.9
Rwanda	0.2	0.2	-0.1
Sierra Leone	1.9	3.3	1.4
Togo	5.2	3.4	-1.8
Zambia	3.8	2.1	-1.6
Deterioration[a] (continued)			
Mozambique	-0.9	4.3	5.2
Congo	2.3	4.2	1.9
Côte d'Ivoire	-4.0	4.2	8.2
Cameroon	3.6	-1.1	-4.7
Gabon	1.4	2.9	1.5
Mean	**1.9**	**2.6**	**0.6**
Median	**2.3**	**3.3**	**-0.1**
Unclassified			
Chad	2.0	8.9	6.9
Guinea	—	2.5	—
Guinea-Bissau	7.7	2.7	-5.0
Medians			
All countries	3.1	2.8	-0.1
Low-income countries	3.1	2.7	-0.1
Middle-income countries	2.3	2.9	1.5
Countries with fixed exchange rates	3.2	3.0	-0.1
Countries with flexible exchange rates	2.5	2.5	0.4
Oil-exporting countries	1.8	3.4	1.7

— Not available.

a. Classifications are based on the overall scores reported in table B.1.

b. 1987–90 average annual growth rate.

c. 1984–86 average annual growth rate.

Sources: IMF and World Bank data.

Table A.21 Growth in Industry and Manufacturing

	Industry			Manufacturing		
	Average annual growth rate (percent)		Difference between 1981–86 and 1987–91 (percentage points)	Average annual growth rate (percent)		Difference between 1981–86 and 1987–91 (percentage points)
Country	1981–86	1987–91		1981–86	1987–91	
Large improvement in macroeconomic policies[a]						
Ghana	-1.8	6.4	8.2	-0.4	4.5	4.9
Tanzania	-9.2	2.8	12.1	-4.5	3.3	7.8
The Gambia	5.2	2.8[b]	-2.3	—	—	—
Burkina Faso	2.5	5.0	2.5	-0.3	6.3	6.6
Nigeria	-5.0	5.1	10.1	0.6	—	—
Zimbabwe	-0.2	3.8	3.9	2.7	4.2	1.5
Mean	**-1.4**	**4.3**	**5.7**	**-0.4**	**4.6**	**5.2**
Median	**-1.0**	**4.4**	**6.1**	**-0.3**	**4.4**	**5.8**
Small improvement[a]						
Madagascar	-2.8	1.1	3.9	—	—	—
Malawi	1.0	5.9	5.0	3.0	5.4	2.4
Burundi	5.7	5.5	-0.2	6.1	6.6	0.5
Kenya	3.0	5.0	2.0	4.2	5.3	1.2
Mali	11.2	2.1	-9.1	—	—	—
Mauritania	5.2	—	—	—	—	—
Senegal	2.1	4.8	2.8	5.8	5.6	-0.3
Niger	-3.0	—	—	—	—	—
Uganda	-3.7	13.7[c]	17.3	-6.3	17.2[c]	23.6
Mean	**2.1**	**5.5**	**3.1**	**2.6**	**8.0**	**5.5**
Median	**2.1**	**5.0**	**2.8**	**4.2**	**5.6**	**1.2**

(Table continues on the following page.)

Table A.21 *(continued)*

Country	Industry			Manufacturing		
	Average annual growth rate (percent)		Difference between 1981–86 and 1987–91 (percentage points)	Average annual growth rate (percent)		Difference between 1981–86 and 1987–91 (percentage points)
	1981–86	1987–91		1981–86	1987–91	
Deterioration[a]						
Benin	8.3	4.0	-4.4	7.8	5.8	-2.0
Central African Republic	0.5	5.2	4.7	—	—	—
Rwanda	2.6	-1.5	-4.1	3.2	-0.2	-3.4
Sierra Leone	-3.5	4.3	7.8	5.2	6.3	1.1
Togo	-2.6	4.7	7.4	-0.4	8.3	8.7
Zambia	0.0	1.7	1.7	2.0	4.7	2.8
Mozambique	-6.7	1.1	7.8	—	—	—
Congo	8.3	4.1	-4.1	11.2	3.3	-7.9
Côte d'Ivoire	-1.2	-2.2	-1.1	—	—	—
Cameroon	12.5	-4.0	-16.5	17.2	—	—
Gabon	1.8	3.6	1.8	4.8	20.0	15.3
Mean	**1.8**	**1.9**	**0.1**	**6.4**	**6.9**	**2.1**
Median	**0.5**	**3.6**	**1.7**	**5.0**	**5.8**	**1.1**
Unclassified						
Chad	16.0	-0.1	—	1.9	—	—
Guinea	—	5.0	—	4.6	—	—
Guinea-Bissau	4.5	5.2	0.7	—	—	—
Medians						
All countries	1.4	4.1	2.5	3.0	5.5	1.9
Low-income countries	1.0	4.8	3.4	2.0	5.6	2.4
Middle-income countries	1.8	3.6	-1.1	8.0	4.2	1.5
Countries with fixed exchange rates	2.3	4.0	0.4	5.3	6.1	3.2
Countries with flexible exchange rates	-0.1	4.6	3.9	2.7	5.0	1.9
Oil-exporting countries	5.0	3.9	-1.2	8.0	11.7	3.7

— Not available.

a. Classifications are based on the overall scores reported in table B.1.

b. 1987–90 average annual growth rate.

c. 1984–86 average annual growth rate.

Sources: IMF and World Bank data.

Table A.22 Growth in Exports

Country	Average annual growth rate (percent) 1981–86	1987–91	Difference between 1981–86 and 1987–91 (percentage points)
Large improvement in macroeconomic policies[a]			
Ghana	4.5	8.1	3.5
Tanzania	—	—	—
The Gambia	-0.6	11.3	11.9
Burkina Faso	0.0	5.3	5.4
Nigeria	-5.5	4.9	10.3
Zimbabwe	—	—	—
Mean	**-0.4**	**7.4**	**7.8**
Median	**-0.3**	**6.7**	**7.9**
Small improvement[a]			
Madagascar	-7.6	6.1	13.7
Malawi	1.6	3.6	2.0
Burundi	11.8	4.9	-6.9
Kenya	2.3	6.3	4.0
Mali	2.6	6.7	4.2
Mauritania	8.9	-0.8	-9.7
Senegal	6.1	0.9	-5.2
Niger	-7.1	0.2	7.3
Uganda	—	—	1.2
Mean	**2.3**	**3.5**	**1.2**
Median	**2.5**	**4.3**	**3.0**
Deterioration[a]			
Benin	2.2	-4.1	-6.3
Central African Republic	-3.6	-4.4	-0.8
Rwanda	4.5	2.1	-2.4
Sierra Leone	-10.5	-0.8	9.7

Country	Average annual growth rate (percent) 1981–86	1987–91	Difference between 1981–86 and 1987–91 (percentage points)
Deterioration[a] *(continued)*			
Togo	-1.4	2.7	4.1
Zambia	-2.2	-2.8	-0.5
Mozambique	—	—	—
Congo	5.9	2.0	-3.9
Côte d'Ivoire	3.9	4.9	1.0
Cameroon	13.7	-11.8	-25.4
Gabon	0.4	11.4	11.0
Mean	**1.3**	**-0.1**	**-1.4**
Median	**1.3**	**0.6**	**-0.7**
Unclassified			
Chad	14.8	5.0	-9.7
Guinea	—	—	—
Guinea-Bissau	—	—	—
Medians			
All countries	2.2	3.6	2.0
Low-income countries	0.8	4.2	3.8
Middle-income countries	5.9	2.0	-3.9
Countries with fixed exchange rates	2.4	2.4	0.1
Countries with flexible exchange rates	1.6	4.9	3.5
Oil-exporting countries	3.2	3.4	3.2

— Not available.

a. Classifications are based on the overall scores reported in table B.1.

Sources: IMF and World Bank data.

Table A.23 Investment

Country	Gross domestic investment			Public investment[a]		
	Percentage of GDP		Difference between 1981–86 and 1987–91 (percentage points)	Percentage of GDP		Difference between 1981–86 and 1987–91 (percentage points)
	1981–86	1987–91		1981–86	1987–91	
Large improvement in macroeconomic policies[b]						
Ghana	6.3	15.1	8.8	1.7	3.2	1.5
Tanzania	18.3	26.9	8.7	6.8	5.3	-1.5
The Gambia	19.0	18.4	-0.6	12.4	10.3	-2.1
Burkina Faso	20.0	20.9	0.9	15.7	10.4	-5.3
Zimbabwe	19.6	20.7	1.1	6.0	8.0	2.1
Mean	**16.6**	**20.4**	**3.8**	**8.5**	**7.5**	**-1.1**
Median	**19.0**	**20.7**	**1.1**	**6.8**	**8.0**	**-1.5**
Nigeria[c]	16.5	15.4	-1.1	9.5	5.6	-3.9
Small improvement[b]						
Madagascar	9.1	12.4	3.3	6.6	7.5	1.0
Malawi	17.6	18.7	1.1	8.7	6.7	-2.1
Burundi	16.4	18.0	1.6	13.7	13.7	0.0
Kenya	23.1	23.7	0.5	7.1	6.0	-1.1
Mali	17.2	21.6	4.4	10.5	11.1	0.6
Mauritania	29.8	16.6	-13.2	2.5	5.7	3.3
Senegal	11.2	13.0	1.7	3.8	2.8	-1.0
Niger	12.9	10.0	-2.9	8.7	8.2	-0.5
Uganda	7.8	11.1	3.3	2.2	5.0	2.8
Mean	**16.1**	**16.1**	**0.0**	**7.1**	**7.4**	**0.3**
Median	**16.4**	**16.6**	**1.6**	**7.1**	**6.7**	**0.0**
Deterioration[b]						
Benin	16.0	12.4	-3.6	11.0	6.2	-4.9
Central African Republic	11.0	12.1	1.0	6.9	12.1	5.2
Rwanda	15.6	14.4	-1.2	8.2	8.1	-0.1

Sierra Leone	13.9	11.6	-2.3	4.3	3.2	-1.1
Togo	25.3	22.7	-2.6	10.7	7.4	-3.3
Zambia	17.2	12.8	-4.4	4.9	5.4	0.5
Mozambique	12.8	34.6	21.8	13.8	22.7	8.9
Côte d'Ivoire	17.9	11.5	-6.4	10.0	3.5	-6.5
Mean	**16.2**	**16.5**	**0.3**	**8.7**	**8.6**	**-0.2**
Median	**15.8**	**12.6**	**-2.4**	**9.1**	**6.8**	**-0.6**
Cameroon[c]	24.8	17.8	-7.0	10.6	8.6	-2.0
Congo[c]	39.4	16.1	-23.4	18.7	5.0	-13.7
Gabon[c]	37.2	29.0	-8.3	16.7	6.0	-10.7
Unclassified						
Chad	5.9	8.9	3.1	—	—	—
Guinea	—	—	—	—	—	—
Guinea-Bissau	27.2	31.1	4.0	—	—	—
Medians						
All countries	17.2	16.3	0.8	8.7	6.4	-1.0
Low-income countries	16.4	16.0	1.1	8.5	7.0	-0.3
Middle-income countries	22.2	16.9	-6.7	10.3	5.5	-4.2
Countries with fixed exchange rates	17.6	14.5	-1.3	10.6	7.4	-3.3
Countries with flexible exchange rates	16.9	17.3	1.1	6.8	6.0	0.0
Oil-exporting countries	31.0	16.9	-7.7	13.7	5.8	-7.3

— Not available.

a. Capital expenditures and net lending.

b. Classifications are based on the overall scores reported in table B.1.

c. Data for Cameroon, Congo, Gabon, and Nigeria are not counted in the group means and medians because of the strong influence of oil exports on investment levels in these countries.

Sources: IMF and World Bank data.

Table A.24 Savings

	Gross domestic savings			Public savings[a]		
	Percentage of GDP		Difference between 1981–86 and 1987–91 (percentage points)	Percentage of GDP		Difference between 1981–86 and 1987–91 (percentage points)
Country	1981–86	1987–91		1981–86	1987–91	
Large improvement in macroeconomic policies[b]						
Ghana	5.6	7.5	2.0	-1.7	2.6	4.3
Tanzania	9.7	-2.6	-12.3	-4.2	-1.6	2.6
The Gambia	6.2	8.2	2.1	-1.4	1.0	2.4
Burkina Faso	-4.9	1.5	6.4	-1.1	0.5	1.5
Nigeria	14.4	22.8	8.4	3.6	-1.2	-4.9
Zimbabwe	17.9	22.3	4.5	-3.7	-2.5	1.3
Mean	**8.1**	**10.0**	**1.8**	**1.4**	**-0.2**	**-1.2**
Median	**7.9**	**7.9**	**3.3**	**-1.6**	**-0.4**	**2.0**
Small improvement[b]						
Madagascar	1.9	5.9	4.0	0.2	1.5	1.3
Malawi	13.3	9.0	-4.3	-2.7	-0.3	2.4
Burundi	3.1	1.8	-1.3	1.4	1.5	0.1
Kenya	20.7	18.8	-1.9	-0.1	-1.1	-0.9
Mali	-3.7	5.3	9.0	-2.3	0.8	3.1
Mauritania	4.3	8.1	3.8	-2.8	3.1	5.9
Senegal	-0.4	7.9	8.3	-3.3	-0.1	3.2
Niger	5.1	4.6	-0.5	0.3	-2.7	-2.9
Uganda		—	—	-3.9	-0.7	3.1
Mean	**5.5**	**7.7**	**2.1**	**-1.5**	**0.2**	**1.7**
Median	**3.7**	**6.9**	**1.6**	**-2.3**	**-0.1**	**2.4**
Deterioration[b]						
Benin	0.7	3.1	2.4	-2.6	-3.5	-0.9
Central African Republic	-2.0	-0.7	1.4	-0.7	-1.3	-0.6

Rwanda	6.0	4.8	-1.2	1.1	-2.1	-3.2
Sierra Leone	7.4	6.8	-0.6	-8.9	-8.0	0.9
Togo	18.8	13.4	-5.4	3.7	0.9	-2.7
Zambia	14.1	13.4	-0.7	-10.3	-7.4	2.8
Mozambique	—	—	—	-2.5	-2.7	-0.3
Congo	35.7	23.1	-12.7	11.1	-6.7	-17.8
Côte d'Ivoire	21.3	15.4	-6.0	3.2	-9.8	-13.0
Cameroon	29.1	15.6	-13.4	10.6	0.3	-10.2
Gabon	50.1	36.3	-13.9	16.0	-1.0	-17.0
Mean	**18.1**	**13.1**	**-5.0**	**1.9**	**-3.7**	**-5.6**
Median	**16.4**	**13.4**	**-3.3**	**1.1**	**-2.7**	**-2.7**
Unclassified						
Chad	-11.6	-15.7	-4.1	—	—	—
Guinea	—	—	—	—	—	—
Guinea-Bissau	-4.7	-6.2	-1.5	—	—	—
Medians						
All countries	6.1	7.7	-0.7	-1.2	-1.0	0.5
Low-income countries	5.3	5.6	-0.6	-1.6	-0.9	1.1
Middle-income countries	25.2	19.0	-9.3	6.9	-1.7	-11.6
Countries with fixed exchange rates	2.9	6.6	-2.3	0.3	-1.0	-2.7
Countries with flexible exchange rates	6.8	7.8	-0.7	-2.5	-1.1	1.3
Oil-exporting countries	32.4	22.9	-13.1	10.8	-1.1	-13.6

— Not available.

a. Current revenue (excluding grants) minus current expenditure.

b. Classifications are based on the overall scores reported in table B.1.

Sources: IMF and World Bank data.

Table A.25 Sources of Income of Poor, Rural Smallholders in Selected Countries *(percent)*

Country	Agricultural income[a]			Off-farm earned income[b]	Nonearned income[c]	Total income
	Foods for home consumption	Foods sold	Total			
Burkina Faso, 1984–85						
Sahelian zone	—	—	49	20	31	100
Sudanian zone	—	—	59	25	16	100
Guinean zone	—	—	56	38	6	100
Côte d'Ivoire, 1985–86						
Forest	31	45	76	21	3	100
Savannah	40	41	81	17	2	100
The Gambia, 1991						
Various regions	22	35	57	22	21	100
Ghana, 1988						
Forest	37	20	57	40	3	100
Savannah	54	14	68	31	1	100
Kenya, 1985–87						
South Nyanza Province	40	14	54	42	4	100
Madagascar, 1984						
Coast	25	17	42	55	3	100
Plateau	31	8	39	58	3	100
South	37	11	48	49	3	100
Malawi, 1988						
South	37	14	51	13	36	100
Rwanda, 1985–86						
Northwest	33	12	45	38	17	100
Tanzania, 1976	50	23	73	25	2	100

— Not available.

Note: Data may not add up to totals because of rounding.

a. Includes income from livestock.

b. Includes wages, salaries, and earnings from self-employment.

c. Includes income from transfers, remittances, and other nonearned sources.

Source: Dorosh and Sahn (1993), table 1.

Table A.26 Sources of Agricultural Income of Poor, Rural Smallholders in Selected Countries *(percent)*

Country	Traded foods[a]			Nontraded foods[b]			Export crops[c]	Total agricultural income
	For home consumption	Sold	Total	For home consumption	Sold	Total		
Côte d'Ivoire, 1985–86								
Forest	8	6	14	32	9	41	45	100
Savannah	18	14	32	31	14	46	22	100
The Gambia, 1991								
Various regions	19	44	63	20	17	37	0	100
Ghana, 1988								
Forest	9	9	18	57	13	70	12	100
Savannah	16	10	26	63	10	73	1	100
Kenya, 1985–87								
South Nyanza Province	—	—	35	—	—	45	20	100
Madagascar, 1984								
Coast	23	..	23	35	11	46	31	100
Plateau	28	2	30	51	18	69	1	100
South	33	3	36	44	15	58	6	100
Malawi, 1988								
South	52	1	53	20	4	24	23	100
Tanzania, 1976	27	9	35	42	18	61	4	100

.. Neglible (less than 1 percent).

— Not available.

Note: Data may not add up to totals because of rounding.

a. Such as rice, maize, and groundnuts.

b. Such as millet, cassava, sweet potatoes, and yams.

c. Such as cocoa, tobacco, cotton, coffee, cola nuts, rubber, and sugar.

Source: Dorosh and Sahn (1993), table 2.

Table A.27 Expenditures of Poor, Rural Smallholders in Selected Countries (*percent*)

Country	Traded foods					Nontraded foods				Total food expenditures	Nonfood expenditures	Total expenditures
	Rice	Maize	Ground-nuts	Other	Total	Millet	Cassava	Other	Total			
Côte d'Ivoire, 1985–86												
Forest	6	5	1	2	15	0	4	46	50	65	35	100
Savannah	11	10	5	3	28	3	3	37	42	70	30	100
The Gambia, 1991												
Various regions	15	..	2	16	34	—	—	—	33	67	33	100
Ghana, 1988												
Forest	2	6	1	1	10	0	12	51	63	73	27	100
Savannah	8	16	1	1	26	16	5	33	54	80	20	100
Kenya, 1985–87												
South Nyanza Province	1	31	—	1	33	2	45	2	49	82	18	100
Madagascar, 1984												
Coast	13	..	..	5	19	..	(— 40 —)		40	59	41	100
Plateau	16	..	1	0	16	..	(— 49 —)		49	65	35	100
South	13	..	..	3	16	..	(— 46 —)		46	62	38	100
Malawi, 1988												
South	0	33	2	0	35	1	1	25	26	61	39	100
Tanzania, 1976	5	17	1	0	23	4	2	41	48	71	29	100

.. Negligible (between 0 and 0.5 percent).

— Not available.

Note: Data may not add up to totals because of rounding.

Source: Dorosh and Sahn (1993), table 4.

Table A.28 Allocation of the Education Budget in Selected Countries

Country and year	Type of expenditure	Percentage of budget allocated to specific education levels[a]	Distribution of allocated budget (percent)		
			Primary education	Secondary education	Higher education
Benin, 1988	Both recurrent and development	79.0	54.4	27.8	17.7
Burkina Faso, 1990	Recurrent	94.0	45.7	24.5	29.8
Cameroon, 1992	Recurrent	100.0	42.1	25.0	32.9
Central African Republic, 1990	Both	100.0	54.0	25.0	21.0
Chad, 1988	Recurrent	75.2	3.2	68.1	28.7
Côte d'Ivoire, 1990	Recurrent	100.0	52.0	32.5	15.5
	Development	100.0	27.4	52.8	19.8
	Both	100.0	51.8	32.7	16.5
The Gambia, 1989	Both	84.0	48.8	39.3	11.9
Ghana, 1988	Both	100.0	85.9	(——— 14.1 ———)	
Guinea, 1990	Recurrent	92.8	36.0	32.3	31.7
Guinea-Bissau, 1989	Recurrent	71.2	76.3	21.3	2.4
Kenya, 1990	Recurrent	94.0	57.1	24.7	18.3
	Development	83.5	0.0	27.4	72.6
	Both	92.6	49.8	25.1	25.2
Madagascar, 1990	Both	100.0	(——— 72.0 ———)		28.0
Malawi, 1988	Recurrent	81.5	58.0	16.3	25.6
	Development	87.4	4.1	21.5	74.4
	Both	82.8	45.7	17.5	36.8
Mali, 1988	Recurrent	92.0	38.0	41.4	20.7
Mozambique, 1990	Recurrent	100.0	37.2	42.7	20.1
	Development	100.0	8.2	59.9	31.9
Nigeria, 1984	Both	100.0	(——— 81.2 ———)		18.8
Senegal, 1991	Recurrent	94.0	48.9	25.5	25.5
Tanzania, 1986	Recurrent	91.2	62.1	24.2	13.7
	Development	76.1	15.9	63.7	20.4
	Both	87.9	52.7	32.7	14.7
Togo, 1990	Recurrent	97.0	38.9	33.6	27.5
Uganda, 1989	Recurrent	89.1	29.9	51.0	19.1
	Development	93.0	41.6	14.6	43.8
	Both	90.0	32.9	42.0	25.2
Zambia, 1986	Recurrent	90.1	45.0	30.9	24.1
Zimbabwe, 1990	Both	95.8	55.3	30.4	14.3
Median	Recurrent	93.4	47.3	29.6	20.4
	Development	90.2	12.1	40.1	37.9
	Both	94.2	52.3	30.4	18.8

a. Excludes nonallocable items such as general administrative expenditures.
Source: Sahn and Bernier (1993), table 1.

Table A.29 Change in Net External Transfers as a Share of GDP, 1981–86 to 1987–91

(percentage points)

	Countries with improvement in macroeconomic policies		Countries with deterioration in macroeconomic policies	
Countries with increases in net external transfers	Tanzania	19.7	Mozambique	42.0
	Malawi	8.4	Cameroon	2.9
	Madagascar	4.7	Central African Republic	2.8
	Kenya	4.3	Gabon	2.7
	Uganda	4.2	Sierra Leone	2.6
	Burundi	3.9	Benin	2.4
	Ghana	2.7	Rwanda	1.7
	Mean	**6.9**	Zambia	0.4
	Median	**4.3**	**Mean**	**7.2**
			Median	**2.6**
Countries with decreases in net external transfer	Burkina Faso	−1.9	Togo	−0.8
	Zimbabwe	−2.5	Côte d'Ivoire	−1.3
	Nigeria	−3.4	Congo	−9.2
	The Gambia	−5.5	**Mean**	**−3.8**
	Niger	−0.7	**Median**	**−1.3**
	Senegal	−4.2		
	Mali	−6.2		
	Mauritania	−12.1		
	Mean	**−4.6**		
	Median	**−3.8**		

Note: Chad, Guinea, and Guinea-Bissau are excluded because of insufficient data.
Source: World Bank data.

Appendix B

The Indexes of Macroeconomic Policy Change and Stance

THIS APPENDIX HAS TWO OBJECTIVES. ONE IS TO explain how the index of change in macroeconomic policies and the index of macroeconomic policy stance were constructed. The second objective is to explore the robustness of our findings about the relation between policies and GDP per capita growth.

Change in Macroeconomic Policies and Change in Growth

THE INDEX OF CHANGE IN MACROECONOMIC POLICIES MEAsures the changes in three policy indicators: fiscal, monetary, and exchange rate policies between 1981–86 and 1987–91. Numerical scores from –3 to +3 were assigned to each country based on the size of the change in each indicator, with a higher score indicating more improvement in policy (table B.1).

- For fiscal policy, the index scores were based on the change in the budget deficit *excluding* grants, which provides a more accurate measure of the domestic fiscal effort than does the deficit including grants. Changes in domestic tax revenue were also taken into account, because they are a proxy for the quality of the fiscal adjustment: the index score was increased (or decreased) by one point if revenue as a share of GDP rose (or fell) by more than 3 percentage points.

Table B.1 Change in Macroeconomic Policies, 1981–86 to 1987–91

Country	Fiscal policy					Monetary policy			
	Change in overall fiscal balance excluding grants		Change in total revenue		Change in fiscal policy (score)[c]	Change in seigniorage[d]		Change in inflation	
	Percentage points	Score[a]	Percentage points	Score[b]		Percentage points	Score[e]	Percentage points	Score[f]
Benin	4.0	2	–3.6	0	2.0	3.6	–2	–2.7	1
Burkina Faso	6.8	3	0.4	0	3.0	–0.7	1	–5.2	1
Burundi	0.1	0	2.0	0	0.0	—	—	0.2	0
Cameroon	–8.3	–2	–6.2	–1	–3.0	–0.5	0	–7.1	1
Central African Republic	–5.9	–2	–1.9	0	–2.0	–1.1	1	–11.6	2
Congo	–4.2	–1	–12.8	–1	–2.0	0.2	0	–7.9	1
Côte d'Ivoire	–6.5	–2	–6.0	–1	–3.0	–1.7	1	–3.8	1
Gabon	–6.3	–2	–10.7	–1	–3.0	–0.2	0	–7.9	1
The Gambia	4.5	2	2.6	0	2.0	–0.4	0	–7.9	1
Ghana	2.8	1	5.7	1	2.0	–1.0	1	–25.7	2
Kenya	0.2	0	–0.5	0	0.0	–0.3	0	–1.9	0
Madagascar	0.3	0	–0.7	0	0.0	0.7	0	–6.7	1
Malawi	4.4	2	0.0	0	2.0	0.7	0	5.9	–1
Mali	2.5	1	2.3	0	1.0	–2.5	2	–3.8	1
Mauritania	2.6	1	2.0	0	1.0	–0.2	0	–3.0	1
Mozambique	–9.2	–2	–0.5	0	–2.0	—	—	47.1	–3
Niger	–2.4	–1	–1.0	0	–1.0	–0.9	1	–10.0	1
Nigeria	–1.0	0	3.7	1	1.0	1.4	–1	9.9	–1
Rwanda	–3.1	–1	0.7	0	–1.0	0.0	0	1.1	0
Senegal	4.1	2	–0.6	0	2.0	–1.6	1	–12.4	2
Sierra Leone	2.0	1	–0.5	0	1.0	0.2	0	40.7	–3
Tanzania	4.1	2	1.0	0	2.0	2.4	–2	–4.8	1
Togo	0.6	0	–6.2	–1	–1.0	–2.9	2	–6.5	1
Uganda	0.3	0	–2.6	0	0.0	—	—	27.6	–2
Zambia	2.4	1	–3.8	0	1.0	1.1	–1	60.3	–3
Zimbabwe	–0.8	0	5.8	1	1.0	1.3	–1	–0.1	0

— Not available.   n.a. Not applicable.

Note: Chad, Guinea, and Guinea-Bissau are excluded because of insufficient data.

a. A score of –2 reflects a change in the fiscal balance of –9.9 to –5.0 percentage points; –1, a change of –4.9 to –2.0 percentage points; 0, a change of –1.9 to 0.9 percentage points; 1, a change of 1.0 to 2.9 percentage points; 2, a change of 3.0 to 4.9 percentage points; and 3, a change of 5.0 percentage points or more.

b. A score of –1 reflects a change in total revenue of –4.0 percentage points or more; 0, a change of –3.9 to 3.0 percentage points; 1, a change of 3.1 percentage points or more.

c. Calculated by adding the scores for change in overall fiscal balance and change in revenue.

d. Seigniorage is based on M1; however, for Tanzania in 1985–86 and 1990, it is based on M2.

e. A score of 2 reflects a change in seigniorage of –3.0 to –2.1 percentage points; 1, a change of –2.0 to –0.6 percentage points; 0, a change of –0.5 to 0.9 percentage points; –1, a change of 1.0 to 1.9 percentage points; and –2, a change of 2.0 to 3.9 percentage points.

f. A score of 2 reflects a change in inflation of –49.0 to –10.0 percentage points; 1, a change of –9.9 to –2.5 percentage points; 0, a change of –2.4 to 4.9 percentage points; –1, a change of 5.0 to 9.9 percentage points; –2, a change of 10.0 to 30.9 percentage points; and –3, a change of 31.0 percentage points or more.

Change in monetary policy (score)[g]	Change in the real effective exchange rate[b]		Change in the parallel market exchange rate premium		Change in exchange rate policy (score)[k]	Overall change in macroeconomic policies score)[l]	Country
	Percentage points	Score[i]	Percentage points	Score[j]			
−0.5	−12.2	−2	n.a.	n.a.	−2.0	−0.2	Benin
1.0	−5.7	−1	n.a.	n.a.	−1.0	1.0	Burkina Faso
0.0	56.7	3	−4.9	0	1.5	0.5	Burundi
0.5	−27.1	−2	n.a.	n.a.	−2.0	−1.5	Cameroon
1.5	1.4	0	n.a.	n.a.	0.0	−0.2	Central African Republic
0.5	−6.7	−1	n.a.	n.a.	−1.0	−0.8	Congo
1.0	−20.8	−2	n.a.	n.a.	−2.0	−1.3	Côte d'Ivoire
0.5	−19.2	−2	n.a.	n.a.	−2.0	−1.5	Gabon
0.5	16.7	2	3.1	0	1.0	1.2	The Gambia
1.5	283.7	3	−1,080.6	3	3.0	2.2	Ghana
0.0	42.7	3	−4.6	0	1.5	0.5	Kenya
0.5	99.2	3	−28.0	1	2.0	0.8	Madagascar
−0.5	8.4	1	−27.1	1	1.0	0.8	Malawi
1.5	−9.2	−1	n.a.	n.a.	−1.0	0.5	Mali
0.5	31.7	3	52.3	−3	0.0	0.5	Mauritania
−3.0	86.9	3	−2,039.5	3	3.0	−0.7	Mozambique
1.0	4.3	1	n.a.	n.a.	1.0	0.3	Niger
−1.0	404.4	3	−197.4	3	3.0	1.0	Nigeria
0.0	8.1	1	−7.0	0	0.5	−0.2	Rwanda
1.5	−14.0	−2	n.a.	n.a.	−2.0	0.5	Senegal
−1.5	34.6	3	398.1	−3	0.0	−0.2	Sierra Leone
−0.5	255.4	3	−164.1	3	3.0	1.5	Tanzania
1.5	−4.7	−1	n.a.	n.a.	−1.0	−0.2	Togo
−2.0	46.5	3	−41.3	2	2.5	0.2	Uganda
−2.0	65.0	3	239.8	−3	0.0	−0.3	Zambia
−0.5	49.9	3	−37.2	2	2.5	1.0	Zimbabwe

g. Calculated by averaging the scores for change in seigniorage and change in inflation.

h. An increase in the real effective exchange rate constitutes a depreciation; a decrease constitutes an appreciation.

i. A score of −2 reflects a change in the real effective exchange rate of −10.0 percentage points or more; −1, a change of −9.9 to −5.0 percentage points; 0, a change of −4.9 to 2.0 percentage points; 1, a change of 2.1 to 14.9 percentage points; 2, a change of 15.0 to 30.9 percentage points; and 3, a change of 31.0 percentage points or more.

j. A score of 3 reflects a change in the premium of −100 percentage points or more; 2, a change of −99 to −30 percentage points; 1, a change of −29 to −10 percentage points; 0, a change of −9 to 4 percentage points; −1, a change of 5 to 15 percentage points; −2, a change of 16 to 50 percentage points; and −3, a change of 51 percentage points or more.

k. Calculated by averaging the scores for change in the real effective exchange rate and change in the parallel market exchange rate premium.

l. Calculated by averaging the scores for change in fiscal policy, change in monetary policy, and change in exchange rate policy. A score of 1.0 or more reflects large improvement; 0 to 0.9, small improvement; and below 0, deterioration.

Sources: World Bank data; IMF data; staff estimates.

- For monetary policy, the index scores were based on the average of changes in seigniorage and inflation.[1] Changes in real interest rates were not factored in because they are very similar to changes in inflation.
- For exchange rate policy, the index scores for the fixed exchange rate countries were based on the change in the real effective exchange rate (REER); for the flexible exchange rate countries, the scores were based on a simple average of the change in the REER and the change in the parallel market exchange rate premium.

The individual scores for each of the three indicators were then aggregated by simple averaging to arrive at a composite score for overall change in macroeconomic policies. Based on their composite scores, the adjusting countries of Sub-Saharan Africa were divided into three groups: countries that had large improvement in macroeconomic policies (scores above or equal to 1), small improvement (scores below 1 but above 0), or deterioration (scores below 0).

Before deciding upon this methodology, we experimented with other ways of scoring countries. For example, we used weighted averages that gave more importance to the REER and inflation, and we widened the range of scores from –9 to +9 so as to give more weight to large distortions. While country rankings were somewhat altered as a result, the overall picture did not change significantly. We are thus confident that the scoring procedures themselves were robust.

To check the robustness of the results obtained using this index, we explored two other ways of constructing an index of overall change in macroeconomic policies.

Substituting other policy indicators. The first approach was to use alternative indicators of change in macroeconomic policies. For fiscal policy, changes in three different indicators were used: the fiscal deficit including grants, the primary deficit including grants, and the primary deficit excluding grants. For monetary policy, an indicator was developed based only on the rate of inflation. For exchange rate policy, we continued to use the change in the REER for the fixed exchange rate countries, and, for the flexible exchange rate countries, the change in the REER together with the change in the parallel market premium. These indicators were then combined in various ways to create eight variants on the measure of overall policy change (table B.2).

Table B.2 Alternative Approaches for Calculating Overall Change in Macroeconomic Policies

	Indicators used		
Approach	*Change in fiscal policy*	*Change in monetary policy*	*Change in exchange rate policy*
Approach used in the study	Change in the overall fiscal balance excluding grants, plus change in total revenue	Average of the changes in seigniorage and inflation	Change in the real effective exchange rate (for countries with fixed exchange rates) *or* the average of the changes in the parallel market premium and the real effective exchange rate (for countries with flexible exchange rates)
Alternative 1	Change in the overall fiscal balance including grants	See above	See above
Alternative 2	Change in the overall fiscal balance excluding grants	See above	See above
Alternative 3	Change in the primary fiscal balance including grants	See above	See above
Alternative 4	Change in the primary fiscal balance excluding grants	See above	See above
Alternative 5	Change in the overall fiscal balance including grants	Change in inflation only	See above
Alternative 6	Change in the overall fiscal balance excluding grants	See above	See above
Alternative 7	Change in the primary fiscal balance including grants	See above	See above
Alternative 8	Change in the primary fiscal balance excluding grants	See above	See above

Comparing different time periods. The second approach was to retain the original indicators of policy change, but to calculate the change over alternative time periods: first, between 1981–86 and 1990–91, and second, between 1985–86 and 1990–91. The choice of time period depends on whether one is interested in period averages or endpoints in time. We had opted to compare the policies during 1981–86 with those during 1987–91 because we were interested in the average change from the pre-reform period to the adjustment period. But for countries that have only recently begun to make reforms, the change in policies from 1981–86 to 1990–91 may be more meaningful. And if one wants to track progress starting from a time when many countries had very poor policies, it might be more appropriate to look at the change between 1985–86 and 1990–91.

Robust outcomes. Although choosing different policy indicators or time periods does shift some countries from one group to the next, the correlation between policy reform and growth remains robust. The evidence indicates that the group of countries with the largest improvement in macroeconomic policies consistently had the largest increase in economic performance, while the countries whose macroeconomic policies deteriorated generally fared the worst (tables B.3 and B.4). The major exception to this pattern is in agricultural growth, which exhibits no clear-cut link to policy change in any of the three time periods used. Also, when we assess the change in policies between 1981–86 and 1990–91, the group with deterioration in policies did better in GDP, export, and manufacturing growth than the group whose policies improved slightly.

The country groupings themselves exhibit a certain amount of robustness. Regardless of the policy indicators used, six of the countries in the study (Burkina Faso, The Gambia, Ghana, Nigeria, Tanzania, and Zimbabwe) consistently showed a large improvement in overall macroeconomic policies, while four countries (Mali, Niger, Senegal, and Uganda) were always among the group with small improvement. Five countries (Cameroon, Congo, Côte d'Ivoire, Gabon, and Togo) consistently appeared among the countries with deterioration in policies. Of the remaining ten countries with data available, four (Kenya, Madagascar, Malawi, and Mauritania) switched between the large- and small-improvement groups. Five countries (Benin, the Central African Republic, Rwanda, Sierra Leone, and Zambia) shifted between the group with small improvement and the group with deterioration. Only Mozambique jumped between the top and bottom groups, showing a large improvement in policies if grants were included in the fiscal indicator and a deterioration in policies if they were not. Country groupings exhibited a similar robustness across time periods, with the same core groups of countries consistently registering large improvement or deterioration in overall policies.

Table B.3 Economic Outcomes Using Alternative Approaches for Calculating Overall Change in Macroeconomic Policies

Approach used to calculate overall change in macroeconomic policies[a]	Median change between 1981–86 and 1987–91 (percentage points)						
	GDP per capita growth	Agricultural growth	Industrial growth	Manufacturing growth	Export growth	Gross domestic investment[b]	Gross domestic savings
Approach used in the study							
Countries with large improvement	1.8	–0.2	6.1	5.8	7.9	1.0	3.3
Countries with small improvement	1.5	0.3	2.8	1.2	3.0	1.6	1.6
Countries with deterioration	–2.6	–0.1	1.7	1.1	–0.7	–3.6	–3.3
Alternative 1							
Countries with large improvement	1.9	1.4	4.5	4.9	7.9	1.1	3.1
Countries with small improvement	0.4	–1.6	2.4	1.2	–0.7	1.3	0.4
Countries with deterioration	–2.8	0.7	–2.6	–0.4	–0.7	–5.0	–5.7
Alternative 2							
Countries with large improvement	1.8	–0.2	6.1	5.8	7.9	1.0	3.3
Countries with small improvement	1.5	0.3	2.8	1.2	3.0	1.6	1.6
Countries with deterioration	–2.6	–0.1	1.7	1.1	–0.7	–3.6	–3.3
Alternative 3							
Countries with large improvement	1.5	0.3	3.9	3.2	5.4	1.4	2.1
Countries with small improvement	0.4	–0.1	3.8	1.7	–0.5	–0.1	–0.5
Countries with deterioration	–2.8	0.7	–2.6	3.3	–1.5	–6.7	–9.3
Alternative 4							
Countries with large improvement	1.5	0.3	3.9	4.9	7.9	1.0	3.1
Countries with small improvement	1.0	1.4	3.9	1.1	2.0	1.4	–0.5
Countries with deterioration	–2.6	–0.1	0.3	0.4	–0.8	–4.0	–5.4
Alternative 5							
Countries with large improvement	1.6	0.9	4.5	4.9	5.4	1.1	3.8
Countries with small improvement	–0.6	–0.2	2.4	0.5	–0.8	1.6	1.4
Countries with deterioration	–0.8	0.7	0.3	1.9	0.2	–5.4	–5.7
Alternative 6							
Countries with large improvement	1.6	0.9	3.9	5.8	10.3	1.1	4.0
Countries with small improvement	–0.4	–0.3	2.4	0.8	–0.8	1.1	1.4
Countries with deterioration	0.9	1.4	1.7	1.9	0.2	–4.4	–5.7
Alternative 7							
Countries with large improvement	1.5	–0.3	3.9	3.2	4.7	1.1	2.9
Countries with small improvement	–0.6	0.7	3.8	0.4	0.6	1.0	0.4
Countries with deterioration	–0.8	–0.1	0.3	5.7	0.2	–6.7	–9.3
Alternative 8							
Countries with large improvement	1.5	–0.3	3.9	4.9	5.4	0.9	3.8
Countries with small improvement	–0.6	0.7	3.8	0.8	0.6	1.1	0.4
Countries with deterioration	–0.8	0.7	0.3	2.8	–0.5	–5.4	–6.0

a. See table B.2 for a description of the policy indicators used under each alternative approach.
b. Calculations include the oil-exporting countries (Cameroon, Congo, Gabon, and Nigeria), in contrast to table A.23.
Source: World Bank data.

Table B.4 Economic Outcomes Using Alternative Time Periods for Calculating Overall Change in Macroeconomic Policies

Time period used to calculate overall change in macroeconomic policies	GDP per capita growth	Agri-cultural growth	Industrial growth	Manu-facturing growth	Export growth	Gross domestic investment[a]	Gross domestic savings
	Median change (percentage points)						
Period used in the study (1981–86 to 1987–91)							
Countries with large improvement	1.8	–0.2	6.1	5.8	7.9	1.0	3.3
Countries with small improvement	1.5	0.3	2.8	1.2	3.0	1.6	1.6
Countries with deterioration	–2.6	–0.1	1.7	1.1	–0.7	–3.6	–3.3
Alternative 1 (1981–86 to 1990–91)							
Countries with large improvement	2.9	2.2	8.2	6.4	10.3	3.3	2.0
Countries with small improvement	–0.8	–1.9	2.0	0.8	–3.9	1.0	4.1
Countries with deterioration	0.9	–0.1	1.8	1.9	0.2	–2.9	–0.9
Alternative 2 (1985–86 to 1990–91)							
Countries with large improvement	2.9	2.2	8.2	6.4	3.5	1.1	1.7
Countries with small improvement	0.9	0.3	2.6	1.5	5.4	0.9	1.8
Countries with deterioration	–2.8	–0.9	–4.1	–2.0	–5.1	–5.0	–3.3

a. Calculations include the oil-exporting countries (Cameroon, Congo, Gabon, and Nigeria), in contrast to table A.23.
Source: World Bank data.

Policy Stance and GDP per Capita Growth

THIS REPORT ALSO USES AN INDEX OF POLICY STANCE TO assess the relation between macroeconomic policy stance and growth. The index, which reflects the state of macroeconomic policies in adjusting countries as of 1990–91, uses the following policy indicators:

- Fiscal policy stance is based on the budget deficit including grants, because this provides a good measure of the current fiscal imbalance. In using this indicator, we implicitly assume that grants will continue in the short term.
- Monetary policy stance is based on seigniorage, inflation, and the real interest rate.[2]
- The exchange rate policy stance is based on the change in the REER between 1980 and 1990–91 for the countries with fixed exchange rates; for the countries with flexible exchange rates, the stance is based on the parallel market exchange rate premium.

For each policy, each country was classified as having a good/adequate, fair, poor, or very poor stance and assigned a numerical score from 1 to 4, with a smaller number indicating a better policy stance (table B.5). The individual scores were then aggregated by simple averaging to arrive at a composite score for overall macroeconomic policy stance. The cutoff points were unavoidably arbitrary, since there is no solid analytical basis for differentiating sharply between fair and poor policy stances, or between adequate and fair. For example, there is probably little difference in the macroeconomic policy environment in Burundi and Ghana: Burundi had a larger parallel market exchange rate premium and a slightly bigger budget deficit in 1990–91, but lower inflation. And yet Burundi fell into the fair category, while Ghana was classified as adequate. The labels—*adequate*, *fair*, *poor*, and *very poor*—provide a useful basis for ranking countries according to generally accepted standards, but not too much weight should be attached to the precise rankings.

To test the robustness of the index of macroeconomic policy stance, we recomputed the index using the primary deficit, rather than the overall deficit, as an indicator of fiscal policy stance. Again, there was some movement of countries from one group to the next. The main change was that Congo and Zimbabwe shifted from the groups rated poor or very poor to those with fair or adequate stance. With respect to the mean and median growth rates for each group, however, there was little noticeable change, indicating that the choice of indicator for fiscal policy stance does not make much difference for our results.

Notes

1. Although inflation is an outcome, rather than an indicator, of monetary policy, it is useful to include it as an indicator in the index, because it reflects the effectiveness of monetary policy. The effectiveness of monetary policies in controlling inflation is as important as the monetary policies themselves.

2. Interest rates are included in the stance index because they generally do not follow the same pattern as the rates of inflation. (Interest rates were *not* taken into account in the index of overall change in macroeconomic policies because changes in the interest rate are closely related to changes in the rate of inflation.)

Table B.5 Components of Macroeconomic Policy Stance, 1990–91

Country	Fiscal policy Overall fiscal balance including grants (percentage of GDP)	Fiscal policy (score)[a]	Seigniorage Percent	Seigniorage Score	Monetary policy Inflation Percent	Monetary policy Inflation Score
Benin	−6.3	3	2.7	3	0.1	1
Burkina Faso	−3.4	2	−0.1	1	1.9	1
Burundi	−3.3	2	—	—	8.0	1
Cameroon	−8.6	4	0.0	1	0.5	1
Central African Republic	−6.5	3	−0.6	1	0.3	1
Congo	−7.7	4	0.8	2	−0.3	1
Côte d'Ivoire	−13.0	4	0.4	1	0.6	1
Gabon	−1.7	2	0.2	1	5.2	1
The Gambia	2.7	1	1.8	3	10.4	1
Ghana	0.8	1	0.4	1	27.6	3
Kenya	−5.6	3	1.8	3	13.3	2
Madagascar	−5.1	3	1.5	2	6.5	1
Malawi	−2.5	2	1.0	2	12.2	2
Mali	−5.3	3	−0.6	1	3.3	1
Mauritania	−0.9	1	1.1	2	6.6	1
Mozambique	−8.9	4	—	—	35.9	3
Niger	−7.2	4	−0.7	1	−4.3	1
Nigeria	−4.5	3	2.9	3	10.2	1
Rwanda	−7.0	3	0.8	2	11.9	2
Senegal	−1.1	1	−0.8	1	−0.7	1
Sierra Leone	−7.7	4	6.2	4	106.8	4
Tanzania	−0.9	1	7.6	4	21.0	2
Togo	−3.3	2	1.4	2	1.0	1
Uganda	−4.1	3	—	—	32.2	3
Zambia	−8.5	4	4.0	4	101.8	4
Zimbabwe	−8.3	4	2.5	3	20.8	2

— Not available.

n.a. Not applicable.

Note: Chad, Guinea, and Guinea-Bissau are excluded because of insufficient data.

a. A score of 1 is considered good or adequate; 2, fair; 3, poor; and 4, very poor.

b. A score of 1.0 to 1.3 is considered adequate; 1.4 to 2.3, fair; 2.4 to 3.0, poor; and 3.1 and above, very poor.

c. An increase in the real effective exchange rate constitutes a depreciation; a decrease constitutes an appreciation.

Sources: IMF data; World Bank data; staff estimates.

Real interest rate		Monetary policy (score)[b]	Exchange rate policy		Exchange rate policy (score)[a]	Overall macro-economic policies (score)[b]	Country
Percent	Score		Parallel market exchange rate premium (percent)	Change in the real effective exchange rate since 1980 (percent)[c]			
6.6	2	2.0	n.a.	10.8	3	2.7	Benin
2.6	1	1.0	n.a.	10.3	3	2.0	Burkina Faso
—	—	1.0	20.9	n.a.	2	1.7	Burundi
8.7	3	1.7	n.a.	−18.0	4	3.2	Cameroon
6.8	2	1.3	n.a.	9.1	3	2.4	Central African Republic
8.7	3	2.0	n.a.	−9.2	4	3.3	Congo
5.4	2	1.3	n.a.	2.8	4	3.1	Côte d'Ivoire
6.7	2	1.3	n.a.	7.8	3	2.1	Gabon
3.2	2	2.0	21.3	n.a.	2	1.7	The Gambia
2.8	1	1.7	3.4	n.a.	1	1.2	Ghana
−1.0	1	2.0	7.3	n.a.	1	2.0	Kenya
—	—	1.5	7.1	n.a.	1	1.8	Madagascar
−0.3	1	1.7	29.4	n.a.	2	1.9	Malawi
2.8	1	1.0	n.a.	10.8	3	2.3	Mali
—	—	1.5	166.6	n.a.	4	2.2	Mauritania
—	—	3.0	62.6	n.a.	4	3.7	Mozambique
16.0	3	1.7	n.a.	28.0	2	2.6	Niger
1.7	1	1.7	25.1	n.a.	2	2.2	Nigeria
−9.9	2	2.0	47.5	n.a.	3	2.7	Rwanda
8.9	3	1.7	n.a.	−4.0	4	2.2	Senegal
−30.7	3	3.7	104.4	n.a.	4	3.9	Sierra Leone
—	—	3.0	74.5	n.a.	4	2.7	Tanzania
5.9	2	1.7	n.a.	9.7	3	2.2	Togo
−2.9	1	2.0	24.6	n.a.	2	2.3	Uganda
—	—	4.0	149.7	n.a.	4	4.0	Zambia
−12.5	2	2.3	23.5	n.a.	2	2.8	Zimbabwe

Appendix C
Agricultural Policy Indicators

DECOMPOSING THE REAL PRODUCER PRICE INTO its policy and exogenous components shows how policy and world price trends interact in determining real producer prices for agricultural exports. The equation is as follows:

$$RPP = \frac{P_F}{CPI} = \frac{P_F}{P_B e} \cdot e \frac{WPI}{CPI} \cdot \frac{P_B}{WPI} = NPC \cdot RER \cdot p_B \ ,$$

where RPP is the real producer price for export crops, P_F is the farmgate producer price, P_B is the border price in dollars, e is the nominal exchange rate, CPI is the consumer price index for the country in question, and WPI is the U.S. wholesale price index.

Let us look more closely at the three terms of the decomposition. The first term, $P_F/P_B e$, is the nominal protection coefficient (NPC). An NPC of less than 1 means that producers are being taxed rather than protected.[1] An increase in the NPC means that the producer's share of the border price is increasing, and thus that explicit taxation is decreasing. All other things being equal, this will raise the RPP. The second term in the decomposition, $e(WPI/CPI)$, is the bilateral real exchange rate (RER). If the real exchange rate depreciates and the depreciation is passed back to the producer, the RPP will increase. The third term in the decomposition, P_B/WPI, is the price of the country's exports (at the border) deflated by the WPI, which we call the real border price, p_B. A fall in the real border price will result in a decline in the RPP, unless the fall is offset by a sufficiently large reduction in explicit taxation or by a depreciation of the real exchange rate.

Because real prices for export producers are influenced by world price trends as well as domestic variables, shifts in the real price for export producers do not tell us whether overall taxation of agricultural producers has increased or decreased. For this we need a measure combining explicit taxation (from policies that affect the producer price) and implicit taxation (through overvaluation of the real exchange rate).[2] The real protection coefficient (RPC) measures overall taxation. It is identical to the nominal protection coefficient (NPC), except that it calculates the border price at the equilibrium exchange rate instead of at the official exchange rate. It is defined as follows:

$$RPC = \frac{P_F}{P_B E} = \frac{P_F}{P_B e} \cdot \frac{e}{E} = NPC \cdot \frac{e}{E},$$

where E is the equilibrium exchange rate. The first term, $P_F/P_B e$, is the nominal protection coefficient, which shows how much producers are being taxed explicitly by governments. The second term, e/E, is the ratio of the nominal exchange rate to the equilibrium exchange rate, which shows how much producers are being taxed implicitly by overvalued exchange rates.

The change in the RPC is a better proxy for assessing the change in taxation than the change in the product of the NPC and the RER (the first two terms in the decomposition of the real producer price). This is illustrated by the following example. Suppose the real exchange rate depreciates by a small amount at the same time that the equilibrium exchange rate moves increasingly out of line (because of a large terms-of-trade shock, for example). Producers would be implicitly taxed more by the more overvalued exchange rate (indicated by a decrease in the RPC), while at the same time the real producer price would improve because of the depreciation in the real exchange rate. Hence, using the change in the product of the NPC and the RER does not show how much the level of taxation has changed, but rather how much of the change in the real exchange rate is transferred back to producers, taking into account changes in direct taxation.

In practice, the RPC is not easy to compute because the equilibrium exchange rate is not an observable variable. It can only be estimated. We used the parallel market premium as a rough proxy for the real exchange rate misalignment in the flexible exchange rate countries. As a very rough proxy for the misalignment in the countries with fixed exchange rates, we compared the change in each country's real effective exchange rate between 1980 and 1990–91 with the extent of real exchange rate depreciation in the reference group of countries over the same period (see chapter 2). This gives a crude indication of how much additional depreciation was needed in 1990–91 to restore competitiveness.

Notes

1. Generally, the producer price is calculated at the border price equivalent—that is, transportation and marketing costs are added to the producer price. Our estimates of the NPC do not include transportation and marketing costs because of a lack of data. Also, we did not want to add in marketing and distribution costs, because they may reflect substantial inefficiencies due to parastatal and other interventions in these services. It would be important to take account of differences in these costs in comparing NPCs across countries.

2. Ideally, a method similar to that of Kreuger, Schiff, and Valdés (1988) would be used to calculate total taxation—something beyond the scope of this study.

References

Akiyama, Takamasa, and Donald F. Larson. 1989. "Recent Trends and Prospects for Agricultural Commodity Exports in Sub-Saharan Africa." PPR Working Paper 348. World Bank, International Economics Department, Washington, D.C.

——. 1993. "Adding Up Problem—Strategies for Primary Commodity Exports in Sub-Saharan Africa." PPR Working Paper 1245. World Bank, International Economics Department, Washington, D.C.

Alderman, Harold, Sudharshan Canagarajah, and Stephen D. Younger. 1993. *Consequences of Permanent Layoff from the Civil Service: Results from a Survey of Retrenched Workers in Ghana.* Cornell Food and Nutrition Policy Program Working Paper 35. Ithaca, N.Y.: Cornell University.

Barrett, Scott. 1990. "Macroeconomic Policy Reforms and Third World Soil Conservation." Draft. London Business School, Department of Economics.

Barro, R. J. 1991. "Economic Growth in a Cross-Section of Countries." *Quarterly Journal of Economics* 106(2):407–43.

Bates, Robert H., and Paul Collier. 1993. "The Politics and Economics of Policy Reform in Zambia." In Robert H. Bates and Anne O. Krueger, eds., *Political and Economic Interactions in Economic Policy Reform.* Oxford, U.K., and Cambridge, Mass.: Basil Blackwell.

Berg, Elliot. 1993. "Privatization in Sub-Saharan Africa: Results, Prospects, and New Approaches." Consultant's report prepared for World Bank, Policy Research Department, Transition and Macro-Adjustment Division, and for Financial Sector Development Department, African Economies in Transition Project, Washington, D.C.

Binswanger, Hans. 1989. "The Policy Response of Agriculture." In World Bank, *Proceedings of the World Bank Annual Conference on Development Economics 1989*, pp. 231–58. Washington, D.C.

Birdsall, Nancy, and Richard Sabot. 1993. "Virtuous Circles: Human Capital, Growth and Equity in East Asia." Background paper for *The East Asian Miracle.* World Bank, Policy Research Department, Washington, D.C.

Blejer, Mario I., and Adrienne Cheasty, eds. 1993. *How to Measure the Fiscal Deficit: Analytical and Methodological Issues.* Washington, D.C.: International Monetary Fund.

Bond, Marian E. 1983. "Agriculture Responses to Prices in Sub-Saharan African Countries." *International Monetary Fund Staff Papers* 20(4): 703–36.

Chamley, Christophe, and Patrick Honohan. 1992. "Taxation of Financial Intermediation: Measurement Principles and Application to Five African Countries." PRE Working Paper 421. World Bank, Policy Research Department, Washington, D.C.

Cleaver, Kevin M. 1993. *A Strategy to Develop Agriculture in Sub-Saharan Africa and a Focus for the World Bank.* Technical Paper 203. Washington, D.C.: World Bank.

Cleaver, Kevin, and Gotz Schreiber. 1993. "The Population, Agriculture and Environment Nexus in Sub-Saharan Africa." Africa Technical Department working paper. World Bank, Washington, D.C.

Collins, Susan M., and Won-Am Park. 1989. Book II, "External Debt and Macroeconomic Performance in South Korea." In Jeffrey D. Sachs and Susan M. Collins, eds., *Developing Country Debt and Economic Performance.* Vol. 3, *Country Studies–Indonesia, Korea, Philippines, Turkey.* Chicago: University of Chicago Press.

Conservation International. 1989. *The Debt for Nature Exchange.* Washington, D.C.

Corbo, Vittorio, and Klaus Schmidt-Hebbel. 1991. "Public Policies and Savings in Developing Countries." *Journal of Development Economics* 36(1):89–115.

Cromwell, C., and J. T. Winpenny. 1991. *Has Economic Reform Harmed the Environment? A Review of Structural Adjustment in Malawi.* London: Overseas Development Institute.

Delgado, Christopher L. 1992. "Why Domestic Food Prices Matter to Growth Strategy in Semi-Open West African Agriculture." *Journal of African Economies* 1(3):446–71.

Demery, Lionel. Forthcoming. "Côte d'Ivoire: Fettered Adjustment." In Ishrat Husain and Rashid Faruqee, eds., *Adjustment in Africa: Lessons from Country Case Studies.* A Regional and Sectoral Study. Washington, D.C.: World Bank.

Demery, Lionel, and Ishrat Husain. 1993. "Assessment of the Interrelation between Adjustment Financing and Economic Performance in SPA Countries." Draft. World Bank, Africa Region, Washington, D.C.

Denizer, Cevdet, and Alan Gelb. 1992. "Mongolia: Privatization and System Transformation in an Isolated Economy." Policy Research Working Paper 1063. World Bank, Policy Research Department, Washington, D.C.

Devarajan, Shantayanan, and Jaime de Melo. 1991. "Membership in the CFA Zone: Odyssean Journey or Trojan Horse?" In Ajay Chhibber and Stanley Fischer, eds., *Economic Reform in Sub-Saharan Africa.* A World Bank Symposium. Washington, D.C.: World Bank.

Devarajan, Shantayanan, Jeffrey D. Lewis, and Sherman Robinson. 1993. "External Shocks, Purchasing Power Parity, and the Equilibrium Real Exchange Rate." *World Bank Economic Review* 7(1):45–63.

Dia, Mamadou. 1993. *A Governance Approach to Civil Service Reform in Sub-Saharan Africa.* Technical Paper 225. Washington, D.C.: World Bank.

Dollar, David. 1992. "Outward-Oriented Developing Economies Really Do Grow More Rapidly: Evidence from 95 LDCs, 1976–1985." *Economic Development and Cultural Change* 40(April):523–44.

Dornbusch, Rudiger, and Stanley Fischer. 1993. "Moderate Inflation." *World Bank Economic Review* 7(1):1–44.

Dorosh, Paul A., and David E. Sahn. 1993. *A General Equilibrium Analysis of the Effect of Macroeconomic Adjustment on Poverty in Africa.* Cornell Food and Nutrition Policy Program Working Paper 39. Ithaca, N.Y.: Cornell University.

Dutz, Mark, and Claudio Frischtak. 1993. "Industrial Adjustment in Tanzania: An Enterprise-Level Analysis." Working paper. World Bank, Private Sector Development Department, Washington, D.C.

Easterly, William. 1992. "Projection of Growth Rates." Outreach 5. World Bank, Policy Research Department, Washington, D.C.

Easterly, William, and Ross Levine. 1993. "Is Africa Different? Evidence from Growth Regressions." Draft. World Bank, Policy Research Department, Washington, D.C.

Easterly, William, Michael Kremer, Lant Pritchett, and Lawrence H. Summers. 1993. "Good Policy or Good Luck: Country Growth Performance and Temporary Shocks." *Journal of Monetary Economics* 32(3).

Easterly, William, and Klaus Schmidt-Hebbel. 1991. "The Macroeconomics of Public Sector Deficits: A Synthesis." PRE Working Paper 775. World Bank, Policy Research Department, Washington, D.C.

Elbadawi, Ibrahim A. 1992. "Have World Bank–Supported Adjustment Programs Improved Economic Performance in Sub-Saharan Africa?" Policy Research Working Paper 1001. World Bank, Policy Research Department, Washington, D.C.

← Evidence de l'
de l'orientat macro

Elbadawi, Ibrahim, and Nader Majd. 1992. "Fixed Parity of the Exchange Rate and Economic Performance in the CFA Zone: A Comparative Study." Policy Research Working Paper 830. World Bank, Policy Research Department, Washington, D.C.

Fischer, Stanley. 1982. "Seigniorage and the Case for a National Money." *Journal of Political Economy* 90(April):295–313.

Fosu, Augustin Kwasi. 1992. "Political Instability and Economic Growth: Evidence from Sub-Saharan Africa." *Economic Development and Cultural Change* 40(July):829–41.

Fry, Maxwell J. 1988. *Money, Interest, and Banking in Economic Development.* Baltimore, Md.: Johns Hopkins University Press.

Gelb, Alan. 1988. *Oil Windfalls: Blessing or Curse?* New York: Oxford University Press.

Giovannini, Alberto. 1983. "The Interest Elasticity of Savings in Developing Countries: The Existing Evidence." *World Development* 11(7):601–07.

———. 1985. "Saving and the Real Interest Rate in LDCs." *Journal of Development Economics* 18(2–3):197–217.

Giovannini, Alberto, and Martha de Melo. 1993. "Government Revenue from Financial Repression." *American Economic Review* 83(4):953–63.

Glickman, Joan, and Darius Teter. 1991. "Debt, Structural Adjustment, and Deforestation: Examining the Links—A Policy Exercise for the Sierra Club." Consultants' report. Sierra Club, Washington, D.C.

Godfrey, Martin. 1985. "Trade and Exchange Rate Policy: A Further Contribution to the Debate." In Tore Rose, ed., *Crisis and Recovery in Sub-Saharan Africa.* Paris: Development Centre of the Organization for Economic Cooperation and Development.

Grootaert, Christiaan. 1993. "The Evolution of Welfare and Poverty under Structural Change and Economic Recession in Côte d'Ivoire, 1985–88." Policy Research Working Paper 1078. World Bank, Policy Research Department, Washington, D.C.

Grut, Mikael, John A. Gray, and Nicolas Egli. 1991. *Forest Pricing and Concession Policies: Managing the High Forests of West and Central Africa.* Technical Paper 143. Washington, D.C.: World Bank.

Gupta, Kanhaya L. 1987. "Aggregate Savings, Financial Intermediation, and Interest Rate." *Review of Economics and Statistics* 69(2):303–11.

Haggard, Stephan, and Steven B. Webb. 1993. "What Do We Know about the Political Economy of Economic Policy Reform?" *World Bank Research Observer* 8(2):143–68.

Hardin, Garrett. 1968. "The Tragedy of the Commons." *Science* 162: 1243–48.

Helleiner, G. K. 1992. "The IMF, the World Bank and Africa's Adjustment and External Debt Problems: An Unofficial View." *World Development* 20 (June):779–92.

Hodd, Michael. 1991. *The Economies of Africa: Geography, Population, History, Stability, Structure, Performance Forecasts.* Aldershot, U.K.: Dartmouth Publishing.

Husain, Ishrat. 1993. "Trade, Aid and Investment in Sub-Saharan Africa." Paper presented at Royal African Society Conference on Africa '93: Governance, Business Aid, in Oxford, U.K., March 21–23.

Husain, Ishrat, and Rashid Faruqee, eds. Forthcoming. *Adjustment in Africa: Lessons from Country Case Studies.* A Regional and Sectoral Study. Washington, D.C.: World Bank.

IMF (International Monetary Fund). Various issues. *International Financial Statistics.* Washington, D.C.

International Currency Analysis, Inc. Various years. *World Currency Yearbook.* Brooklyn, N.Y.

Jaeger, William K. 1992. *The Effects of Economic Policies on African Agriculture.* Discussion Paper 147. Washington, D.C.: World Bank.

Kessides, Christine. 1993. *Institutional Options for the Provision of Infrastructure.* Discussion Paper 212. Washington, D.C.: World Bank.

Kiguel, Miguel, and Stephen A. O'Connell. 1993. "Parallel Exchange Rates in Developing Countries: Lessons from Eight Case Studies." Draft. World Bank, Policy Research Department, Transition and Macro-Adjustment Division, Washington, D.C.

Kikeri, Sunita, John Nellis, and Mary Shirley. 1992. *Privatization: The Lessons of Experience.* Washington, D.C.: World Bank.

Killick, Tony. 1992. *Explaining Africa's Post-Independence Development Experiences.* Working Paper 60. London: Overseas Development Institute.

King, Robert G., and Ross Levine. 1992. "Financial Indicators and Growth in a Cross Section of Countries." PRE Working Paper 819. World Bank, Policy Research Department, Washington, D.C.

Krueger, Anne O. 1978. *Liberalization Attempts and Consequences.* Published for the National Bureau of Economic Research. Cambridge, Mass.: Ballinger.

Krueger, Anne O., Maurice Schiff, and Alberto Valdés. 1988. "Agricultural Incentives in Developing Countries: Measuring the Effect of Sectoral and Economywide Policies." *World Bank Economic Review* 2(3):255–71.

Lall, Sanjaya. 1992. "Structural Problems of African Industry." In Frances Stewart, Sanjaya Lall, and Samuel Wangwe, eds., *Alternative Development Strategies in Sub-Saharan Africa.* London: Macmillan.

Lambert, Sylvie, Hartmut Schneider, and Akiko Suwa. 1991. "Adjustment and Equity in Côte d'Ivoire: 1980–86." *World Development* 19(11): 1563–76.

Lopez, Ramon. 1992. "The Environment as a Factor of Production: The Economic Growth and Trade Policy Linkages." In Patrick Low, ed., *International Trade and the Environment.* Washington, D.C.: World Bank.

Maddison, Angus. 1989. *The World Economy in the 20th Century.* Paris: Development Centre of the Organization for Economic Cooperation and Development.

Mayfield, Malcolm R. 1992. "The Effects of Policy Reforms on the Performance of Agriculture in Tanzania." Consultant's report. World Bank, Eastern Africa Department, Agriculture and Environment Division, Washington, D.C.

McKinnon, Ronald. 1973. *Money and Capital in Economic Development.* Washington, D.C.: Brookings Institution.

Meade, J. E. 1967. "Population Explosion, the Standard of Living and Social Conflict." *Economic Journal* 77(June):233–55.

Mills, Bradford, David Sahn, E. E. Walden, and Stephen Younger. Forthcoming. *Public Finance and Public Employment: An Analysis of the Public Sector Retrenchment Programs in Guinea and Ghana.* Cornell Food and Nutrition Policy Program Working Paper. Ithaca, N.Y.: Cornell University.

Mosley, Paul, Jane Harrigan, and J. F. J. Toye. 1991. *Aid and Power: The World Bank and Policy-Based Lending.* London and New York: Routledge.

Narasimhan, Bhanu, and Lant Pritchett. 1993. "The Evolution of Import Restrictions in Sub-Saharan Africa in the 1980's: An Empirical Analysis." Draft. World Bank, Washington, D.C.

Nashashibi, Karim, and Stefania Bazzoni. 1994. "Alternative Exchange Rate Strategies and Fiscal Performance in Sub-Saharan Africa." *International Monetary Fund Staff Papers* 41(1).

Nellis, John R. 1989. *Contract Plans and Public Enterprise Performance.* Discussion Paper 48. Washington, D.C.: World Bank.

OED (Operations Evaluation Department). 1993. "Adjustment in Sub-Saharan Africa: Selected Findings from OED Evaluations." Report 12155. World Bank, Washington, D.C.

Pack, Howard. 1993. "Productivity and Industrial Development in Sub-Saharan Africa." *World Development* 21(1):1–16.

Perrings, Charles, Hans Opschoor, Jaap Arntzen, A. Gilbert, and David W. Pearce. 1988. *Economics for Sustainable Development—Botswana: A Case Study.* Gaborone: Ministry of Finance and Development Planning.

Pimentel, David, Beth Floyd, Wayne Teel, and Julie Bourns. 1991. "Deforestation, Biomass Depletion, and Land Degradation: Linkages to Policy Reform in Sub-Saharan Africa." Paper presented at a seminar. Cornell University, Department of Natural Resources, Ithaca, N.Y.

Pritchett, Lant. 1991. "Measuring Outward Orientation in Developing Countries: Can It Be Done?" PRE Working Paper 566. World Bank, Policy Research Department, Trade Policy Division, Washington, D.C.

Reed, David, ed. 1992. *Structural Adjustment and the Environment.* Boulder, Colo.: Westview.

Repetto, Robert. 1989. "Economic Incentives for Sustainable Production." In Gunter Schramm and Jeremy J. Warford, eds., *Environmental Management and Economic Development.* Baltimore, Md.: Johns Hopkins University Press.

Rutihinda, G. 1992. "Tanzania's Experience." In I. G. Patel, ed., *Policies for African Development: From the 1980s to the 1990s.* Washington, D.C.: International Monetary Fund.

Sahn, David E. 1992. "Public Expenditures in Sub-Saharan Africa during a Period of Economic Reforms." *World Development* 20(5):673–93.

Sahn, David E., and René Bernier. 1993. *Evidence from Africa on the Intrasectoral Allocation of Social Sector Expenditures.* Cornell Food and Nutrition Policy Program Working Paper 45. Ithaca, N.Y.: Cornell University.

Sarris, Alexander H., and Rogier van den Brink. 1993. *Economic Policy and Household Welfare during Crisis and Adjustment in Tanzania.* New York: New York University Press.

Schadler, Susan, Franek Rozwadowski, Siddarth Tiwari, and David Robinson. 1993. *Economic Adjustment in Low-Income Countries: Experience under the Enhanced Structural Adjustment Facility.* IMF Occasional Paper 106. Washington, D.C.: International Monetary Fund.

Schiff, Maurice, and Alberto Valdés. 1992. *The Plundering of Agriculture in Developing Countries.* Washington, D.C.: World Bank.

Schloss, Miguel. 1993. "Does Petroleum Procurement and Trade Matter? The Case of Sub-Saharan Africa." *Finance and Development* 30(1):44–46.

Schwartz, Gerd, and Paulo Silva Lopes. 1993. "Privatization: Expectations, Trade-Offs, and Results." *Finance and Development* 30(2):14–17.

Seckler, David, ed. 1993. *Agricultural Transformation in Africa.* Arlington, Va.: Winrock International Institute for Agricultural Development.

Selowski, Marcelo, and Herman G. van der Tak. 1986. "The Debt Problem and Growth." *World Development* 14(9):1107–1124.

Serven, Luis, and Andrés Solimano. 1992. "Private Investment and Macroeconomic Adjustment: A Survey." *World Bank Research Observer* 7(1): 95–114.

Shaikh, Hafeez, Sunita Kikeri, and Daniel Swanson. 1993. "Privatization and Public Enterprise Reform in Africa." Background paper prepared for *Adjustment in Africa: Reforms, Results, and the Road Ahead.* World Bank, Washington, D.C.

Sherif, Khaled Fouad. 1993. "Public Enterprise Reform and Privatization in Africa." Working paper. World Bank, Africa Technical Department, Washington, D.C.

Stein, Howard. 1992. "Deindustrialization, Adjustment, the World Bank and the IMF in Africa." *World Development* 20(Jan.):83–95.

Stewart, Frances, Sanjaya Lall, and Samuel Wangwe, eds. 1992. *Alternative Development Strategies in Sub-Saharan Africa.* London: Macmillan.

Stryker, J. Dirck, Robert L. West, Jeffery C. Metzel, B. Lynn Salinger, Peter M. Haymond, Alison T. Slack, and Bruce Aylward. 1989. "Linkages between Policy Reform and Natural Resource Management in Sub-Saharan Africa." Draft. Fletcher School, Tufts University, Somerville, Mass., and Associates for International Resources and Development, Cambridge, Mass.

Summers, Lawrence H., and Lant H. Pritchett. 1993. "The Structural Adjustment Debate." *American Economic Review, Papers and Proceedings* 83(May):383–89.

Tan, Jee-Peng, and Alain Mingat. 1992. *Education in Asia: A Comparative Study of Cost and Financing.* Washington, D.C.: World Bank.

Tanzi, Vito. 1978. "Inflation, Real Tax Revenue, and the Case for Inflationary Finance: Theory with an Application to Argentina." *International Monetary Fund Staff Papers* 25(3):417–51.

——. 1991. "Fiscal Policy, Growth, and Design of Stabilization Programs." In Ana María Martirena-Mantel, ed., *External Debt, Savings, and Growth in Latin America,* pp. 121–41. Washington, D.C.: International Monetary Fund.

Tenconi, Roland. 1992. "The African Banking Systems in the 1980s and Early 1990s." Draft. World Bank, Occidental and Central Africa Department, Industry and Energy Operations Division, Washington, D.C.

Torfs, Marijke. 1991. "Effects of the IMF Structural Adjustment Programs on Social Sectors of Third World Countries." Discussion paper. Friends of the Earth, Washington, D.C.

UNCTC (United Nations Centre on Transnational Corporations). 1991. *Accountancy Development in Africa: Challenge of the 1990s.* New York: United Nations.

Valdés, Alberto. 1989. "Comment on 'The Policy Response of Agriculture' by Binswanger." In World Bank, *Proceedings of the World Bank Annual Conference on Development Economics 1989,* pp. 263–68. Washington, D.C.

van den Brink, Rogier. 1993. "A Review of Agricultural Statistics of Mainland Tanzania." Revised version of background paper for Agricultural Sector Memorandum for Tanzania. World Bank, Eastern Africa Department, Agriculture and Environment Division, Washington, D.C.

von Braun, Joachim, and Eileen Kennedy. 1987. "Cash Crops versus Subsistence Crops: Income and Nutritional Effects in Developing Countries." In J. Price Gittinger, Joanne Leslie, and Caroline Hoisington, eds., *Food Policy: Integrating Supply, Distribution, and Consumption.* Baltimore, Md.: Johns Hopkins University Press.

WCED (World Commission on Environment and Development). 1987. *Our Common Future.* Oxford: Oxford University Press.

World Bank. 1989a. *Sub-Saharan Africa: From Crisis to Sustainable Growth.* Washington, D.C.

———. 1989b. *World Development Report 1989: Financial Systems and Development.* New York: Oxford University Press.

———. 1990. *World Development Report 1990: Poverty.* New York: Oxford University Press.

———. 1991a. *The African Capacity Building Initiative: Toward Improved Policy Analysis and Development Management.* Washington, D.C.

———. 1991b. *Reform of Public Sector Management: Lessons from Experience.* Policy and Research Series Paper 18. Washington, D.C.

———. 1991c. *World Development Report 1991: The Challenge of Development.* New York: Oxford University Press.

———. 1992a. *Adjustment Lending and Mobilization of Private and Public Resources for Growth.* Policy and Research Series Paper 22. Washington, D.C.

———. 1992b. *Governance and Development.* Washington, D.C.

———. 1992c. *World Debt Tables 1992–93: External Finance for Developing Countries.* Washington, D.C.

———. 1992d. *World Development Report 1992: Development and the Environment.* New York: Oxford University Press.

———. 1993a. *The East Asian Miracle: Economic Growth and Public Policy.* New York: Oxford University Press.

———. 1993b. "Ghana 2000 and Beyond—Setting the Stage for Accelerated Growth and Poverty Reduction." Economic Report 11486. Washington, D.C.

———. 1993c. *Implementing the World Bank's Strategy to Reduce Poverty: Progress and Challenges.* Washington, D.C.

———. 1993d. *World Development Report 1993: Investing in Health.* New York: Oxford University Press.

Young, Crawford. 1982. *Ideology and Development in Africa.* New Haven, Conn.: Yale University Press.

Younger, Stephen D. 1992. "Aid and the Dutch Disease: Macroeconomic Management When Everybody Loves You." *World Development* 20(11): 1587–97.